BARTER IN THE
WORLD ECONOMY

BARTER IN THE WORLD ECONOMY

Edited by
Bart S. Fisher
Kathleen M. Harte

PRAEGER SPECIAL STUDIES • PRAEGER SCIENTIFIC

New York • Philadelphia • Eastbourne, UK
Toronto • Hong Kong • Tokyo • Sydney

Library of Congress Cataloging in Publication Data
Main entry under title:

Barter in the world economy.

    Bibliography: p.
    Includes indexes.
    1. Barter--Addresses,   essays,   lectures.
I. Fisher, Bart S.   II. Harte, Kathleen M.
HF1019.B37   1985   382   85-6257
ISBN 0-03-071609-8 (alk. paper)

Published in 1985 by Praeger Publishers
CBS Educational and Professional Publishing, a Division of CBS Inc.
521 Fifth Avenue, New York, NY 10175 USA

© 1985 by Praeger Publishers

56789 052 987654321

Printed in the United States of America on acid-free paper

INTERNATIONAL OFFICES

Orders from outside the United States should be sent to the appropriate address listed below. Orders from areas not listed below should be placed through CBS International Publishing, 383 Madison Ave., New York, NY 10175 USA

Australia, New Zealand
Holt Saunders, Pty. Ltd., 9 Waltham St., Artarmon, N.S.W. 2064, Sydney, Australia

Canada
Holt, Rinehart & Winston of Canada, 55 Horner Ave., Toronto, Ontario, Canada M8Z 4X6

Europe, the Middle East, & Africa
Holt Saunders, Ltd., 1 St. Anne's Road, Eastbourne, East Sussex, England BN21 3UN

Japan
Holt Saunders, Ltd., Ichibancho Central Building, 22-1 Ichibancho, 3rd Floor, Chiyodaku, Tokyo, Japan

Hong Kong, Southeast Asia
Holt Saunders Asia, Ltd., 10 Fl, Intercontinental Plaza, 94 Granville Road, Tsim Sha Tsui East, Kowloon, Hong Kong

 Manuscript submissions should be sent to the Editorial Director, Praeger Publishers, 521 Fifth Avenue, New York, NY 10175 USA

ACKNOWLEDGMENTS

This study grew out of a workshop seminar conducted at the Georgetown University School of Foreign Service from September, 1982, through May, 1983. The authors gratefully acknowledge the assistance of all the participants in the workshop seminar, and wish particularly to thank Dr. Peter Krogh, Dean, School of Foreign Service, and Dr. Allan Goodman, Associate Dean, School of Foreign Service, for their assistance in encouraging the flexible format of the workshop seminar program.

The authors also express their appreciation for Michael D. Esch's contribution to several chapters.

Thanks are due also to Mrs. Deborah Wharton and Kathi Waters, who so conscientiously typed the final manuscript.

Bart S. Fisher
Kathleen M. Harte

CONTENTS

1

Barter in the World Economy: INTRODUCTION

Bart S. Fisher

Barter, the oldest form of commercial transaction, consists of the direct exchange of goods or commodities of equal value without the use of currency.[1] It is a growing phenomenon in the world economy, and may now account for 20-30 percent of world trade[2] and 5-10 percent of domestic U.S. commerce.[3]

Barter is frequently associated with trade among primitive peoples,[4] and its limited but defined presence in East-West trade and trade among developing countries has been a longstanding, well-described phenomenon. What is new is the growth in pressures on U.S. private enterprises and the U.S. government to retreat from commerce based on money as the medium of exchange, and revert to trade based on the direct transfer of goods against goods. How should the United States respond to the challenge of barter on a unilateral, bilateral or multilateral basis?

The purpose of this volume is to cast some light on the shadowy world of international barter. As pressures on international liquidity have intensified and recessionary pressures in the world economy have increased, barter has intruded on the scene of world commerce as a necessary evil—an alternative to having no sales in a given market for U.S. business.

However, very little has been written in the United States about barter, and for a very good reason. Knowledge about barter is in itself a competitive advantage in a period when competitive advantages are hard to obtain. Accordingly, those fortunate enough to complete barter deals are very reluctant to explain publicly how to consummate such transactions.

1

This volume is intended to be more than merely an addition to the limited store of anecdotal information that exists on barter. It presents an overall approach to barter, in terms of how it works, where it works, and the economic, legal, and policy problems traders will confront when using it.

MECHANICS OF BARTER

Thomas McVey, in his chapter, "Overview of the Commercial Practice of Countertrade," introduces the subject of barter by defining its many forms. He expertly explains some of the many variations on the barter theme, including counterpurchase, compensation, "straight" barter, import entitlement programs, offsets, clearing arrangements, switch trading, "progressive" countertrade, develop-for-import transactions, performance requirements, and collection-through-export transactions. He presents barter as an alternative form of financing for deals that would otherwise not have taken place, and concludes by describing the hesitant response of U.S. firms to countertrade.

David Koschik's chapter, "Structuring Barter and Countertrade Transactions," builds on McVey's definitions describing, in very precise legalistic fashion, how to put together barter and countertrade transactions. An important disadvantage of barter is its inordinate complexity, compared to the simple sale of an item for money. Lawyers will be required to draw up contracts for linked transactions that protect the interests of traders, and Koschik's chapter provides actual contracts and checklists that can be used to guide participants in barter negotiations.

BARTER SCENARIOS

Until 1982 the international barter focus was on East-West trade. The practices of the Foreign Trade Organizations (FTOs) of Eastern Europe are described in "Countertrade—As Practiced in Eastern Europe" by Gerhart Vogt and Heinrick Nowak, both of Centrobank in Vienna.

In 1983 the primary scenario for barter shifted to North-South trade, as credit and liquidity tightened in the context of a global recession. Millicent H. Schwenk's chapter, "North-South Barter Trade," explains how developing countries are using barter to promote their exports by analyzing in detail the cases of Indonesia and Malaysia.

Indonesia's experience indicates that mandated counterpurchase requirements will face resistance from businessmen and governments and are likely to be unsuccessful. The pragmatic, "wait-and-see" approach of the government of Malaysia is more likely to be the developing countries' attitude toward mandated counterpurchase re-requirements.

The third international scenario for barter is South-South barter, i.e., barter among developing nations. This form of exchange has primarily involved the barter of agricultural commodities for desired goods, as explained in Donna Vogt's chapter, "Barter of Agricultural Commodities Among Developing Countries."

The chapter by James Higgiston, "Domestic Barter" examines the role barter now plays in the United States. Higgiston describes the "underground economy" of barter clubs, media barter, corporate barter, and personal barter in a fascinating exposition of the U.S. barter explosion. The size of the underground economy has been estimated to be $176 billion, or approximately 10 percent of the gross national product, and growing.[5] The Internal Revenue Service has cast a wary eye on barter and indicated that barter is perhaps being used as a means of tax evasion by many U.S. participants.

Donna Vogt's second contribution to the volume, "U.S. Government International Barter," examines bartering by the U.S. government. Her opening sentence says it all: "Public barter by the U.S. Government is a complicated way of doing business and is not an actively pursued goal at this time." The Reagan administration has resolutely opposed public barter, despite intense pressure from U.S. agricultural interests. Mrs. Vogt, however, does examine in detail the exception to the general disposition of the Reagan administration to view barter as a sin against free enterprise, the 1982 U.S.-Jamaica Barter Agreements.

PROBLEMS WITH BARTER

The problems with barter at the level of the private trader abound. Apart from getting stuck with unwanted goods of low quality, the businessman has to worry about the application of the U.S. tax, antitrust, and trade laws to the proposed transaction. Barter is so full of problems in the contract, tax, antitrust, and trade regulation areas as to make most lawyers palpitate with excitement. Kathleen Harte considers the domestic legal consequences of barter in her chapter, "Legal Aspects of Barter and Countertrade Transactions."

R. Michael Gadbaw examines the problems posed by barter and countertrade for the General Agreement on Tariffs and Trade (GATT). Gadbaw's selection casts into bold relief the tension between countertrade and the underlying premises of the GATT, which was established to promote commerce on an open, nondiscriminatory, multilateral basis. The essence of barter is that it is, on the contrary, a nontransparent, discriminatory, bilateral transaction which tends to be trade-distorting. Whereas the GATT looks to Ricardo's "Law of Comparative Advantage" model as its normative objective, countertrade is a recognition of the reality that governmental intervention is becoming the norm in international trade.

What Gadbaw gently suggests is developed further by Thomas McVey in the concluding chapter, "Policy Issues in Countertrade." Simply put, the case can be cogently made that countertrade is a coercive, anticompetitive practice standing in the way of efficiency and the free flow of commerce. McVey's selection describes the agonizing that is now going on inside the U.S. government regarding how to respond to the increasing international pressures towards barter.

WHITHER BARTER?

Recent news suggests that the bloom is off the rose so far as barter advocates in the U.S. business community are concerned. The most prominent U.S. retailer to enter the barter business has been Sears, which established an affiliate, Sears World Trade, to pursue countertrade transactions. In 1984 its staff was slashed by 10 percent, due to its disappointing performance. Within two months, two U.S. banks, the European American Bank and Trust Co. and J. Henry Schroder Bank and Trust Co. shut down their countertrade operations. The failure of Sears and many U.S. banks and trading houses profitably to undertake countertrade is becoming apparent.

What is not clear is whether the failures of U.S. business in the world of barter and countertrade will continue, or whether we are witnessing only a hiatus brought about by a slowly improving world economy. While barter has typically been an outgrowth of recessionary conditions, there are probably deeper reasons for the failure of U.S. businesses at barter. McVey correctly identifies the primary ones: the lack of experience in countertrade, the substantial risks involved in acquiring the unneeded goods, and the aversion to the complexity of countertrade. Can U.S. firms overcome their natural reluctance to engage in barter and countertrade when faced with the unpalatable alternative of losing sales? There may be guidance in Will Rogers' observation about growing old: "Distasteful as it is," he commented, "it is preferable to the alternative."

NOTES

1. This chapter uses the term *barter* to mean all forms of barter and countertrade.

2. U.S. Int'l Trade Comm., Analysis of Recent Trends in U.S. Countertrade (1982), USITC Publication 1237, prepared principally by Ronald J. DeMarines.

3. In 1976 Peter Gutmann estimated the size of the underground economy to be $176 billion or approximately 10 percent of the GNP. Gutmann, "The Subterranean Economy," *Financial Analysts Journal* 27 (November-December, 1977).

4. The principle of the reciprocal exchange of goods, of giving and taking, appears to be deeply rooted in human nature. Commerce in the form of regular acts of exchange appears even in the lowest level of primitive peoples, those who live by collecting the forest's bounties. Variations on the direct exchange of goods against goods include "silent trade," or dumb barter, with neither party holding any communication with the other, and the "gift-exchange," in which the transaction takes the form of present and counter-present.

5. See Gutmann, "The Subterranean Economy."

PART ONE
MECHANICS OF BARTER

2
OVERVIEW OF THE COMMERCIAL PRACTICE OF COUNTERTRADE

Thomas B. McVey

WORKING DEFINITION OF COUNTERTRADE

As a general working definition, countertrade is a practice in international trade in which two parties link an import transaction and an export transaction in a reciprocal fashion. In most instances, a private firm agrees to sell certain goods to a sovereign nation and simultaneously agrees to purchase certain goods from the nation in a parallel transaction. In recent years, however, the term countertrade has been expanded to refer to a broad range of additional practices in which a seller conveys other types of benefits to a purchasing nation to induce the sale of its goods such as the hiring of subcontractors located in the purchasing nation, the transferring of technology to the nation or the undertaking of an investment in the nation.

As mentioned above, the parties will probably engage in countertrade upon the insistence of the importing nation which states that it will not purchase the goods from the private firm unless the firm agrees to export a corresponding amount of products from the nation. Once the private firm has acquired quantities of the nation's goods, the firm must devise means of disposing of these goods, generally through resale on the world market to third parties, in order to end up in a positive cash position. Frequently, the U.S. firm will be required to locate a Western bank willing to loan the nation funds to pay for the firm's products for the period of time between when the private firm delivers its goods and when it fulfills its purchase commitment.

9

Countertrade is frequently confused with the concept of barter. Barter is an exchange of goods effectuated without the use of currency. As mentioned above, countertrade is most frequently used to refer to two reciprocal sales transactions in which each party is paid in currency. Despite this technical distinction, most observers view barter transactions as a subcategory of countertrade, especially in cases in which barter requirements are imposed by nations in a coercive fashion for purposes of disposing of goods which they cannot otherwise sell.

REASONS BEHIND THE RECENT INCREASE IN COUNTERTRADE

The question is often asked why nations do not merely sell their goods on the open market in conventional transactions instead of imposing them upon private companies through barter/countertrade requirements. In most cases, this is because they are unable to do so or, in limited instances, because the other party considers the goods in question to be more valuable than currency.

Countertrade requirements are imposed by nations as a mechanism to assist in expanding their exports and in generating sufficient amounts of hard currency to finance their import transactions. In most cases, these requirements are imposed by nations which are experiencing shortages in foreign exchange reserves, low currency values or similar economic difficulties. In essence, the nation uses its purchasing power as leverage to generate the currency it needs to finance its purchases from a private firm and to force that private firm to accept the responsibility (and corresponding risk) of marketing the nation's marginally undesirable goods in the world marketplace.

Countertrade practices have been increasing at a dramatic rate in recent years due to the heightened problems of many nations in dealing with world economic pressures. Throughout the last decade, radical changes in the price of key commodities including crude oil and other natural resources have left many non-industrialized nations with severe balance of payments problems, seriously restricting their abilities to finance their ever-expanding industrial and social needs. Most recently, the dramatic cutback in sovereign lending and prolonged world recession have increased the Third World's economic turmoil. Countertrade has been relied upon at an increasing rate as a means of dealing with these economic pressures because it permits nations to sustain their importing activities without depleting foreign exchange reserves or by guaranteeing the replacement of hard currency within a relatively short period of time. Consequently, these nations are relieved of the burdens of additional international borrowing or restrictive internal economic measures. As these economic pressures become more severe, countertrade is becoming an especially important tool in assisting the economic survival of developing and developed nations.

EXAMPLES OF COUNTERTRADE TRANSACTIONS

Examples of the involvement of U.S. firms in countertrade are abundant.

- In a $12 million sale of locomotive and diesel engines by a U.S. automobile manufacturer to the government of Yugoslavia, the U.S. firm reportedly agreed to purchase $4 million in Yugoslav cutting tools that it then exported and sold to a U.S.-based tool manufacturer for cash.
- A major U.S. manufacturer of farm equipment sold tractor design and technology to the government of Poland and agreed to purchase a portion of the tractor components built in Poland utilizing the purchased design and technology; the components were slated for use in the U.S. firm's sub-assembly plant in Europe.
- The government of Indonesia awarded contracts to ten fertilizer suppliers from several countries, including the United States, for the sale of $127.7 million in fertilizer to Indonesia; each of these firms agreed to purchase quantities of Indonesian products including rubber, coffee, and cement.
- A well-known U.S. apparel manufacturer sold the Hungarian government equipment and design necessary to manufacture blue jeans, and also agreed to purchase a portion of the jeans produced in the plant; the U.S. firm reportedly purchases approximately 60 percent of the annual output of the plant for resale in other parts of the world.
- In a $2.37 billion sale of fighter aircraft to Canada by a major U.S. aerospace firm, the firm reportedly has agreed to hire Canadian subcontractors, transfer proprietary aerospace and electronics technology to Canadian firms, establish Canadian plants, promote the Canadian tourist industry, and develop the export marketing program for Canadian goods.
- In a transaction between another U.S. aerospace firm and the government of The Netherlands, the U.S. firm is reported to have sold

communications equipment to The Netherlands and agreed to purchase Dutch-produced metal castings, cables, and electronic parts.
- In an agreement with the Rumanian government to sell soft-drink concentrates, a U.S. soft drink manufacturer consented to purchase quantities of Rumanian wine. In a similar sale of concentrates to the Soviet Union, the firm received the exclusive right to import Soviet vodka into the United States.
- To increase sales of its soft drink products, another U.S. soft drink manufacturer frequently purchases or barters for products such as toys from Korea, glasswork from Thailand, honey, wine, and cashmere from China, wines from Yugoslavia, and beer from Poland.
- In an arrangement between a major U.S. industrial company and Poland, the U.S. company is reported to have sold equipment and technology to manufacture electrocardiogram meters in Poland, and agreed to purchase a portion of the meters produced over a period of years.

COUNTERTRADE IN EAST-WEST, NORTH-SOUTH AND WEST-WEST TRADE TRANSACTIONS

Despite the fact that countertrade remains relatively unheard of in the United States, it has been a permanent fixture in East-West trade for decades. The Soviet Union and Eastern European nations have long employed countertrade in dealing with their private Western trading partners. Similarly, the People's Republic of China has placed great emphasis on countertrade requirements in importing technology and equipment, although these requirements have been reduced within the past year due to the recent availability of foreign exchange in China. In a recent analysis of countertrade trends in East-West trade, the Organization for Economic Cooperation and Development (OECD) has estimated that as much as $35 billion worth of Western exports could have been involved in countertrade transactions between 1969 and 1979. As mentioned above, the U.S. International Trade Commission has reported in a more recent study the involvement of countertrade in the financing and development of a substantial number of industrial facilities in a variety of industries in Eastern Europe and the USSR.

Countertrade is not restricted to East-West trade, however. Countertrade requirements are being imposed with increasing frequency by the Third World nations, by "partly-industrialized" nations and, in certain instances, by Western industrialized nations. In a recent survey undertaken by a private trade association, 88 nations were identified as requesting countertrade in some form. Non-Communist nations that have implemented or are about to introduce some form of countertrade program include Brazil, India, Costa Rica, Israel, Chile, Indonesia, Colombia, Mexico, Austria, Sweden, Switzerland, Australia, Belgium, The Netherlands, Spain, Canada, South Korea, New Zealand, Malaysia, Guatemala, Argentina, Jamaica, Nigeria, Iran, Angola, and the United States.

In the case of non-OPEC Third World nations, where the use of countertrade is growing most rapidly, countertrade practices are utilized to finance imports, to promote the sale of traditional Third World exports and to accelerate industrial development. Countertrade permits the transfer of technology to the Third World from the West with minimal investment by the host nations. In addition, the practice establishes markets for both traditional products such as agricultural goods and natural resources as well as the output of the newly acquired equipment and technology. Most importantly, however, countertrade assures the continuity of essential imports at times when no foreign exchange is available to the importing nation.

Examples of Third World countertrade requirements are as varied as the nations imposing them. In a program initiated by the Department of Trade and Cooperatives of the Republic of Indonesia in 1981, for example, a requirement is in effect which provides that all foreign firms selling products to the Indonesian government must purchase equal amounts of specified Indonesian goods including rubber, coffee, pepper, tobacco, cement, sawn timber, plywood and textile products. Guatemala recently announced that it would be enacting a countertrade program within the near future, and the Government of Kenya recently transmitted a request to the United States government through diplomatic channels for assistance in evaluating the feasibility of initiating a countertrade program. As mentioned, Jamaica entered barter agreements with Chrysler Corp. and General Motors Corp. under which Jamaican alumina and bauxite were traded for commercial vehicles and numerous countries, including Nigeria, Iran, and Angola, are known to have been bartering crude oil for non-petroleum products for a number of years.

Countertrade is also finding increasing acceptance among many partly-industrialized nations, including Mexico, Brazil, Switzerland, and Sweden. Mexico, for example, published a decree in 1983 sanctioning barter transactions in lieu of conventional transactions which normally would involve foreign exchange. In Brazil, where the granting of import licenses has been on a steep decline, an "unofficial" policy has been implemented under which favorable treatment of import license applications will be granted to parties who generate a corresponding amount of exports. Additionally, the Brazilian Central Bank presently is undertaking a study of whether to expand and formalize its current countertrade activities. Numerous countries in Southeast Asia, including New Zealand, South Korea and Australia, have been reviewing countertrade offers as a part of bid proposals submitted by private contractors for major government procurement projects and indications are that many other neighboring nations are not far behind in establishing such practices. Products exported from partly-industrialized nations, including advanced machinery and electronic components, are often more sophisticated than those from the developing industries of most Third World nations and consequently pose more of a threat to competing producers in Western Europe and the United States.

Finally, countertrade practices have long been utilized by certain Western industrialized nations in the narrow context of military sales. Countertrade in weapons production, frequently referred to as "offset" trade, has developed out of the Western military practice known as "coproduction" in which allies jointly produce weapons and related military systems. Under the policy of coproduction, a number of Western nations each produce different components for a weapons system which is to be purchased by each of the member nations. In addition to fostering standardization and other efficiencies in weapons procurement, coproduction allows each nation to "offset" against its cost of an imported weapon the value of the components for the weapon which companies within that nation produce. As a result of the widespread use of coproduction in Western procurement activities, it has become common for nations purchasing weapons systems from foreign private contractors to require that the contractor agree to purchase a predetermined level of components from subcontractors located within the purchasing nation, to fulfill other portions of the private firm's international purchasing requirements from firms within that nation, or even to assist the nation in selling its unrelated products to third parties. Today, offset requirements are an integral part of many of the largest weapons procurement transactions between sovereign purchasers and private defense contractors.

TYPES OF COUNTERTRADE

Countertrade exists in a variety of forms. The two most common types of countertrade are known as counterpurchase and compensation trade. Barter has also been growing in prominence in Latin America following the recent liquidity crisis in the region. In addition, myriad other variations of countertrade have developed in response to specific conditions surrounding individual transactions and the particular needs of the parties involved. A number of these forms are discussed below.

Counterpurchase

In a *counterpurchase* agreement, the private firm agrees to sell products to the sovereign nation and to purchase from the nation products which are unrelated to the items which it is selling. For example, in a series of transactions between a major U.S. manufacturer of commercial aircraft and the government of Yugoslavia, the U.S. firm sold jet aircraft to the Yugoslavians and agreed to purchase substantial quantities of Yugoslavian crystal glassware, cutting tools, leather coats, and canned hams.

In a counterpurchase transaction, each party is paid in currency upon its delivery of its products to the other party. It is common in such transactions for the private firm to be allowed a period of time following the delivery of the goods that it is selling in which to fulfill its purchase obligation. Periods from three to five years, for example, are not uncommon in counterpurchase obligations imposed by the Soviet Union and Eastern European nations. Frequently, the parties agree upon a list of goods from which the private firm will later be able to select the items which it will be purchasing.

The goods which the nation will be offering for the counterpurchase will often be of low quality or in excess supply. Private firms resort to a variety of methods to dispose of the goods which they are forced to purchase, but most frequently resell the goods to trading companies or directly to end users, often at a discount or *disagio*. In certain instances, the private firm will resell the countertraded goods at a price below that which it paid for them, seeking to offset this loss by larger profits generated by the sale of its own product to the nation. Finally, except in rare instances, the nation imposing the countertrade requirement will insist that its private trading partner agree to pay a penalty, backed by security acceptable to the nation, in the event the firm defaults on its purchase obligation. Counterpurchase is most frequently used in transactions involving the Soviet Union, Eastern Europe, the People's Republic of China and Indonesia.

Compensation

The most common form of countertrade is referred to as *compensation* or *buy-back*. In a compensation transaction, the private firm will sell equipment, technology and/or an entire turnkey plant to the sovereign nation and agree to purchase a portion of the output produced from the use of the equipment of technology. For example, in the celebrated $20 billion Occidental Petroleum ammonia barter/ countertrade transaction with the Soviet Union, Occidental assisted the Soviets in constructing and financing ammonia plants and agreed to purchase quantities of ammonia produced in these plants over a 20-year period.

Compensation transactions frequently involve significantly longer periods of time during which the private firm will be permitted to fulfill its purchase obligation than in counterpurchase, commonly ten years or more. In addition, compensation transactions are generally of larger dollar value than counterpurchase transactions. As with counterpurchase, the private firm most often is paid in currency when it takes possession of its portion of the output. An agreement providing for the payment of a penalty by the private firm in the event of default is common as well. Unlike counterpurchase transactions, however, the products that the private firm purchases in compensation trade are frequently of marketable quality and in demand in the international marketplace. In addition, Western firms frequently are able to negotiate a purchase price for the output that is below the world market price so that the firm can earn a profit in reselling the product.

Barter

Barter, swap, and other types of noncurrency transactions are frequently viewed as forms of countertrade. Of course, many noncurrency transactions are entered into for convenience, to provide transportation efficiencies or for similar reasons, and as such, lack the coercive overtones characteristic of typical countertrade transactions. In many cases, however, the sovereign nation will impose a barter requirement in a coercive fashion for purposes of disposing of a surplus of low quality goods that it otherwise cannot sell. In such instances, however, barter, swap, and other noncurrency transactions are correctly characterized as countertrade transactions.

Barter transactions are frequently utilized in crude oil transfers as a means of conveying crude below official OPEC prices. Similarly, barter is occasionally used as a means of "liberating" blocked currencies or otherwise circumventing foreign exchange controls. As pointed out above, barter transactions are increasing in prominence in trade with Latin American and Southeast Asian nations due to recent restrictions on international lending. Unlike classic East-West and Indonesian counterpurchase transactions, however, barter often is not required by the purchasing nation. Rather, the concept of barter frequently is introduced by the private firm selling to the nation as a means of "financing" an otherwise unfinanceable transaction.

Import Entitlement Programs

An *import entitlement* is a government-imposed mechanism under which a party is afforded preferential treatment in obtaining an import license if it arranges an export transaction of equivalent value. In many partly industrialized and Third World nations, hard currency shortages have forced national governments to impose import-licensing programs under which only essential goods are allowed to be imported. Under such programs, exceptions will be made for nonessential items if the importer also arranges an export from that country of equivalent value. An "informal" program of this nature is currently in effect in Brazil on an ad hoc basis. While under an import entitlement program the responsibility to arrange the parallel purchases is placed upon the importer in the foreign nation and not upon the foreign private supplier, the importer will frequently shift the burden of arranging the export purchase to the private supplier. Consequently, the private foreign supplier confronts what amounts to a countertrade requirement. In these situations, while it may not be technically necessary for the foreign private firm to export goods from the host nation, a private firm which is capable of undertaking such exports will be more successful in selling its product to the purchasers in that nation.

Offsets

The term *offsets* is frequently used to describe the practice where the private firm hires subcontractors located within the purchasing nation or uses components or raw materials originating from within the nation. For example, in a railway electrification project recently under bid in New Zealand, bidding consortia offered to purchase certain design, engineering, and construction services locally and substitute locally produced components for items which they would normally import into New Zealand.

Clearing Agreements

While countertrade is conducted most frequently between a sovereign nation and a private firm, countertrade arrangements also occur between and among sovereign nations. Nations have historically entered into bilateral or multilateral *clearing agreements* under which they agree to purchase equal values of each other's products over an agreed period of time. This is a form of reciprocal trading not unlike the private firm-sovereign nation relationships discussed above. Under such arrangements, the participants frequently open reciprocal lines of credit and exchange quantities of goods during a predetermined "clearing period." Clearing accounts are established at international banks and balances kept out of quantities sold or exchanged. At the end of the clearing period, the nations balance the accounts. When an imbalance develops in an account which a nation cannot rectify, private firms known as *switch trading* firms step in to assist a recalcitrant nation in disposing of the goods which it is required to purchase, usually for a fee. Bilateral clearing agreements are most common among Third World and Communist nations, although such arrangements occasionally appear in other contexts as well.

Switch Trading

A *switch trade* is a device used to balance a bilateral clearing agreement. In a bilateral clearing arrangement between Rumania and Brazil, for example, Rumania may have taken more products from Brazil than Brazil has taken from Rumania at the end of the clearing period. In this instance, Brazil will have a "credit" in its "clearing account," or as is frequently described, a surplus of Rumanian "clearing dollars." The problem will arise when there are no available Rumanian products that Brazil is interested in taking. In a switch trade, Brazil will locate a third party which is interested in purchasing Rumanian goods and substitute this third party's purchase of Rumanian goods for its own. Technically, Brazil sells its clearing dollars to the third party and the third party uses these credits to pay for exports from Rumania. Brazil sells the credits at a discount (discounts of up to 30 percent are not uncommon) and receives hard currency from the third party. It is common for a trading intermediary to assist Brazil in locating the third party purchaser. This intermediary, known as a *switch trader*, would generally receive a portion of the discount for its services.

Progressive or Proactive Countertrade

In *progressive* or *proactive* countertrade, a firm purchases goods from a nation prior to the point in time at which it is selling its product to the nation. This is done for the specific purpose of developing the right or opportunity to sell products to the nation in the future. This practice differs from traditional types of countertrade discussed above in that the private firm generates the hard currency for the purchasing nation prospectively, rather than simultaneously or over a period of time subsequent to the sale of its products to the nation. In addition to inducing future sales or otherwise generating goodwill with the nation, the private firm will be in a position to sell its products to the nation without the delay and inconvenience of negotiating post hoc countertrade requirements. Under variations of this type of arrangement, the firm may obtain the right to utilize its credits in serving as an agent for selling the products of other firms to the nation, or if the nation approves, the firm may transfer these credits to other private firms for a fee. Indonesia, for example, has announced that it will allow the crediting of Indonesian exports generated by one firm against the countertrade commitments of another from selling to Indonesia. In cases where the private firm is unable to locate desirable locally produced products for export from the nation to develop countertrade credits, firms have been known to transfer technology and/or establish plants in the nation in an effort to assist the nation to produce items for which the private firm has an established overseas market. The term proactive countertrade is also frequently used to refer to the practice in which the private firm voluntarily offers countertrade to the nation as an inducement to conclude a sale in cases where countertrade is not required.

Framework Agreements

In a countertrade *framework agreement* a private firm establishes a formal, long-term "crediting" mechanism with the host nation under which exports generated by the private firm are routinely credited to the countertrade commitments of numerous third-party firms on an ongoing basis. Under a variation of this type of arrangement, foreign exchange earned by exports generated by the private party is automatically placed in an escrow account and earmarked for payment to private third parties selling to the nation. In these instances, the private party generating the exports is generally paid a fee (for example, 3 to 10 percent) by the third party seller for allowing its "credits" to be utilized by the third party. The key to a framework agreement is that the "crediting" (or escrowing and payment of funds) is undertaken on a routine and ongoing basis under a prearranged agreement rather than on the more common case-by-case basis.

Positive or Reverse Countertrade

In certain instances, private firms prefer countertrade arrangements over conventional transactions. In so-called *positive* or *reverse* countertrade, the private firm views the goods which it will be required to purchase as more valuable than hard currency. This is most often the case when a firm seeks to establish a guaranteed supply of a necessary commodity or production components when it anticipates future shortages of these items. For example, in one of the proposed East-West "gas-for-pipes" transactions known as the North Star Project, a group of private firms was negotiating with the Soviet Union to transfer gas transportation and production equipment and technology to the Soviets in return for guarantees of quantities of natural gas produced through the use of this equipment and technology. In a similar transaction, a U.S. oil firm was reported to have assisted in the development of a $300 million export refinery and a separate $300 million petrochemical complex in Saudi Arabia in exchange for the right to purchase 1.4 billion barrels of Saudi Arabian crude oil over a 15-year period.

Develop-For-Import Transactions

Develop-For-Import transactions are a specialized type of positive countertrade undertaken between an industrialized nation and a developing or Communist nation for the specific purpose of guaranteeing sufficient future supplies of strategic minerals or other scarce resources for the industrialized nation. Under such arrangements, nations such as Germany, France, and Japan will provide the capital, equipment, and technology to develop mining and energy projects in nations rich in resources but lacking the economic and technological capability to develop the same. In exchange, the transferring nation will be guaranteed a long-term supply of the mineral or hydrocarbon produced from the mine or well which it assisted in developing. Develop-For-Import transactions differ from other positive compensation transactions discussed above in that the primary motive of the projects' proponents in undertaking these projects is to establish guaranteed future supplies of the strategic commodity rather than to effectuate the sale of the equipment or technology. In a draft report on Develop-For-Import projects prepared by James I. Walsh of the Office of the U.S. Trade Representative, the author estimates that Germany, Japan, and France will collectively receive over 79 million tons of various minerals, including iron ore, nickel ore, manganese ore, bauxite, alumina, aluminum, chromite and tungsten in 1984 pursuant to Develop-For-Import projects. Similarly, it is estimated that Western European nations will receive some 35 billion cubic meters of Soviet gas per year as a result of the sale of gas production and transportation equipment in the Yamal "gas-for-pipes" transaction with the Soviet Union.

Performance Requirements

A *performance requirement* is a condition imposed by a sovereign government which requires that foreign parties who wish to undertake an investment in that nation agree to take certain steps to increase exports from the nation. Such steps include the agreement by the foreign investors to export a certain percentage of the output from the investment project, to employ a certain level of local inhabitants in the project, to use a predetermined level of locally produced components in the manufactured product and to transfer certain technology to the host nation. Performance requirements are distinguishable from countertrade requirements in that the former involve the private firm's investment in the imposing nation rather than the sale of goods to the nation. Both practices involve intervention by the host nation in the free market process, however, and in light of their similarity, are frequently treated as one and the same phenomenon.

One of the most frequently cited performance requirements is the "Mexican Automotive Decree" pursuant to which foreign-owned automobile assembly enterprises operating in Mexico are required to generate sufficient exports to cover the value of all Mexican imports which occur as part of their respective assembly operations. Another example is a requirement by the Canadian government that in order for a U.S. multinational firm to be permitted to acquire a Quebec truck-body manufacturer, the U.S. firm had to commit to export 80 percent of the plant's output. In testimony on trade-related performance requirements before the Subcommittee on International Economic Policy of the Senate Foreign Relations Committee Alan W. Wolff, counsel to the Labor-Industry Coalition for International Trade, stated that approximately 40 countries impose some form of trade-related performance requirements in connection with automotive production alone. Similarly, the U.S. Department of Commerce Benchmark Survey of U.S. Direct Investment Abroad—1977, reported that 19 percent of U.S.-owned affiliates in developing countries were subject to trade-related performance requirements in 1977.

Collection-Through-Export Transactions

A major problem currently experienced by U.S. firms doing business overseas has been the collection of overseas funds which have been restricted from repatriation due to foreign exchange controls. In such instances, a private firm might be owed funds by a foreign party as a result of a trade debt or have profits in local currency earned by a foreign subsidiary. The private firm will have possession of the local currency, but due to foreign exchange shortages will be unable to convert this currency into dollars. In a *collection-through-export transaction*, the firm will use the local currency to purchase locally produced goods from the host nation and sell the goods overseas for dollars or another convertible currency. The success of this type of transaction is limited due to restrictions on such activities by many host nations, although a limited number of these transactions have nonetheless been successfully concluded.

Miscellaneous Countertrade Variations

Not all countertrade transactions result in the requirement that the private firm purchase goods. The purchasing nation may occasionally require the private firm to establish a plant within the nation, transfer technology to the nation or engage in similar economic practices on a reciprocal basis. Similarly, firms may limit the scope of their obligation merely to "assist" the nation in marketing its products or agreeing to a purchase obligation on a "best efforts" basis, avoiding the payment of a penalty if it is unable to locate purchasers for the nation's products.

HOW U.S. FIRMS ARE RESPONDING TO COUNTERTRADE

Hesitant Response by U.S. Firms

As might be expected, most U.S. firms are hesitant to become involved in countertrade. With the exception of a limited number of major U.S. exporters in the aerospace, automotive, construction, chemical, heavy manufacturing, and high technology fields, most U.S. firms are unaccustomed to countertrade and recognize the substantial risks involved in purchasing quantities of marginally undesirable goods which they have no interest in owning. They recognize as well how countertrade injects layers of complexity into otherwise normal transactions and consumes vast amounts of personnel time. This is in contrast to many West European firms which, due to their greater involvement in East-West trade, have considerably more experience with countertrade. As was the case with their Western European and Japanese counterparts years ago, however, U.S. firms are slowly acknowledging the fact that the risks and inconveniences of countertrade may be acceptable if they serve as the means through which new sales relationships can be established or existing ones retained in the lucrative Third World and Communist markets.

In most cases, the nation will not offer products for barter or countertrade that can be readily sold for cash on the world markets since the nation generally can sell these products to generate foreign exchange. Consequently, the goods that a private firm will be required to take frequently will be of low quality or otherwise not in demand in the world markets. While in a few instances the private firm can use the countertraded goods in-house or may know of a purchaser of such products, most firms are unwilling to assume the risk of purchasing and reselling large quantities of unwanted products. Consequently, firms are faced with the difficult dilemma of either losing traditional markets or being exposed to substantial risks in purchasing untold quantities of undesirable goods. This situation has become particularly severe since countertrade and barter are now becoming an important element in business with most of the Third World nations, major markets for U.S. exporters.

U.S. firms are dealing with countertrade requirements in a variety of ways. As discussed further below, firms occasionally use the countertraded goods in-house. More frequently, however, they utilize the services of brokers to locate third party purchasers or the services of independent trading houses or other "counterpartners" to dispose of the goods. In many instances, the firm will be required to pay a discount or disagio of between one percent to 30 percent of the value of the resold goods as compensation to the trading company or other purchaser. The firm may take title to the products and resell them to the trading company or bring in the trading house to purchase the goods directly from the nation. Firms which are inexperienced in countertrade frequently rely upon the advice of outside trade consultants and legal counsel to assist in negotiating and structuring these arrangements. Multinational corporations frequently reorganize their sales and purchasing activities to maximize benefits in the new countertrading environment.

Companies that have been active in countertrade over a period of time frequently develop in-house trading divisions or subsidiary companies to resell their countertraded goods. Examples of such trading subsidiaries include Motors Trading Corp., a subsidiary of General Motors Corp., and Commerce International Inc., a subsidiary of Control Data Corp. In a number of instances, these in-house countertrading organizations have developed into separate profit centers in the corporate hierarchy by trading in goods unrelated to the parent's countertrade commitments and by assisting other U.S. firms in dealing with their countertrade commitments. This trend toward the establishment of Fortune-500 "Sogo Shoshba" trading houses is seen in the recent establishment of export trading companies by General Electric Co. and Sears, Roebuck and Co.

Services Available to U.S. Firms to Deal with Countertrade

A number of U.S. and foreign trading companies have begun offering services to assist private firms in successfully dealing with countertrade requirements and related trade finance problems. In addition to purchasing countertraded goods from private firms at a discount, trading companies frequently provide services such as structuring the countertrade transaction, negotiating with the host government pertaining to the "linkage" of the various commodities involved, and financing of the transactions. The trading company frequently will enter into an agreement to purchase the countertraded commodities from the private firm before the firm enters into the transaction with the foreign nation, thus substantially reducing the firm's risk of being left holding the unwanted product. In addition, the trading company may even purchase the private firm's export product, sell the product to the purchasing nation and purchase the countertraded goods. In such a case, the U.S. firm is paid in dollars in the United States and avoids the complexity of dealing with the foreign nation in either the primary sale or the countertrade. The fees charged for such services generally range from 1 to 10 percent of the value of the countertraded goods but may be higher in instances involving certain countries or commodities. In addition to trading companies, countertrade brokers and consultants provide many of the same services described above without taking title to the goods.

Similarly, a number of these trading companies provide services related to the "liberation" of blocked currencies. These firms have developed various techniques for purchasing local currencies from U.S. exporters for hard currency at a discount and using these currencies in their trading operations. The likelihood of success of these transactions and the fees charged for such services, however, vary considerably depending upon the country and currency involved, the capability of the trading company, the size of the transaction and the time during which the transaction is taking place.

Banks have become intimately involved in countertrade as well. Many of the largest U.S.-based international banks as well as a surprising number of small and regional banks have established countertrade departments. The purposes of these departments are not only to finance countertrade transactions but also to advise customers regarding the structuring and execution of such transactions and even to assist customers in locating purchasers for their countertraded products. With the enactment of the Export Trading Company Act of 1982, bank holding companies now are permitted to acquire equity interests in trading companies and indirectly to take title to countertraded goods for resale on behalf of their customers. Banks that have established countertrade units within the recent past for one or more of these purposes include Citicorp, European American Bank, Manufacturer's Hanover Trust Company, Chemical Bank, Bank of America, and First Chicago.

Opportunities for Importers, Trading Companies and End Users Arising Out of Countertrade

The recent rise in countertrade has presented significant opportunities for U.S. trading companies, multinationals, importers/distributors and end-users that purchase goods offered by countertrade nations. In most cases, U.S. exporters have no use for the goods that they are forced to purchase and consequently must find markets for these goods elsewhere. With the exception of the largest U.S. manufacturing companies, however, most of these firms do not have the expertise to dispose of such goods alone and frequently look to locate *counterpartners*, parties that will purchase goods offered by these nations. In most instances, parties that agree to purchase the countertraded goods are paid a fee or subsidy by the private firms as compensation for their involvement in the transaction. Hence, a firm that purchases products from a countertrade country and links such purchases with an export to that country can receive products at a price substantially below the world market. Trading companies and importers/distributors will sell these goods for a profit; end-users will have acquired products at substantial savings. As pointed out above, the fees or discounts paid to the counterpartner in such transactions can range up to 10 percent or more of the value of the counterpurchase depending upon the commodity and the country in question. Additionally, firms that purchase products from countertrade nations, especially Rumania, Yugoslavia, Hungary, Poland and Czechoslovakia, are sought after by switch trading houses, firms that assist Third World nations in fulfilling bilateral trade commitments. Such trading firms offer fees of between 1 and 10 percent for being able to link such purchases to bilateral purchasing agreements of their client nations. The danger exists, however, that the U.S. exporter looking to unload unwanted countertrade imports at significant discounts could depress the U.S. price for the commodity, causing injury to other U.S. importers or competing domestic manufacturers. In addition, the linkage of exports and imports in countertrade and switch transactions raises a variety of antitrust and other legal issues which should be adequately addressed by all of the parties to the transaction.

METHODS FOR DISPOSING OF COUNTERTRADED GOODS

Although there is no established procedure for disposing of countertraded goods, U.S. exporters have employed a number of methods for dealing with this problem. A sample of these methods is set forth below.

Use in Production Process

To start, a firm would first look to see if the goods offered are materials or components that it would normally purchase from another source for use in its manufacturing process. If the quality and price of the available goods meet the company's purchasing requirements, the countertraded items could be substituted for the goods which it is currently purchasing with no negative financial effect upon the company.

Nonproduction In-house Use

As in the case with production-related purchasing, the company may be able to substitute a portion of the countertraded goods for goods which it is already purchasing for nonproduction purposes such as office equipment and supplies, construction and maintenance materials, transportation equipment, food products, and employee incentive items. Recent examples of the in-house use of goods purchased by U.S. firms pursuant to countertrade obligations include the use of Polish hams in the company cafeteria and vacation trips to the second party nation for employee incentive purposes.

Already Purchasing Products from the Country in Question

Large manufacturing companies frequently purchase materials and supplies from a variety of foreign sources. Occasionally, these companies will already be purchasing goods from countries that are imposing a countertrade requirement on them in connection with an unrelated sale. It is often possible to obtain a credit for the existing purchasing practices to be applied against a countertrade requirement.

Countertraded Goods to Be Used by Subcontractors

Even though the company may not be able to use all or a portion of the offered goods, other companies with which it works closely, including subcontractors or suppliers, may be able to use a portion of these goods either in their manufacturing process or for other in-house purposes. Occasionally, U.S. firms have requested that such companies assist them in meeting countertrade obligations. As stated above, parties should use considerable care in communicating these requests and establishing these relationships, in order not to violate U.S. antitrust laws or similar legal proscriptions.

Specification Production

The second party nation may agree to manufacture goods according to specifications that the first party company provides. These goods would then be used in the company's manufacturing process, for other in-house purposes, or disposed of by other methods discussed above and below.

Sale of Goods to U.S. Importers, Distributors, or Ultimate Purchasers

The predominant method of fulfilling barter/countertrade obligations is for companies to locate an independent party to purchase the countertraded goods. This purchaser can be the ultimate user of goods in question or a distributor or importer who is in the business of purchasing these goods for resale. Obviously, it is preferable to have the third party purchaser available prior to entering into the countertrade agreement.

Transfer to Trading Company

Finally, it is common for U.S. companies to utilize the services of an independent trading company in disposing of countertraded goods. This can be undertaken in a number of ways, including taking title to the goods in question and reselling them to the trading company, assigning the counterpurchase agreement to the trading company without taking title to the goods, or utilizing the trading company as a broker or finder in locating foreign buyers. It is not uncommon for the private first party actually to bring a representative of the trading company to the negotiations with the second party nation in order to determine at an early stage the economic feasibility of proposed countertrade requirements.

APPENDIX A

Appendix Table 2.1 Identified Chemical Compensation Agreements with Eastern Europe

Western Company	Year Contract Signed	Eastern Country	Equipment Supplied	Total Value of Eastern Export ($ million)	Planned Yearly Value of Exports ($ million)	Time-span of Buy-back Deliveries
Occidental Petroleum (USA)	1978	Poland	Phosphate rock	670	33.5	1978-97
Rhone Poulenc/Institut Francais du Petrole (France)	1975	,,	Chemicals and textile fibres	*	*	*
Ugine Kuhlmann (France)	1976	,,	Unspecified cooperation in chemical production	*	*	*
Uhde/Hoechst (Germany)	1976	East Germany	Complex of 4 plants including 1 for producing caustic soda	32	4	1980-87
Catalytic (United Kingdom)	1977	East Germany	Chlorine plant	11.5	2.3	*
Petrocarbon Developments (United Kingdom)	1975	Poland	Chlorine plant (part of larger deal)	*	*	1980-89
Krebs, Klockner (France and Germany)	1975	Poland	Soda ash plant	180	30	1980-85
De Nora (Italy)	1978	Rumania	2 chlorine plants	*	*	*
Chemie Linz (Austria)	1976	East Germany	Pesticides, herbicide agents and fertilizers	58.58	*	*
Vereinigte Edelstahlwerke (Austria)	1977	East Germany	Fine steel products	*	*	*
Haldor Topsoe (Denmark)	1978	Bulgaria	Ammonia plant	7	1	1978-84
Creusot Loire (France)	1976	Poland	2 ammonia plants	520	52	1983-92
Creusot Loire (France)	1974	USSR	4 ammonia plants	270	27	1980-89

(Table 2.1 continues)

29

Appendix Table 2.1 (Continued)

Western Company	Year Contract Signed	Eastern Country	Equipment Supplied	Total Value of Eastern Export ($ million)	Planned Yearly Value of Exports ($ million)	Time-span of Buy-back Deliveries
Occidental Petroleum (USA)	1974	USSR	Building facilities for storing and handling fertilizers, including ammonia and deliveries of super phosphoric acid	10,000	441	1978-97
Klockner-Davy Powergas (West Germany)	1977	"	Phtalic anhydride plant and maleic anhydride plant	20	2	1980-89
Snamprogetti/Anic (Italy)	1975	"	3 urea plants	115	11.5	1979-88
Montedison (Italy)	1973	"	3 urea plants	287	28.7 (ammonia)	1978-87
				78	7.8 (urea)	1976-85
Mitsui/Toyo (Japan)	1976	"	4 ammonia plants	240	11	1977-97
Klockner-Davy Powergas (Germany)	1976	"	Phthalic anhydride plant, fumaric acid unit	20	2	1980-89
Krupp led consortium (Germany)	1976	Poland	Coal gasification plants	*	*	*
ENI (Italy)	1975	USSR	2 urea plants	*	*	*
Lurgi (Germany)	1976	Bulgaria	Polypropylene plant	*	*	*
Mitsui (Japan)	1977	East Germany	Benzene plant (part of aromatics complex)	150	25	1983-88
Technip (France)	1976	USSR	2 aromatics complexes	950	95	1980-89

30

				($ million)	($ million)	
Krupp-Koppers (Germany)	1976	USSR	Dimethylterephthalate plant	100	10	1981-90
Uhde/Hoechst (Germany)	1977	"	Polyester staple fiber plant	*	9	1981-87
Rhone-Poulenc (France)	1976	"	Complex deal including supply of equipment and chemicals	*	*	1984-93
Chisso (Japan)	1972	Czechoslovakia	Polypropylene plant	*	5	*
Salzgitter (Germany)	1972	USSR	Polyethylene plant	170	13	1971-83
same	1973	"	"	225	25	1978-86
CJB/Union Carbide (United Kingdom)	1974	"	"	70	7	1980-89
same	1977	"	"	162	16	1983-93
Litwin (France)	1973	"	Plants to produce styrene and polystyrene	160	19	1979-87
Marubeni (Japan)	1975	"	Extension of plant to 75,000 t/yr of acrylonitrile	30	6	1978-82
Montedison (Italy)	1973	"	Acrylonitrile plant	150	15	1980-90
Krupp-Koppers (Germany)	1976	"	2 DMT plants	100	10	1981-90
same	1978	"	"	150	15	1981-
Uhde-Hoechst (Germany)	1977	"	Polyester staple fiber plant	*	9	
Technip/Technipetrol (France-Italy)	1972	Bulgaria	Ethylene plant	10	2.2	1979-83
Salzgitter (Germany)	1976	USSR	Ethylene oxide plant	100	10	1979-88
Lummus-Monsanto (USA)	1975	"	Acetic acid plant	*	*	*
Snia Viscosa (Italy)	1975	"	Caprolactam plant	224	28	*

(Table 2.1 continues)

31

Appendix Table 2.1 (Continued)

Western Company	Year Contract Signed	Eastern Country	Equipment Supplied	Total Value of Eastern Export ($ million)	Planned Yearly Value of Exports ($ million)	Time-span of Buy-back Deliveries
Klockner-Davy Powergas (Germany)	1976	USSR	Phthalic anhydride plant and fumaric acid unit	50	7	1980-89
same	1977	"	Phthalic anhydride plant and maleic anhydride plant	50	7	1980-89
Hoechst-Uhde-Wacker (Germany)	1974	"	VCM plant	66	16.5	1976-79
Klockner-Hols (Germany)	1974	"	PVC plant	33	3.30	*
same	1974	Bulgaria	PVC plant	25	3.5	1980-88
same	1974	USSR	PVC plant	54	5.4	1978-87
Uhde/Hoechst (Germany)	1976	East Germany	PVC plant in complex	80	10	1980-87
Kommerling (Germany)	1977	Hungary	License and equipment for making windows from synthetic materials	*	*	*
Chemie Linz/Voest Alpine (Austria)	1974	Poland	Melamine resin plant	*	*	*
Dow Chemical Europe (West Germany)	1977	East Germany	Propylene oxide	85	*	1979-88
Montedison (Italy)	1973	USSR	11 chemical plants	57.5	5.75	1980-90

32

Rhone-Poulenc (France)	1976	”	Complex deals including supply of equipments and chemicals	34.5	3.45	1981-90
Krupp-Koppers (Germany)	1976	”	Dimethylterephthalate plant	100	10	1981-90
Davy-Powergas/ICI/Klockner (United Kingdom-Germany)	1977	”	2 methanol plants	345	34.5	1981-90
Uhde-Hoechst (Germany)	1977	”	Polyester staple fiber plant	*	9	1981-87

*Not available.

Sources: Compiled from various published sources including "Soviet Chemical Equipment Purchases from the West: Impact on Production and Foreign Trade," *Central Intelligence Agency*, October 1978, and "East-West Trade in Chemicals," *Organization for Economic Co-operation and Development*, 1980. Reprinted from *Analysis of Recent Trends in U.S. Countertrade*, Report in Investigation No. 332-125 Under Section 332 of the Tariff Act of 1930., USITC Publication, March 1982.

APPENDIX B

Appendix Table 2.2 Examples of Countertrade Transactions Involving U.S. Companies

U.S. Company	Product Sold	Product Returned	Date of Contract	Country
Airco, Inc.	1,500 tons/yr. steel mill	Chromium	1971	USSR
Ashland Oil, Inc. and General Dynamics	F-16 Fighter jets	Oil	*	Iran
China Trade Corp. (U.S.) Konrad Hornschuch AG (FGR)	2 plants for the production of PVC foils	Artificial leather	Nov. 1978	China
Clarke Equipment Credit	Machinery, know-how	Rear axles	†	China
Clark Equipment	License for manufacture of construction equipment	Axles	1972	Poland
Container Transport Int'l (U.S.) and Givet (HK)	Container plants (2) Guangdong, Tianjin	Marine containers used in int'l shipping	Feb. 1979	China
Coco-Cola	Syrup/technology	Krakus beer	*	Poland
DeKalb Agresearch (U.S.)/ Nichimen (Japan)	Technical advice, agricultural training	Soybeans	†	China
Do All	Machinery, know-how	Saws	†	China
Dow Chemical	Propylene oxide	Propylene	*	East Germany
FMC	300 mt./yr. powdered pectin plant	*	1973	Poland
General Electric	License and machines for production of medical equipment	Electrocardiogram meters	1976	Poland
General Motors	Technology for building vans	Lightweight vans	1975	Poland
General Motors	Earth-moving trucks	Timber	*	USSR
General Tire and Rubber Co.	Equipment and technology to build truck tires	Truck tires	*	Rumania

Company	Description	Product	Year	Country
Gettys Inc.	Technology and gear box components	Electrical motors and drive systems for incorporation into machine tools	1978	Hungary
Goodyear	Materials, equipment training for printing plant	Labels, packing material, etc.	1979	China
Hesston	Harvesters and hay-handling	Heads and gear boxes for harvesters	1977	Hungary
International Harvester	Design and technology for tractor production	Tractor components	*	Poland
International Harvester	License for manufacture of tractors and accessories	Tractors and accessories	1972	Poland
Katy Industries	Machinery and technology for shoe production	Shoes	1976	Poland
Katy Industries	Technology for manufacturing women's shoes	Women's shoes	1976	Hungary
Levi Strauss	Technology for producing jeans	Jeans	*	Hungary
Marathon Mfg. Co.	Offshore drilling rigs	Petroleum	*	China
McDonnell Douglas Aircraft Co.	DC 9 aircraft	Hams and other products	*	Yugoslavia
McGraw-Edison	Power system electronics plants	Electronic goods	†	China
Mego Cor.	Industrial sewing machines	Doll costumes	†	China
Norton	Supply of machines and equipment for production of abrasive discs	*	1975	Poland
Occidental Petroleum	Ammonia, urea complex	Ammonia, urea, potash	*	USSR
Occidental Petroleum	Phosphate rock	Sulphur	1978	Poland
Oxford Industries	Apparel finishing equipment	Suits	1978	China
Pepsico	Cola concentrate bottling facilities	Soviet vodka	*	USSR

(Table 2.2 continues)

35

Table 2.2 (Continued)

U.S. Company	Product Sold	Product Returned	Date of Contract	Country
Pepsico	Bottling plant and cola syrup	Vodka	*	USSR
Philip-Morris (via European subsidiaries)	Tobacco production machinery	Tobacco	1978	USSR
Prestige	Textile machines	Resultant product	Nov. 1978	China
Pullman Kellogg (U.S.) DAYY Int'l (U.K.)	Technology for aromatics plant	Chemicals	*	East Germany
Steiger Tractor, Division of International Harvester	Component technology	Tractor axles	*	Hungary
Textron	Supply of plant for brass and copper strip mill	Copper and brass mill products	1973	Poland
Thyssen, Inc. (U.S.)	U.S. scrap	Steel (Korean)	*	Korea, et al.
Union Carbide	Chemical technology	Polyethylene	*	USSR
Union Carbide, et al.	Technology	Unspecified chemicals	1977	USSR
Universal Machinery Equipment Co.	Technology for producers' electrical furnaces	Electrical furnaces	1977	Hungary
Waterbury Farrell	Steel rolling mill	Surface-grinding machinery	1973	Poland
Waterbury Farrell	Brass and copper strip mill	Miscellaneous products, including copper and brass	1975	Poland
Westinghouse	License, equipment	Semiconductors	1974	Poland

*Unknown.

†Under negotiations.

Sources: Compiled from data obtained from personal interviews, and published sources including Pompiliu Verzariu, "Countertrade Practices in East Europe, the Soviet Union, and China: An Introductory Guide to Business," U.S. Department of Commerce, 1980. Reprinted from Analysis of Recent Trends in U.S. Countertrade, Report in Investigation No. 332-125 Under Section 332 of the Tariff Act of 1930., USITC Publication, March 1982.

3
STRUCTURING BARTER
AND
COUNTERTRADE TRANSACTIONS
David N. Koschik

A barter or countertrade contract, like any contract, is the legal instrument that binds two parties to the intentions expressed in negotiations leading up to the finalization of the contract. Any individual barter or countertrade contract is, and should be, unique to the arrangement it covers. No contract is simply a random series of clauses; rather, each is an integrated legal instrument in which every clause affects the interpretation that will be given of the other clauses.

Although the final contract ultimately will depend on the particular individuals and products involved, parties entering a barter or countertrade arrangement share certain common concerns. In response to these concerns, various general provisions have been developed to protect and further the parties' interests.

The discussion and sample clauses presented below are not intended to serve as model contracts, but as aids to the practitioner in spotting issues and to suggest possible methods of dealing with those issues.

Although an actual contract should never be viewed as a sample series of clauses, a great deal of what is presented below is just that— a series of sample clauses that can be examined, analyzed, expanded, and adapted to specific situations. The subject of barter and countertrade contracts, outside of the East-West arena, is quite new and underdeveloped. The "form" contracts that were developed to facilitate East-West countertrade arrangements are used less as developing countries and U.S. firms become increasingly innovative and creative. The methods used in the East-West context are available as a guide but should in no way be seen as restraints in structuring countertrade arrangements.*

Because of the currently evolving nature of barter and countertrade arrangements, opinions on the best method of structuring such transactions vary greatly. This chapter is aimed not at reaching a conclusion regarding the optimal method of structuring a barter or countertrade transaction because there simply is none; rather, it is intended as a guide to the issues and options open to the lawyer drafting such an unfamiliar instrument.

This chapter will examine three types of transactions—barter, counterpurchase, and compensation, providing a diagram of each (along with a brief explanation of the diagram), a contract checklist, and, where appropriate and helpful, sample clauses adapted from actual transactions and explanations of the terms.†

THE BARTER TRANSACTION

The barter transaction provides a means for the exchange of two commodities between two parties. The key to understanding a barter transaction is to recognize that there is no financing involved in the arrangement. The drafter of a barter transaction contract must take a conventional international sales contract designed for the exchange of one commodity for cash, and amend it to cover the exchange of one commodity for another.

In some respects, the barter contract and the transaction it governs will continue to resemble the conventional sales transaction. Like the conventional international sales transaction, the barter transaction generally requires the use of only one contract. In addition, many of the provisions in the barter transaction are the same as those in an international sales contract.

Barter contracts differ from conventional sales contracts in several important respects. First, many of the clauses must be included

---

*For example, the separate contract method, discussed below, is presently being critically evaluated as banks become more experienced in and less skeptical about countertrade transactions.

†Each of the following is an application of the work of Thomas B. McVey. The contract checklists, for example, were developed by Mr. McVey and discussed in a recent article: McVey, "Countertrade and Barter: Alternative Trade Financing by Third World Nations," *Int'l Trade LJ 6* (1980-1981) p. 197. This chapter represents an attempt to expand on the ideas already presented in the literature on barter and countertrade transactions; diagrams and sample provisions are presented in order to illustrate the analysis.

twice since the contract deals with two distinct commodities with distinct characteristics. Second, since there is no conventional financing involved, the contract must be written in such a way that the security normally provided through the use of a letter of credit is provided in other ways. Third, because of the complexity involved in exchanging two goods and the unique way in which the goods are tied to each other (one being the "payment" for the other), it is particularly important that the barter transaction be drafted clearly and precisely, and that it include contingency and escape clauses to protect the parties in case disputes or other difficulties are encountered.

After explaining a diagram of the barter transaction (Figure 3.1) and a suggested checklist, I will set forth a sample barter contract with corresponding explanations of the various provisions. Although some of the clauses found below were modeled on the barter agreement entered into between the government of the United States and the government of Jamaica for the exchange of bauxite for certain agricultural commodities, it is emphasized once again that this is meant not as a model contract but as a *sample* contract. It is useful to see how a barter arrangement might be structured and where certain clauses are needed, but the substance of any particular clause should not be relied upon as a model provision.

EXPLANATION OF BARTER DIAGRAM

1. Country A and Country B enter into a barter contract for the exchange of Commodity 1 for Commodity 2.
2. Commodity 1 is transferred from Country B to Country A. To facilitate this transfer, three separate auxiliary contracts are entered into:
2(a). A contract is entered into with a shipping line for carriage or transportation of the good;
2(b). A contract is entered into with an insurance company to insure the goods in transit; and
2(c). A bank guarantee, or standby letter of credit is obtained as security for performance (that is, timely delivery of conforming goods).
3. Commodity 2 is transferred from Country A to Country B. This transfer also calls for three additional auxiliary contracts:
3(a). A contract of carriage for Commodity 2;
3(b). An insurance contract for Commodity 2; and
3(c). A bank guarantee or standby letter of credit securing delivery of Commodity 2.

Figure 3.1 Barter transaction.

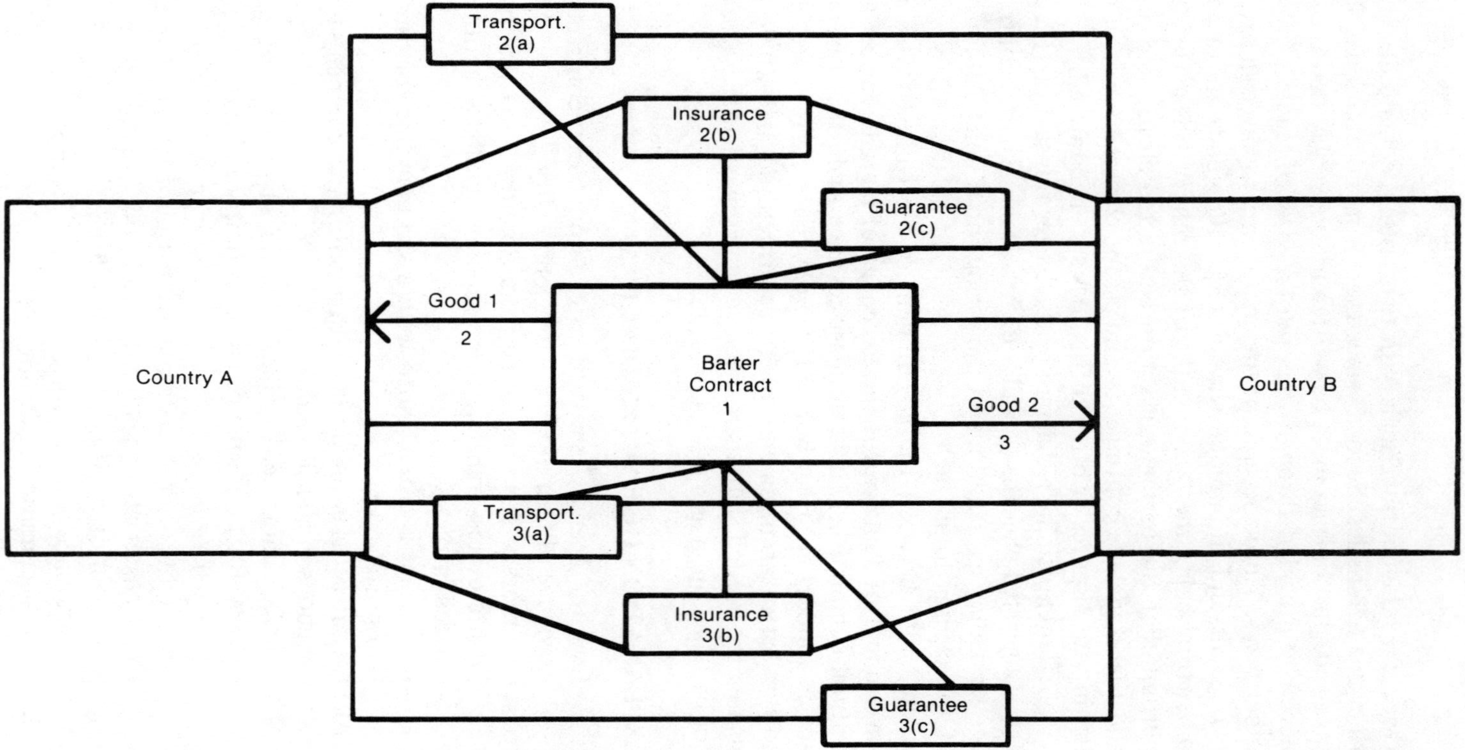

Sample Barter Contract
Agreement for the Barter of Commodity 1
for Commodity 2

1. This Agreement is entered into this 21st day of February, 1984, between the Government of the United States of America represented by the Commodity Credit Corporation, an agency and instrumentality of the United States within the Department of Agriculture (CCC) and the Government of Country A represented by Ministry X (Ministry X).

2. *Whereas*, CCC desires to enter into a barter arrangement with Ministry X under which CCC agrees to sell to Ministry X a quantity of Commodity 1 equal to $10,000,000 (total value).
    Whereas, Ministry X desires to enter into a barter arrangement with CCC under which Ministry X agrees to sell to CCC a quantity of Commodity 2 equal to $10,000,000 (total value).
    Now, therefore, CCC and Ministry X agree as follows:

3. CCC acknowledges its obligation to provide the above-stated quantity of Commodity 1 and accept delivery of the above-stated quantity of Commodity 2 in accordance with the terms of this Agreement so long as Ministry X meets its obligations under this Agreement entirely.

4. Ministry X acknowledges its obligation to provide the above-stated quantity of Commodity 2 and accept delivery of the above-stated quantity of Commodity 1 in accordance with the terms of this Agreement so long as CCC meets its obligations under this Agreement entirely.

5. *First Party Goods*
    5(a).   [Description of Goods, Specifications]
    5(b).   CCC shall deliver a quantity of Commodity 1 such that the total value of all shipments will equal $10,000,000. The acceptable international price per ton of Commodity 1 at the time of each shipment shall determine the value of each shipment. Such shipment value shall be subtracted from the total value due to be shipped at the point of acceptance by Ministry X. Shipments shall be made in accordance with the provisions of article 5(c).
    5(c).   CCC shall make 10 approximately equal shipments of Commodity 1 to Country A. The shipments shall be approximately 1 month apart beginning 2 months after the signing of this Agreement. Under no circumstances shall the final shipment be made later than 18 months from the signing of this Agreement.

In accordance with the provisions of article 5(e), CCC is responsible for transporting Commodity 1 to the U.S.A. port. CCC shall notify Ministry X at least 20 days before the date each shipment will reach port. At least 10 days prior to such date Ministry X shall furnish CCC with a notice to deliver listing the vessel name, estimating time of arrival and port.

5(d). Commodity 1 shall be transported in 10' × 5' crates bearing the following markings:

1) Name of product,
2) Name and location of manufacturing plant,
3) Month and year manufactured,
4) Manufacturer's lot number

5(e). CCC shall deliver Commodity 1 to Ministry X f.a.s. U.S.A. port.

Ministry X shall be responsible for all expenses after delivery by CCC of Commodity 1 to f.a.s. U.S.A. port, including any expenses for failure of vessel to lift all or part of the shipment as scheduled, pier or warehouse storage, rail, truck and/or barge demurrage, reinspection, and deterioration.

5(f). Ministry X shall be responsible for entering into an insurance contract that will cover the goods onward from the point where title passes from CCC (f.a.s. U.S.A. port).

5(g). CCC shall furnish to Ministry X an inspection and grading certificate issued by the U.S. Department of Agriculture showing the manufacture date, quality, and origin of each shipment of Commodity 1. The inspection and grading certificate will be the only document required to be presented by CCC evidencing the date of manufacture, quality, and origin of Commodity 1.

CCC shall furnish a copy of: (a) any over, short, or damage report for each shipment; (b) a dock receipt; and (c) a consignee receipt.

Ministry X will furnish to CCC one copy of the signed on-board ocean bill of lading showing the ultimate destination of Commodity 1 in Country A.

CCC shall furnish Ministry X, or its designated agent, with an invoice and a copy of each required document promptly after each shipment.

6. *Second Party Goods*
   6(a). [Description of Goods, Specifications]

6(b). Ministry X shall deliver a quantity of Commodity 2 such that the total value of all shipments will equal $10,000,000. The acceptable international price per ton of Commodity 2 at the time of each shipment shall determine the value of each shipment. Such shipment value shall be subtracted from the total value due to be shipped at the point of acceptance by CCC. Shipments shall be made in accordance with the provisions of article 6(c).

6(c). Ministry X shall make 5 approximately equal shipments of Commodity 2 to CCC. The shipments shall be approximately 2 months apart beginning 2 months after the signing of this Agreement. Under no circumstances shall the final shipment be made later than 18 months from the signing of this Agreement.

In accordance with the provisions of article 6(e), Ministry X is responsible for transporting Commodity 2 to the Country A port. Ministry X shall notify CCC at least 20 days before the date each shipment will reach port. At least 10 days prior to such date CCC shall furnish Ministry X with a notice to deliver listing the vessel name, estimated time of arrival, and port.

6(d). Commodity 2 shall be transported to 2' X 3' cardboard boxes on wooden pallets bearing the following markings:
1) Name of product,
2) Name and location of manufacturing plant,
3) Month and year manufactured,
4) Manufacturer's lot number

6(e). Ministry X shall deliver Commodity 2 to CCC f.a.s. Country A port.

CCC shall be responsible for all expenses after delivery by Ministry X to f.a.s. U.S.A. port, including any expenses for failure of vessel to lift all or part of the shipment as scheduled, pier or warehouse storage, rail, truck and/or barge demurrage, reinspection, and deterioration.

6(f). CCC shall be responsible for entering into an insurance contract that will cover the goods onward from the point where title passes from Ministry X (f.a.s. Country A port).

6(g). Ministry X shall furnish a copy of: (a) any over, short, or damage report for each shipment; (b) a dock receipt, and (c) a consignee receipt;

CCC will furnish to Ministry X one copy of the signed on-board ocean bill of lading showing the ultimate destination of Commodity 2 in the U.S.A.

Ministry X shall furnish CCC, or its designated agent, with an invoice and a copy of each required document promptly after each shipment.

7. *Finance Arrangements*

7(a). CCC shall arrange with its bank in the United States for the issuance of a standby letter of credit in the amount of $10,000,000 as a guarantee of performance of its obligations under the Agreement. Such standby letter of credit shall provide that if CCC fails to meet its obligations under the Agreement, Ministry X is entitled to draw payment in dollars for the goods shipped to CCC. Ministry X shall have the standby guarantee confirmed by its bank in Country A.

In the event that CCC is found, in the arbitration process established in article 16 of this Agreement, substantially to have breached its obligations, Ministry X has the option to be paid in full by drawing payment through the standby letter of credit for the amount found to be still owing Ministry X. If CCC shall later be in a position to perform, Ministry X shall have the option but shall be under absolutely no obligation to purchase the conforming shipments of Commodity 1.

7(b). Ministry X shall arrange with its bank in Country A for the issuance of a standby letter of credit in the amount of $10,000,000 as a guarantee of performance of its obligations under the Agreement. Such standby letter of credit shall provide that if Ministry X fails to meet its obligations under the Agreement, CCC is entitled to draw payment in dollars for the goods shipped to Ministry X. CCC shall have the standby guarantee confirmed by its bank in the United States.

In the event that Ministry X is found, in the arbitration process established in article 16 of this Agreement, to have substantially breached its obligations, CCC has the option to be paid in full by drawing payment through the standby letter of credit for the amount found to be still owing CCC. If Ministry X shall later be in a position to perform, CCC shall have the option but shall be under absolutely no obligation to purchase the conforming shipments of Commodity 2.

8. *Quality Assurance*

    8(a). The goods delivered by both CCC and Ministry X shall be of sufficient quality that they meet all specifications listed and pass all inspection and testing procedures provided for in this Agreement.

        If the goods delivered under the terms of this Agreement are not of sufficient quality to meet all of the listed specifications and requirements, the shipment shall not be accepted. In such case the party refusing to accept the goods shall promptly notify the delivering party of the refusal to accept the goods and shall list in a clear and detailed manner the reasons for the refusal to accept.

        If the delivered goods comply with all specifications listed in this Agreement, the shipment shall be accepted.

9. *Inspection*

    9(a). Ministry X shall have the right to inspect shipments of Commodity 1 at the U.S.A. port of export and the right to reject any portion of the shipment that does not meet the terms and conditions of this Agreement.

    9(b). CCC shall have the right to inspect shipments of Commodity 2 at the Country A port of export and the right to reject any portion that does not meet the terms and conditions of this Agreement.

10. In the event that any shipment fails the testing or inspection requirements of this Agreement, the delivering party may request that a sample of the shipment be sent to a neutral surveyor for analysis. The neutral surveyor shall be mutually acceptable to both CCC and Ministry X. Each party shall send its testing results to the neutral surveyor. The cost of the neutral surveyor shall be paid by the party whose analysis is the farthest from the neutral surveyor's results. If both are of equal difference from the neutral surveyor, the cost will be shared equally.

11. Promptly after the signing of this Agreement, the parties hereto shall establish a Management Committee to oversee the performance of this Agreement. CCC and Ministry X shall each appoint two members to the Committee. Each party shall appoint an alternate member. The Management Committee will not be empowered to revise or amend this Agreement.

    Subject to requirements set forth in this Agreement, the Management Committee will coordinate efforts among the parties and resolve problems which may arise in the administration of this Agreement. Meetings may be called by either party upon seven days notice and will be held at the principal location of the non-requesting party. An agenda will be proposed for each meeting and distributed by the host at least three working days prior to the meeting. Minutes of each meeting will be published by the host within five working days after the meeting.

12. Any disputes arising under this Agreement concerning a question of law or fact shall first be taken to the Management Committee established under article 11 of this Agreement. Any disputes not settled by the Management Committee shall be finally settled in arbitration according to the provisions of article 16 of this Agreement.

13. *Transshipping*

13(a). Ministry X shall export the Commodity 1 delivered by CCC only to Country A. The Commodity 1 shall not be reentered by anyone into the United States nor shall Ministry X cause the Commodity 1 to be transshipped to any other country. If any quantity of Commodity 1 is transshipped or caused to be transshipped by Ministry X to any other country other than Country A, Ministry A shall be in default and shall be subject to the penalties of section (d) of this article of the Agreement.

13(b). CCC shall export the Commodity 2 delivered by Ministry X only to the United States. The Commodity 2 shall not be reentered by anyone into Country A nor shall CCC cause the Commodity 2 to be transshipped to any other country. If any quantity of Commodity 2 is transshipped or caused to be transshipped by CCC to any other country other than the United States, CCC shall be in default and shall be subject to the penalties of section (d) of this Agreement.

13(c). The exchange of Commodity 1 for Commodity 2 covered by this Agreement is made upon condition that both CCC and Ministry X comply with the export requirements of this Agreement.

13(d). If either party is found to be in violation of the export requirements of this Agreement, that party shall be responsible to the other party in the sum of 50 percent of the value of the shipment in question to be paid in dollars.

14. In the event of late delivery, delivery of nonconforming goods, or failure to deliver a particular shipment, the delivering party shall be responsible for all expenses resulting from such failure.

In the event of two consecutive shipments involving late delivery, delivery of nonconforming goods, or failure to deliver, in any combination, the delivering party shall be responsible for all expenses resulting from such failure and shall pay a sum of 20 percent of the value of the shipments in question to the other party.

In the event of three consecutive shipments involving late delivery, delivery of nonconforming goods, or failure to deliver, in any combination, such action shall constitute a substantial breach of the Agreement entitling the nonbreaching party to resort to its remedy under article 7 of this Agreement.

15. Neither CCC nor Ministry X shall be liable for any failure or delay in complying with their respective responsibilities under this Agreement caused in whole or part by force majeure which shall include, but not be restricted to, acts of God or of the public enemy, acts of Government, fires, floods, epidemics, quarantine, restrictions, strikes, freight embargoes, and unusually severe weather; however, in every case the failure to perform must be beyond the control and without the fault or negligence of the party to the Agreement seeking excuse from liability.

16. Disputes arising under this Agreement shall be finally settled under the Rules of Conciliation of the International Chamber of Commerce or by one or more arbitrators appointed in accordance with the rules thereof.

17. The Agreement shall be governed by the laws of the State of New York.

EXPLANATIONS OF BARTER CONTRACT TERMS

1. *Parties.* As in any international sales contract, the parties must be identified at the outset. The agreement shown here is between two sovereign nations: the United States and Country A. Although many barter transactions are intergovernmental in nature, they also can occur between private parties or between a private party and a sovereign nation.

2. *Recitals.* The recitals identify the contract as a barter arrangement and set forth the general desires and intentions of the parties.

3.-4. *Acknowledgment of Obligation of Parties to Provide and Accept Goods.* Conventional international sales contracts include an acknowledgment, generally included in the recitals, of the obligation on the part of the buyer to purchase the goods. Similar recitals in barter contracts acknowledge each party's obligation to carry out the exchange.

5. First Party Goods

5(a). Description of Goods, Specifications. Since this agreement involves a hypothetical commodity, no description is given. In an actual agreement, however, this provision is very important and warrants a great deal of attention.

With two commodities, the risk that the agreement will break over a dispute concerning the goods involved is twice that involved in a conventional international sales contract. For this reason it is crucial that the parties incorporate into the barter arrangement detailed descriptions of both commodities. The description should include any and all specifications that the commodities will be expected to meet. The stipulation of precise specifications will: 1) reduce the possibility of a dispute over the goods tendered since both parties are on notice as to the other's expectations; and 2) make the resolution of any dispute much easier because an arbitration tribunal could look to the actual terms of the contract for guidance rather than having to determine the parties' intentions based on general descriptions of the goods to be exchanged.

5(b). Quantity. Since the agreement has stated a total value for the arrangement, some mechanism is needed to translate the monetary value into a specific quantity of commodity 1. One way to do this is to value each shipment according to the acceptable international price at the time of the shipment. This is particularly important if portions of the total amount due will be shipped in increments over a period of time. The prices for some commodities fluctuate fairly widely according to season and demand and tying the quantity to the world price is a form of protection for both parties.

It should be noted that many barter arrangements are carried out relatively soon after signing. For this reason it is less likely that the price at the time of delivery will vary substantially from the price at the time of the contract signing. Consequently, it is not uncommon for a barter arrangement to incorporate fixed prices for the goods. Accordingly, the quantities to be exchanged would be set out in absolute numbers rather than subject to a pricing formula.

5(c). Time, Terms, and Other Details Regarding Delivery. If the quantities are to be exchanged in their entirety immediately, the contract should set the exact date of delivery or shipment of the goods. If, as here, the commodities will be shipped in increments over a certain period, the parties should try to set out in the contract some type of schedule for deliveries. It is also wise to set a final date for the last shipment so that the contract does not appear open ended.

When delivery is to be made in increments, notice requirements are important to ensure communication between the parties in order to avoid difficulties in transportation of the goods.

5(d). Packing. The packing provision, by its very nature, is rather product specific. The parties must provide in the contract for any particular packaging requirements of the commodities exchanged. This should include the type of packaging (steel drum, wooden pallet, crate, etc.), any particular linings to be used, markings or warnings required, whether the shipment must be kept warm or refrigerated, etc.

5(e). Shipping. The contract must stipulate a delivery term so that it is clear which party is responsible for arranging and paying for the transportation of each commodity. Here f.a.s. ("free along side") U.S.A. port is used. This means that the seller is responsible for delivering the goods along side the vessel in the U.S.A. port. The buyer must arrange and pay for transportation of the goods from that point forward.

Although the delivery term f.a.s. is used here, any term can be used ("ex works," "ex dock," "ex mine," "f.o.b.," "c.i.f.," "c. & f.," and so on). Different terms can be used for the different commodities involved in the exchange. As in any international sale of goods, the crucial point is that the parties realize the impact of the delivery term on price, passing of title, and passing of risk, and take steps to protect themselves.

5(f). Insurance. A party in any large sales transaction probably would enter into an insurance contract for the part of the journey during which it is at risk. An obligation to purchase insurance is particularly important here because the second half of this agreement, i.e., the transfer of commodity 2 to CCC, relies on the successful completion of the first transfer. If one party suffers an uninsured loss in the transfer of the first party goods while the second part of the transaction is partially or entirely executory, there may be a temptation for that party to renege on its obligations in the transfer of the second party goods.

5(g). Documents Required, Documentary Transfer. As in any international sales transaction, the contract must stipulate any particular documents required by either party, as well as a mechanism for the transfer of the required documents.

6. Second Party Goods. The provisions concerning the transfer of the second party goods should contain the same items covered in the section regarding the transfer of the first party goods. The provisions here may differ somewhat since they must be tailored to cover the particular, unique characteristics of the second party goods. There may be some additional clauses as well, but the important point is that both sections be detailed and explicit. Both parties have an interest in having clear, detailed terms for both commodities because each commodity is both a good transferred and a payment received. A problem with the transfer of either good is capable of destroying the entire arrangement.

6(g). Documents Required, Documentary Transfer. It should be noted that this provision does not include the clause requiring a certificate verifying the quality, date of manufacture, and origin of the goods. The U.S. government will generally insist on verifying the quality of the goods on its own, or through an independent inspector, and provision is made for this later in the contract.

7. Bank Guarantees. In conventional international sales transactions the currency portion of the exchange is secured by a letter of credit. In a barter arrangement there is no currency transfer. An alternative source of security is needed to guarantee payment, that is, the receipt of acceptable goods.

One alternative is the use of standby letters of credit. If the first party found it difficult to have the second party's letter of credit confirmed, the first party could request that a performance bond be issued by the second party's bank. U.S. banks are prohibited from issuing guarantees, but foreign branches of U.S. banks can issue such bonds.

The parties may also wish to establish an evidence account at a neutral bank. Upon delivery and acceptance of the goods, a credit would be made in the account in favor of the delivering party. If all works well, the credits will simply negate each other, the parties will be left with the goods each bargained for; because of the standby letter of credit, however, security against default will have been provided in the interim.

In conjunction with the bank guarantees, a contingency, or "escape," clause can be included for the further protection of the parties. This clause allows one party to "bail-out" of the barter arrangement if the other party is found to have materially breached its obligations. The "escape clause" allows the nonbreaching party to force a cash payment for the goods it has transferred rather than wait indefinitely for the breaching party to correct its breach and tender conforming goods.

8. *Quality and Acceptance.* It is very important that the barter contract provide for a guarantee of quality. At the very least, the goods should have to comply with the specifications listed above in the contract. Furthermore this clause should include additional, detailed quality control requirements desired by either party. These detailed quality specifications are necessary to ensure that both parties understand what is expected. Again if either party is dissatisfied with a particular shipment, the entire barter arrangement is endangered.

The quality control provision should include any particular testing or inspection procedures to be used, maximum periods between manufacture and shipment, limitations on manufacturing locations, special shipping instructions pertinent to quality control, etc. In addition, acceptance of the delivered goods should be made contingent on the compliance of those goods with the quality requirements set forth in the contract.

9. *Right to Inspect.* As a corollary to the quality control provisions and detailed specifications, each party should be granted the right to inspect the goods before accepting them. It is in the interests of both parties to allow inspection so as to identify and resolve any problems with the commodities at an early stage.

10. *Right to Neutral Surveyor.* The right to consult a neutral surveyor is included in the contract for the protection of both parties since each will be delivering and receiving shipments. This clause encourages the tendering of conforming goods and discourages unfounded or arbitrary refusals to accept goods.

11. *Formulation of a Joint Committee to Monitor the Agreement.* The parties may decide that it would be useful to establish a joint committee to monitor the agreement. Such a committee offers the parties a means of communicating and dealing with minor problems through an established mechanism rather than resorting to formal arbitration for every issue that arises. The committee would also be able to anticipate possible difficulties and take steps to avoid potentially serious disputes.

A management committee may not be necessary or effective if the terms of the agreement are fixed and the exchange will take place over a very short period. If the exchange occurs over a longer period, however, and the quantity to be exchanged depends on the changing international price for the goods, a management committee may be able to ensure that the arrangement proceeds smoothly. In a fairly short-term barter arrangement the committee will probably not be given the power to amend the agreement, but could be given such power if the parties consider it necessary.

12. Determination and Settlement of Claims. If a management committee is established under the agreement, disputes should be referred there before resorting to formal arbitration. If the dispute can be resolved amicably between the parties there is a much greater chance that the arrangement will proceed smoothly to the end. Any dispute that cannot be resolved by the committee will have to be referred to an arbitration tribunal since both parties probably will want to avoid the possibility of litigation in the other party's national court system.

13. Marketing Restrictions. Governments are often only interested in bartering goods that, for political, economic, or practical reasons, they cannot sell domestically. For this reason, both parties may seek to protect themselves against reentry of the commodities scheduled to be exported. A country may also be concerned that its partner in his barter arrangement may ship the goods to a third country which the first country is interested in negotiating with separately. Consequently, a prohibition on transshipment may be incorporated into the agreement.

If possible transshipment is of sufficient concern to the countries involved, the contract may provide for a sizeable penalty to encourage compliance with these marketing restrictions.

14. Penalties. Penalties can take many different forms and must be tailored to the individual goods, parties, and risk involved. The parties may opt for a simple percentage penalty in the case of any problem concerning the goods or time of delivery, or they may choose penalties in proportion to the degree of severity of the failure to perform. The clause provided here is not meant as a model but simply as a possibility of what might appear in a barter contract.

The important point is that the parties consider various types of failure to perform in accordance with the economic consequences for each type of failure, and adopt penalties that encourage compliance.

15. Force Majeure. As in most international sales transactions, the contract should provide that neither party shall be held responsible for the delay or failure to comply with their respective responsibilities due to force majeure.

16. Arbitration. To avoid the expense and inherent difficulties of conventional litigation, most barter contracts include a clause calling for binding arbitration. The arbitration can take place in a number of locations including the home country of the party complained against, the International Chamber of Commerce, the Stockholm Chamber of Commerce, or a third country.

17. Choice of Law. While a codified legal system is often preferred over a common law system, it is not uncommon for a contract to which the U.S. government is a party to provide that the law of a particular state applies. The parties often select New York for this purpose because that state has a well-developed body of commercial law and jurisprudence.

THE COUNTERPURCHASE TRANSACTION

In a counterpurchase arrangement, one party sells goods to a second party and simultaneously agrees to purchase from its customer goods equal in value to a stated percentage of the goods sold. In a counterpurchase transaction between a Western firm, for example, and an Eastern bloc government foreign trade organization, the Western firm generally will have the option of purchasing any goods that appear on a list drawn up during negotiations preceding the contract. A counterpurchase arrangement thus involves separate but related sales of goods. Separate contracts are used to cover the individual sales. Yet these contracts must be linked so that the country insisting on a counterpurchase arrangement is assured that the Western firm will fulfill its counterpurchase obligation. The counterpurchase transaction provides the means for each party to get what it wants out of the arrangement: the Western firm makes the sale of goods or machinery to the foreign country, and the foreign country is assured that the Western company will make purchases of goods equal to a certain amount over a specified period.

The counterpurchase arrangement can be divided into two parts: (1) the counterpurchase transaction, calling for the foreign country to purchase goods from the Western firm and establishing a broad, general obligation in the Western firm to buy goods from the foreign country; and (2) subsequent sales contracts under which the Western firm buys goods from the foreign country.

The counterpurchase transaction itself consists of two, and sometimes three, separate but simultaneously negotiated and executed agreements. The first contract, or primary sales agreement, provides for the sale of the Western firm's goods to the foreign country for hard currency. The secondary sales agreement is generally a broad, loosely structured contract setting forth the Western firm's obligation to purchase goods from the foreign country. The transaction may include a third contract, or protocol, which links the other two agreements. When a protocol is not used, the secondary sales agreement will include a provision linking it to the primary sales agreement.

While the secondary sales agreement is linked, through its own terms or by a protocol, to the primary sales agreement, for reasons discussed below the primary agreement will never refer to the counterpurchase obligation set forth in the secondary sales agreement.

The subsequent sales contracts involve individual purchases made by the Western firm, for hard currency, pursuant to the obligation it assumed in the secondary sales agreement.

In order to recognize the significance of the various counterpurchase transaction provisions, it is important to understand the approaches that the different parties are likely to take. Any contract, after all, is the product of the goals, intentions, and bargaining power of the parties involved.

The Western firm is likely to try to avoid a counterpurchase obligation altogether, or at the most, enter a *best efforts* agreement. Under a best efforts agreement, the Western firm would not promise unequivocally to purchase its customer's goods, but instead would promise to use its best efforts to meet the purchase goals. The firm would be reluctant to become involved because it is accustomed to making straight goods-for-cash deals and is not interested in obligating itself to purchase, and then somehow dispose of, goods of questionable quality. The foreign country, however, may not be willing to purchase the goods from the Western firm without a counterpurchase element in the arrangement. The foreign country is interested in creating new markets for its products as well as protecting its hard currency and balance-of-payments positions. In short, the Western firm may have to agree to a counterpurchase obligation if it wants to make the primary sale of goods to the foreign country.

The negotiating does not stop at this point, however, since the parties can still further their interests by insisting that certain provisions be included in the transaction. Since it is the secondary sales agreement that establishes the contours of the Western firm's counterpurchase obligation, a good deal of the negotiation will focus on that portion of the transaction. The Western firm is basically interested in *protection* and *flexibility*—protection against goods of inferior quality and flexibility in the list of goods available for purchase, the time period in which to make the purchases, and the disposal or marketing of the goods. The Western firm thus will seek to include various contingency clauses for its protection and keep the counterpurchase obligation as small and easy to fulfill as possible. The foreign country is interested in *improvement* and *progress*—improvement in its hard currency position and real progress in terms of national development—

even if that entails some conflict with the goals of the Western firm. Consequently, the foreign country will attempt to bind the Western firm to as strict an obligation as possible.

After presenting a diagram of a counterpurchase transaction (Figure 3.2) and a suggested checklist, sample provisions from a counterpurchase arrangement will be noted and discussed. Since the primary sales agreement is really no different from a conventional international sales contract, the specific terms of that agreement will not be discussed. The primary sales agreement's role in the counterpurchase arrangement and its relationship to the other agreements, however, will be examined. The discussion below will concentrate on the secondary sales agreement because that agreement contains the clauses unique to a counterpurchase transaction.

The final counterpurchase agreement reached in any particular situation, of course, will depend on the negotiating process and the provisions below are not set forth as model clauses. No two transactions will ever be exactly alike. The sample clauses and explanations, however, identify the areas of concern that should receive attention in the negotiating and drafting stages of the counterpurchase transaction.

EXPLANATION OF COUNTERPURCHASE DIAGRAM

1. A Western firm and a foreign government-owned industry enter into a primary sales agreement* in which the Western firm transfers goods to the foreign industry for cash. To facilitate this transfer, three separate auxiliary contracts are entered into:

1(a). A contract for the transportation of the goods to the foreign country;

1(b). An insurance contract to cover the goods while in transit; and

1(c). A financing arrangement, or letter of credit, as a means for the Western firm to receive payment for the goods.

2. The primary sales agreement is tied to a secondary sales agreement through a separate contract, called a protocol, or

3. The primary sales agreement is tied to the secondary sales agreement through a specific provision in the secondary sales agreement.

---

*The primary sales agreement, secondary sales agreement, and protocol, if one is used, are generally negotiated and signed simultaneously.

Figure 3.2 Counterpurchase transaction.

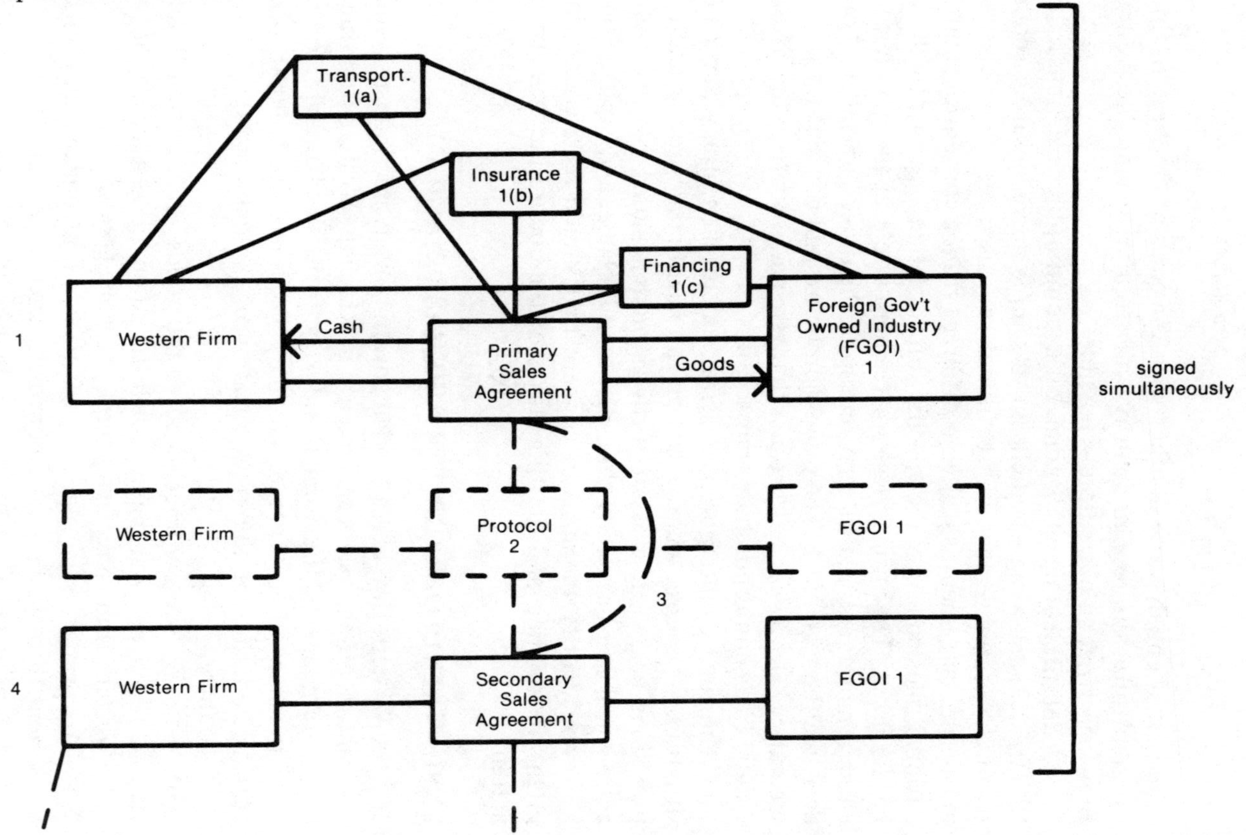

56

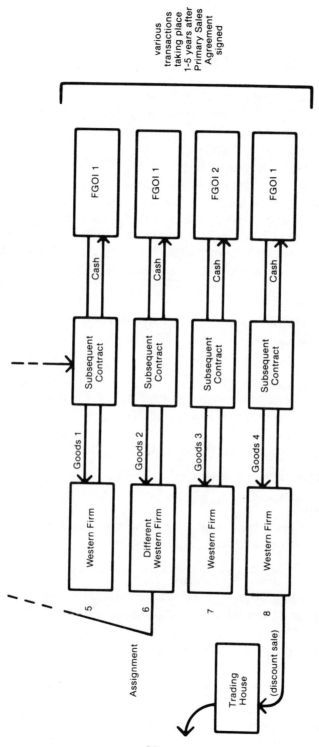

various transactions taking place 1-5 years after Primary Sales Agreement signed

57

4. A secondary sales agreement is signed between the Western firm and the foreign industry, establishing an obligation in the Western firm to counterpurchase goods from the foreign country over a specified period of time (generally 1-5 years).*

5. The Western firm purchases a good from the original industry it contracted with, receiving credit for the amount of the purchase against its total obligation.

6. The Western firm assigns part of its obligation to a different Western firm which purchases a second good from the original foreign industry; the original Western firm nevertheless receives credit for the amount of this purchase against its counterpurchase obligation.

7. The original Western firm purchases a third good from a different foreign industry, nevertheless receiving credit for the amount of the purchase against its obligation under the provisions of a "linkage" term in the secondary sales agreement, a concept which is discussed below.

8. The Western firm purchases a fourth good from the original contracting foreign industry, receives its credit, then sells the goods at a discount to a trading house which subsequently resells the good.

Note: Each subsequent sales contract will also require separate contracts for transportation, insurance, and financing; for simplicity these have been omitted from the diagram.

COUNTERPURCHASE CONTRACT CHECKLIST

1. Primary Sales Agreement
    a) parties
    b) recitals
    c) acknowledgment of obligation to purchase goods
    d) description of goods, specifications
    e) quantity
    f) price, terms of payment
    g) method of payment, guarantee thereof
    h) time, terms and other details regarding delivery
    i) packing
    j) shipping
    k) documents

---

*The four subsequent contracts shown here are merely examples or possibilities of various transactions the Western firm might negotiate pursuant to the counterpurchase obligation outlined in the secondary sales agreement.

l) guarantee of quality, quality control

m) right to inspect

n) right to neutral surveyor

o) determination and settlement of claims

p) penalties, remedies in the event of:
  —late delivery
  —delivery of nonconforming goods
  —failure to deliver

q) force majeure

r) arbitration

s) choice of law

2. Protocol

3. Secondary Sales Agreement
  ([ ] = details possibly in Secondary Sales Agreement, but probably in subsequent contracts)

a) parties

b) recitals

c) acknowledgment of obligation to counterpurchase goods

d) reference to list of available goods

e) quantity of counterpurchase

f) price, terms of payment, guarantee thereof

g) time period in which to fulfill obligation

h) linkage

i) marketing restrictions

j) [specifications, description, quality]

k) [terms and other details regarding delivery]

l) [packing]

m) [shipping]

n) [insurance]

o) [documents, documentary transfer]

p) guarantee of quality, quality control

q) right to inspect

r) right to neutral surveyor

s) determination and settlement of claims

t) first party penalties, remedies

u) second party penalties, remedies

v) cancellation of primary sales agreement

w) transferability of counterpurchase agreement

x) force majeure

y) arbitration

z) choice of law

4. Formulation of joint committee to monitor agreement
5. Additional requirements concerning each individual purchase to be made from the list of available goods

   Appendix: [List of available goods]

Sample Counterpurchase Contract

1. [Primary Sales Agreement]
2. Foreign Government-Owned Industry X (Foreign Industry X) agrees to purchase $X worth of Commodity 1 from Western Firm according to the provisions of the Primary Sales Agreement. Western Firm agrees to make purchases of goods from Foreign Industry X according to the provisions of the Secondary Sales Agreement. Both parties acknowledge their obligations assumed under both Agreements. This Protocol will be fully satisfied at a time when all obligations under both Agreements have been fulfilled to the satisfaction of both parties.
3. Frame Agreement for Counterpurchases by Western Firm from Foreign Industry X.
   3(a). This agreement is entered into this 21st day of February, 1985, between Western Firm, a corporation organized and existing under the laws of the State of Ohio, U.S.A. and Foreign Government-Owned Industry X (Foreign Industry X), organized and existing under the laws of Foreign Country A.
   3(b). *Whereas*, Western Firm and Foreign Industry X have entered into a Primary Sales Agreement pursuant to which Western Firm is to supply Commodity 1 to Foreign Industry X in exchange for cash payment in hard currency.

   Whereas, Western Firm herein obligates itself to undertake a program to achieve a countertrade level in conformity with article 3(e) below.

   Whereas, Foreign Industry X undertakes to cooperate fully with Western Firm in carrying out this program.

   Now, therefore, Western Firm and Foreign Industry X agree as follows:
   3(c). Western Firm acknowledges its obligation to undertake a program to purchase from Foreign Industry X, or other enterprises within Foreign Country A as detailed below, an amount set forth in article 3(e) of this Agreement.

3(d). Western Firm will make its counterpurchases from the goods listed in the Appendix to this Agreement, according to the procedures described in Article 5.

On each anniversary date of this Agreement, Western Firm shall make proposals to Foreign Industry X regarding additions to the product list. Foreign Industry X shall not be unreasonable in declining to add any product to the list. At any other time during the year the Management Committee established in article 4 shall have the authority to add products to the list.

Foreign Industry X may remove a product from the list (on 12 months notice) if it intends to halt production of that product, provided that any existing orders shall be filled.

3(e). Western Firm obligates itself to counterpurchase goods with a value totalling 100 percent of the contract price of the Primary Sales Agreement.

An evidence account is hereby established, the total at this time being 100 percent of the contract price of the Primary Sales Agreement.

Western Firm shall receive a credit against this evidence account when any purchase order is submitted by Western Firm and accepted by Foreign Industry X, in accordance with the procedures set forth in article 5.

Western Firm shall also receive a credit for the dollar amount of the order whenever:

1) Foreign Industry X refuses to cooperate in accordance with the procedures of article 5;
2) Foreign Industry X is unable to fill the order within 60 days following receipt;
3) through the efforts of Western Firm, a third party transferee under article 3(w) places an order which is accepted by Foreign Industry X;
4) force majeure is invoked by Foreign Industry X and this delay lasts more than 6 months;
5) goods of unacceptable quality are delivered to Western Firm.

3(f). Western Firm shall make offers to purchase products on the list of available goods in accordance with the provisions of article 5.

If Foreign Industry X does not accept Western Firm's offer made under article 5 procedures, Western Firm shall have the option of making the particular purchase at a price available to Western Firm from other suppliers in the international market, supported by the appropriate evidence, less 10 percent, at the most competitive international financing terms, also supported by the appropriate evidence, less one percentage point.

As a guarantee of its payment and good faith performance of the remainder of its obligations under this Agreement, Western Firm will open a letter of credit. This obligation is more fully set out in article 3(t).

3(g). The purchase program to be undertaken by Western Firm will be conducted to obtain the desired volume of orders within a period of five years from the effective date of this Agreement.

3(h). The content of the purchase orders referred to in this Agreement will, in the aggregate, involve products of Foreign Industry X, but if Western Firm believes it necessary in order to achieve the purposes of this Agreement, it may make purchases from industries in the foreign country other than Foreign Industry X totalling up to 50 percent of the value of this Agreement, provided Western Firm obtains the approval of the Management Committee which shall not be unreasonably withheld.

3(i). Western Firm hereby agrees not to reenter or cause the reentry of any good purchased in furtherance of this Agreement into Foreign Country A.

Foreign Industry X hereby agrees that Western Firm can otherwise market goods purchased in furtherance of this Agreement without restriction as to geographic markets or resale customer.

3(j). [Specifications, Description, Quality]

3(k). [Terms and Other Details Regarding Delivery]

3(l). [Packing]

3(m). [Shipping]

3(n). [Insurance]

3(o). [Documents, Documentary Transfer]

3(p). The goods purchased by Western Firm shall be of sufficient quality that they meet all specifications listed in the particular sales contract.

If the goods delivered by Foreign Industry X or any other seller Western Firm contracts with under this Agreement are not of sufficient quality to meet all of the listed specifications, the shipment shall not be accepted. In such a case Western Firm shall promptly notify the seller of the refusal to accept the goods, and list in a clear and detailed manner the reasons for refusal to accept.

If the neutral surveyor, consulted through the procedures of article 3(r), determines that the goods are of unacceptable quality, Western Firm shall receive credit against the evidence account for the dollar amount of the order pursuant to article 3(e).

3(q). Western Firm shall have the right to inspect shipments of goods purchased pursuant to this Agreement, and the right to reject any portion of the shipment that does not meet the terms and conditions of this Agreement or the particular sales contract covering the goods in question.

3(r). In the event that Western Firm rejects any shipment because of nonconforming quality, Foreign Industry X (or the supplier if other than Foreign Industry X) shall have the right to request that a sample of the shipment be sent to a neutral surveyor for analysis.

3(s). Any dispute arising under this Agreement or the individual sales contracts entered into in furtherance of this Agreement concerning a question of law or fact shall first be taken to the Management Committee established under article 4 of this Agreement. Any dispute not settled by the Management Committee shall be finally settled in arbitration according to the provisions of article 3(y) of this Agreement.

3(t). In the event that Western Firm fails to fulfill its counterpurchase obligations within five years of the effective date of this Agreement, Western Firm shall pay to Foreign Industry X, as a penalty, a sum equal to 20 percent of the unfulfilled portion of the obligations.

The penalty stated herein shall be the sole remedy for Foreign Industry X, and upon payment of the penalty the obligations of Western Firm under this Agreement terminate.

In order to secure any payment that comes due under this provision, Western Firm will, at its own expense, arrange for an irrevocable letter of credit in a U.S. bank to be opened four years from the effective date of this Agree-

ment in an amount equal to 20 percent of the then unfulfilled portion of the counterpurchase obligation.

Payment of the above-stated penalty by the Western
Firm shall not affect the rights and obligations of the parties under the Primary Sales Agreement.

3(u). [Second Party Penalties]

3(v). This Agreement shall become void if the Primary Sales
Agreement is for any reason cancelled.

3(w). Purchase orders under this Agreement may be placed by
Western Firm, or by any third party designated by Western
Firm so long as that third party transferee is made aware
of and follows the procedures of the provisions of this
Agreement.

Pursuant to article 3(e), Western Firm shall receive credit
for any purchase made by a designated third party transferee.

Neither party shall assign all of its rights or delegate all
of its obligations under this Agreement without the prior
written permission of the other party. Such permission shall
not be unreasonably withheld.

3(x). If the performance by a party to this Agreement is delayed
due to causes beyond its reasonable control, the obligations
of both parties with respect to the delayed performance
shall be suspended for a corresponding period.

3(y). Disputes arising under this Agreement, which are not resolved by the Management Committee, shall be finally settled by arbitration at the International Chamber of Commerce, Paris, France, according to the rules of that body.
Each party shall appoint one arbitrator and the two arbitrators shall select a third arbitrator. All decisions by the
arbitrators shall be made by majority vote.

3(z). The arbitrators selected according to the provisions of article 3(y) shall apply the provisions of the Swiss Federal Code
of Obligations.

4. A Management Committee will be established consisting of six
persons, three of whom will be appointed by each party. The
Committee will have the following functions:

1) To give general supervision to the progress of the primary sale
and counterpurchase program;

2) To facilitate the implementation of the obligations undertaken
by both parties;

3) To conciliate any differences of opinion between the parties informally at the request of either party.

The Committee will convene four times a year, alternating between the U.S.A. and Foreign Country A, to review the progress of both parties in fulfilling their obligations under this Agreement.

5. With regard to purchases to be made by Western Firm in furtherance of the obligations assumed in this Agreement:

1) Western Firm's purchasing program will be fulfilled within the Agreement term of five years.

2) In submitting its purchase orders, Western Firm will act in good faith and consistently with its normal purchasing practices.

3) Purchase orders submitted by Western Firm shall relate to products listed in the Appendix or to products added to the Appendix under article 3(d).

4) Each purchase order submitted by Western Firm shall include detailed specifications for each product ordered, the price of the product, the quantity and delivery dates, and customary payment terms for such products, and if customary in the international markets for such products, the financing conditions.

5) Within 60 days following the receipt by Foreign Industry X of any purchase order submitted by Western Firm, Foreign Industry X shall either accept or reject the offer by written notice to Western Firm; any rejection notice shall specify the reasons for the rejection.

6) If the purchase order is accepted, the parties shall immediately become bound by the terms of such purchase order.

7) If the order is rejected because Foreign Industry X is unable to fill the order, or because Foreign Industry X invokes force majeure and more than six months pass before the situation is resolved, or because of other nonprice reasons, Western Firm shall receive credit for the dollar amount of the order pursuant to and subject to the provisions of article 3(e).

8) If the order is rejected because of dissatisfaction with the price offered, Western Firm shall have the option of:
   a) cancelling the purchase order; or
   b) submitting a new purchase order with a revised price; or
   c) purchasing the product at the price available to the Western Firm in the international market less 10 percent, pursuant to the provisions of article 3(f).

9) If the order is rejected because of the financing terms offered, Western Firm shall have the option of:

a) cancelling the purchase order; or
b) submitting a new purchase order with revised financing terms; or
c) purchasing the product at the offered price and at the most competitive international financing conditions less one percentage point pursuant to the provisions of article 3(f).

Appendix: [List of Available Goods]

EXPLANATION OF COUNTERPURCHASE CONTRACT TERMS

1. Primary Sales Agreement. The primary sales agreement normally consists of a standard international sales contract in which the first party (here the Western firm) agrees to provide a certain product or commodity conforming to certain conditions of quality, quantity, time, and place of delivery. As in any international sales transaction, it is very important that the terms covering the transfer of goods be specific and clear. A fixed price is generally set in the contract and payment is in hard currency upon delivery.

The second party, or buyer (here, the foreign industry), must arrange conventional financing, generally including some type of letter of credit, to pay for the goods. Unlike a barter transaction in which goods are exchanged for other goods, the primary sales agreement portion of the counterpurchase transaction is, then, a simple exchange of goods for hard currency.

The primary sales agreement will generally not refer to the counterpurchase obligation assumed by the Western firm in the secondary sales agreement. While the agreements are negotiated and signed simultaneously and linked by reference to the primary agreement in the protocol or secondary agreement, it is crucial for several reasons that the primary agreement not refer to the counterpurchase obligation. First, the primary agreement must be separately financed because most banks have traditionally not been interested in financing this type of transaction if it is legally connected to the counterpurchase obligation. Banks may be willing to lend based on the buyer's independent ability to repay the borrowed funds, but may not be willing to lend if payment for the goods is legally conditioned upon transactions occurring in the future. That is, the bank may be reluctant to lend funds if the borrower's ability to repay is dependent on what the bank sees as a risky variable—such as expected income from future counterpurchase transactions. It should be noted that as banks become more experienced and accustomed to counterpurchase arrangements their hesitancy toward financing both sides of the arrangement may lapse and with it the need for separate sales agreements.

Second, export risk guarantees such as those offered by the U.S. Export-Import Bank, may be easier to obtain if the primary transaction is free from the added complications of a counterpurchase obligation.

Third, the primary sales agreement is likely to be fully executed before the counterpurchase obligation terminates. Separation of the two agreements allows each to mature independently; thus the obligations of the two transactions are insulated from each other. In this way, if each party has performed satisfactorily its obligations under the primary agreement, that transaction will not be disturbed by any difficulties arising with the counterpurchase obligation.

Thus, although linked to the counterpurchase obligation in ways discussed below, the primary sales agreement must remain a legally separate document and it is critical that the practitioner drafting a counterpurchase transaction not allow the two agreements to merge into one obligation.

2. Protocol. The protocol simply links the obligations assumed under the two sales contracts. The protocol is a separate contract which is fulfilled when both the primary sales agreement and the secondary sales agreement become fully executed.

The counterpurchase transaction can be structured without this separate contract linking the two agreements. In this case, the link is provided by an additional clause in the recitals section of the secondary agreement. Using the latter option may not be desirable, however, if the parties are anxious to emphasize the separateness of the two agreements.

3. Secondary Sales Agreement. As stated above, the purpose of the secondary sales agreement is to establish the counterpurchase obligation of the Western firm. This agreement is generally broader and more loosely worded than the primary sales agreement since it does not deal with the specifics of financing and delivering goods; rather, it establishes a framework for future purchases. In fact, in some cases the secondary agreement may only amount to a broadly worded paragraph establishing the Western firm's obligation to purchase goods totalling a given percentage of the value of the primary agreement.

In some instances the Western firm may determine that such a broadly worded obligation is in its best interests. For example, the firm may decide that vague terms offer flexibility in a certain situation.

But a vaguely-worded provision may not adequately protect the interests of the Western firm. In general, the advantages of a clear, detailed obligation worded to provide the desired flexibility will outweigh the advantages of a vague counterpurchase obligation.

Many of the provisions below, while binding the Western firm to a general counterpurchase obligation and thus meeting the foreign country's needs, nevertheless offer the inducement often needed for the firm to enter into the entire transaction—protection and flexibility.

3(a). Parties. Because the secondary sales agreement is a separate legal instrument, the contract should begin by stating the parties' names. This seeming redundancy is justified because failure to list the parties names (or failure to include any provision present in most contracts) could make the secondary agreement appear dependent on the primary agreement. Such an omission could lead a tribunal to determine that the two had merged into one legal instrument.

The parties involved could be both private, both public, or one public and one private. Because many counterpurchase arrangements presently are between Western firms and foreign government-owned industries, a private-public arrangement is described here.

3(b). Recitals. As noted above, the recital section of the secondary sales agreement may be used to link the agreement to the primary sale of goods. If this is done, a protocol will not be necessary, but careful drafting is crucial to ensure that the agreements remain legally distinct.

3(c). Acknowledgment of Obligation to Counterpurchase Goods. In this provision, the Western firm simply states its obligation to counterpurchase goods. The provision may be short and direct as the one given here, or it may include summaries of the various obligations detailed in the agreement.

3(d). Reference to List of Available Goods. Considerable time may be spent negotiating the list of products available for purchase by the Western firm. The foreign country will be interested in including goods it cannot sell domestically or goods that are not currently exported. The Western firm, however, will seek to have an expansive list of goods to choose from since a larger list affords the firm greater flexibility. The foreign country generally will prefer to include finished goods instead of raw materials. In its recently issued counterpurchase guidelines, for example, the government of Indonesia specifically excluded petroleum natural gas. The Western firm, however, probably will prefer to include raw materials and semiprocessed goods on the list since the latter are considerably more marketable.

The Western firm should also seek to include in the secondary sales agreement a provision for amending the list of available goods. Such a provision could be particularly useful if the Western firm found another Western firm willing to assume a portion of the counterpurchase obligation (see explanation of article 3(w), infra) upon the condition that a certain product is added to the list of available goods.

3(e). Quantity of Counterpurchase. While the quantity of the counterpurchase obligation can be stated in several ways, including an exact quantity of specified products, the most common method is to state the obligation as a percentage of the value of the primary sales agreement.

Many contracts contain the quantity element only, but it is clearly in the Western firm's interest to include a provision whereby it receives credit against its counterpurchase obligation when a third party transferee makes a purchase or when the foreign country cannot deliver goods listed on the available product list.

3(f). Price, Terms of Payment, Guarantee Thereof. Since the counterpurchase transactions will not occur immediately in this example, some type of pricing formula is needed. The pricing formula must be both sufficiently detailed and exact yet flexible and capable of continuing viability even if exchange rates or commodity prices fluctuate widely; thus, a two-tiered system is used here. In the first tier, the parties follow procedures set up in the agreement (see explanation of article 5, infra). These procedures should call for the parties to move through several stages of negotiations or at least one round of offer and counteroffer in an attempt to reach a mutually agreeable price. If this process fails to bring the parties together, the parties would be bound by the current international price for the product—the second tier in this pricing system.

The 10 percent subtracted from the international price and the one percentage point off internationally competitive financing terms will at least partially offset the additional costs such as increased inventories and marketing incurred by the Western firm. This term, of course, is subject to negotiation and the foreign country is unlikely to be enthusiastic about giving a discount. In its counterpurchase guidelines for government procurement, for example, the Indonesian government states simply that "Indonesian exports linked to government procurements must be implemented with international prices prevailing at the time of delivery of the goods." This presumably leaves no room for discounting although the government may have to alter this policy in order to encourage Western firms to enter into counterpurchase transactions.

The Western firm will undoubtedly try to avoid opening a letter of credit as a guarantee of payment but the foreign country may insist on this provision.

3(g). Time Period in Which to Fulfill Obligation. A time period must be designated within which the Western firm will complete its counterpurchase program. The time period allowed will vary depending upon the extent of the obligation and the bargaining power of the parties. While the most common time period allowed is between one and five years, the contract may set the period at up to eight years if the value of the primary sales agreement is very large and the parties contemplate a long-term relationship.

A longer period is generally in the Western firm's best interest because the additional time offers it flexibility in developing markets for the goods or locating third parties willing to assume its obligations to purchase.

3(h). Linkage. In a private-public transaction, the Western firm generally contracts with one particular government agency. The Western firm should insist on a provision allowing it to make purchases from agencies or enterprises other than the one with which it is contracting. This concept is known as *linkage* and gives the Western firm additional flexibility because it increases the pool of potential future suppliers.

The concept of linkage traditionally has been important in contracts with nonmarket countries, but it is also applicable to developing countries which have numerous governmental offices responsible for the sale and control of different commodities. When contracting with a government entity, the Western firm may also seek a specific clause entitling it to purchase from private enterprises within the foreign country.

3(i). Marketing Restrictions. Marketing restrictions must be established in the contract; the exact nature of the provision will depend on the bargaining power of the parties.

The Western firm will seek to limit the number of restrictions because it wants to maximize its ability to resell the goods at a high value. The more markets open to it, the better its chances.

The foreign country, however, will seek, at the very least, a prohibition on reentry. The foreign country may insist that the particular product not be sold in any market where the foreign country already sells that products. The foreign country is trying, after all, to make progress in its balance-of-payments and development positions. Neither will improve if purchases made by the Western firm merely displace other similar goods already exported.

3(j)-3(o). The provisions listed here are those generally covering the transfer of goods. Because this contract calls for purchases of goods in the future and contemplates no immediate transfer of goods, these provisions are not needed in this agreement. These provisions vary depending on the goods involved and would be included in each subsequent contract negotiated under the framework set up in this secondary agreement.

If the secondary agreement contemplated an immediate counterpurchase, or if the first of a number of purchases were to be included here, then these provisions would have to be included. For examples of these provisions, see, supra, articles 5(a)-5(g) of the sample barter transaction and accompanying explanations.

3(p). Guarantee of Quality, Quality Control. While the specific quality specifications for each good purchased will be detailed in the subsequent sales contracts, the secondary sales agreement should establish a procedure to which the Western firm can resort if it is not satisfied with the goods tendered. Inferior goods are a major concern for the Western firm and the firm will undoubtedly seek to have the framework of such a remedy available.

An alternative may be to reduce the price or alter the counterpurchase obligation to compensate for the degree of nonconformity. This may be difficult to administer, however, since the neutral surveyor would have to determine not only whether the goods are unsatisfactory but precisely *how unsatisfactory they are.*

3(q). Right to Inspect. Because of the Western firm's concern over the quality of the goods, it will probably negotiate for the right to inspect the goods before accepting them. This clause is clearly in the Western firm's interest but in order to gain approval for this term, it may have to agree to inspect the goods at the foreign country's port so that the transportation costs are saved if the goods are unsatisfactory.

3(r). Right to Neutral Surveyor. The right to submit part of the shipment to a neutral surveyor may replace the right to inspect clause or it may appear, as here, in conjunction with that clause. If it appears alone, the clause protects the Western firm against nonconforming goods and the foreign supplier against unreasonable rejection of the goods. If it appears along with the right to inspect, the right to a neutral surveyor still protects both parties although it is more likely to be invoked by the delivering party after the Western firm has inspected and rejected the goods.

3(s). Determination and Settlement of Claims. While there is no possible way to anticipate the problems that might arise under this agreement or the subsequent sales contracts, it is essential to establish a mechanism for the settlement of whatever disputes or claims arise. If a joint monitoring committee is established in the agreement, the claim should be aired there first. If no committee is formed, or if the committee cannot resolve the matter, the claim should proceed to binding arbitration rather than to the court system of either party.

3(t). First Party Penalties. The foreign country probably will insist on a penalty provision to ensure performance on the part of the Western firm. The foreign country may also require a bank guarantee for the penalty clause. Although the Western firm may not be able to avoid either of these provisions, it should insist on several additional provisions. The first is that payment of a penalty will not affect the obligations of the parties in the first agreement. This allows the Western firm to gain the benefit of its bargain in the primary sales agreement regardless of what happens concerning the counterpurchase obligation. Second, the agreement should state that if a penalty is paid, the Western firm's counterpurchase obligation terminates. This provision can be used by the Western firm as a type of "escape clause" if it no longer wishes to fulfill its obligation. If, for example, the Western firm faces a 15 percent penalty under the terms of the contract and has determined that it could market the goods purchased at only 80 percent of the price it will have to pay, the Western firm may well decide to pay the 15 percent penalty rather than purchase the goods.

In past countertrade contracts, the size of the penalty has varied widely—from 10 percent to as high as 50 percent. The exact figure agreed upon is, of course, subject to negotiation, but the Western firm should negotiate with the potential use of this provision as an escape clause in mind.

3(u). Second Party Penalties. The Western firm may insist on penalties for the tendering of nonconforming goods, failure to deliver, and so on. No second party penalties are included here because of the inclusion of article 3(e) which provides that in such circumstances the Western firm will receive credit for an order without paying for it.

If the parties decide to include a second party penalty clause, a clause similar to article 14 of the barter contract, supra, may be used. Penalties that vary depending on the degree of nonconformity could be used, but as noted above, there may be problems in administering such a system.

3(v). Cancellation of the Primary Sales Agreement. The Western firm generally agrees to undertake a counterpurchase obligation only as a necessity of making the primary sale. Therefore, the Western firm should insist that if the primary sales agreement is cancelled, the counterpurchase obligation becomes void, or at least voidable, at the Western firm's option.

3(w). Transferability of Counterpurchase Obligation. Since the Western firm is generally concerned with marketing the counterpurchased goods, the firm will seek to include a provision giving it the right to transfer its obligations to a third party interested in purchasing goods from the foreign country. This enables the Western firm to market its goods without handling them at all.

The foreign country may seek to qualify this right to transfer by providing that the obligation can only be transferred to a third party which is not presently purchasing that product from this country. The foreign country is interested in establishing new export markets for its products, and this will not be accomplished if the Western firm gets credit for purchases that a third party would have made anyway.

3(x). Force Majeure. The force majeure clause can be fairly short, as here, or more detailed, as in article 15 of the barter transaction, supra. The more detailed and precise any provision is, however, the less chance there is for disputes in the future.

3(y). Arbitration. To avoid the problems of litigation in a national court system, the parties, as in the barter transaction, supra, will generally consent to binding arbitration.

3(z). Choice of Law. A codified system is generally preferred over a common law system since it offers more certainty. Moreover, most foreign parties are more familiar and comfortable with a codified system.

4. Establishment of a Joint Committee to Monitor the Agreement. If the counterpurchase transaction will be stretched out over several years the parties may well choose to establish a committee to monitor the arrangement. This committee should serve to anticipate and prevent possible difficulties as well as provide the parties with an informal forum in which to air grievances.

5. Additional Requirements Concerning Each Individual Purchase to Be Made from the List of Available Goods. The procedures outlined here form the first tier of the two-tiered pricing system discussed above in article 3(f). By establishing a starting point for the parties, this provision contributes a degree of automaticity to the future negotiations. Negotiations may nevertheless break down. That is the purpose of the second tier, which provides for resort to internationally competitive price and terms, less a discount for the Western firm.

The option of resorting to the international market price is particularly important for the Western firm. The firm is obligated to make purchases totalling a certain amount within a certain period of time. Without this provision the Western firm could find itself faced with a choice of buying inferior goods at high prices or defaulting on its counterpurchase obligation and having to pay a penalty.

Although the procedures set forth in this provision must be as detailed as possible, they will, of course, be supplemented by even more detailed, goods-specific provisions in each subsequent contract. Even though each subsequent contract must be separately negotiated, the importance of setting a strong foundation for those negotiations should not be underestimated. The secondary sales agreement in general, and this provision in particular, set the stage for the future sales contracts, and the ultimate success of the entire purchase and counterpurchase relationship depends a great deal on the clear direction and guidance given by the terms of the secondary sales agreement.

Appendix. Article 3(d) of the secondary sales agreement refers to a list of goods available for purchase by the Western firm. The list will generally be attached to the agreement as an appendix.

THE COMPENSATION TRANSACTION

A *compensation transaction*, also referred to as a buy-back arrangement, involves a sale by a Western firm of machinery, technology, or a turnkey plant to a foreign entity. This sale is tied to a separate agreement under which the Western firm will purchase a specified amount of the product manufactured in the plant. There are essentially two types of compensation arrangements: 1) those providing that the goods received by the Western firm in the future are actual payment for the plant or machinery; and 2) those requiring separate financing and payment for the various transactions. Under the latter arrangement, the Western firm receives hard currency for its machinery immediately, and pays in hard currency for purchases of the plant's output in the future.

The first type of transaction is essentially a modified barter arrangement. The Western firm exchanges plant and technology today for a certain amount of the plant's output in the future. In a simple model at least, no financing or cash enters the transaction. The amount of output to be received in payment must be calculated taking into consideration the Western firm's loss of the use of its money while the plant is under construction.

The second type of compensation transaction is essentially a modified counterpurchase arrangement. The transaction must be tailored to fit the particular machinery or technology transferred and this will undoubtedly call for some very detailed, complex contract terms. Nevertheless, the basic structure, that is, use of separate contracts and financing for separate obligations, is similar to the counterpurchase arrangement discussed above.

Compensation transactions are generally much more complicated than barter or counterpurchase arrangements. But this is not the case because of any additional complex countertrade elements. Rather, it is more complicated because of the difficulties inherent in establishing any turnkey plant or full-scale manufacturing facility in a foreign country.

Because the complexities of building a turnkey plant have been dealt with in detail in other works, and the countertrade elements in a compensation transaction are similar to those discussed regarding barter and counterpurchase arrangements, this transaction will not be discussed as fully as the previous two.

This section opens with a diagram of a compensation arrangement (Figure 3.3) which involves separate financing. A compensation contract checklist follows, along with a brief discussion of several contract terms which are either unique to compensation, or which differ significantly from the other transactions previously discussed. While the discussion will focus primarily on the countertrade type of compensation arrangement (as opposed to the modified barter type), many of the comments will be relevant to both types.

EXPLANATION OF COMPENSATION DIAGRAM

1. A Western firm and a foreign government-owned industry enter into a primary sales agreement* in which the Western firm trans-

---

*The primary sales agreement, secondary sales agreement, and protocol, if one is used, generally are negotiated and signed simultaneously.

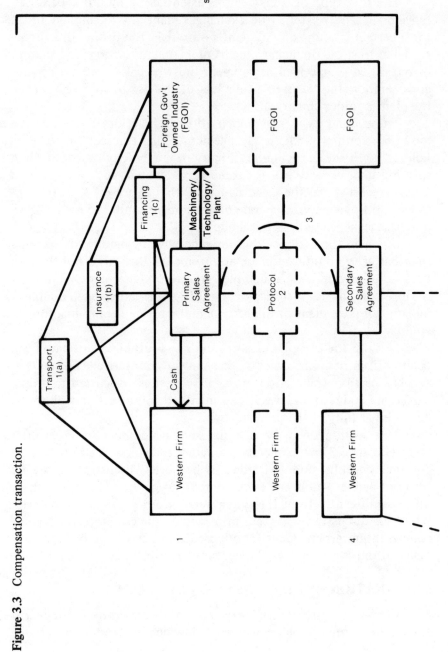

Figure 3.3 Compensation transaction.

76

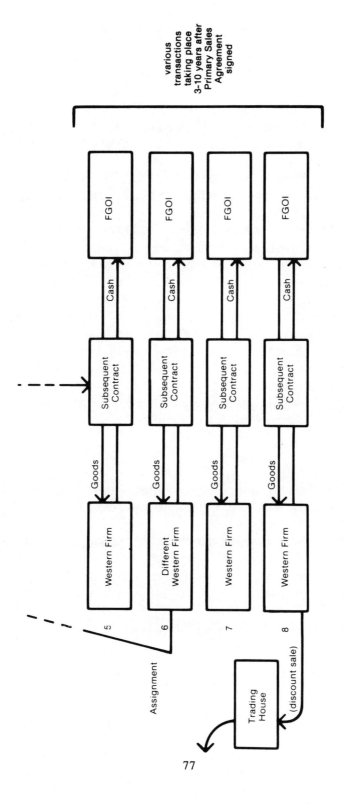

various transactions taking place 3-10 years after Primary Sales Agreement signed

FGOI

FGOI

FGOI

FGOI

Cash

Cash

Cash

Cash

Subsequent Contract

Subsequent Contract

Subsequent Contract

Subsequent Contract

Goods

Goods

Goods

Goods

Western Firm

Different Western Firm

Western Firm

Western Firm

5

6

7

8

Assignment

(discount sale)

Trading House

77

fers to the foreign industry machinery, plant and/or technology in exchange for cash.* To facilitate this transfer, three separate auxiliary contracts are entered into:

1(a). A contract for the transportation of the machinery or construction equipment to the foreign country;

1(b). An insurance contract to cover the machinery or material while in transit; and

1(c). A financing arrangement enabling the Western firm to receive immediate payment for the machinery, plant, or technology transferred.

2. The primary sales agreement is tied to a secondary sales agreement through a separate contract, called a protocol, or

3. The primary sales agreement is tied to the secondary sales agreement through a specific provision in the secondary sales agreement.

4. A secondary sales agreement is signed between the Western firm and the foreign industry, establishing an obligation on the part of the Western firm to purchase a certain amount of output from the plant constructed with the materials and technology transferred in the primary sales agreement.†

5. The Western firm purchases a shipment of the plant's output.

6. The Western firm assigns its obligations to purchase a shipment of output to a different Western firm.

7. The Western firm, again, purchases a shipment of the plant's output.

8. The Western firm purchases a shipment of the plant's output and subsequently sells it at a discount to a trading house which resells the product.

Note: As in the counterpurchase transaction, each subsequent sales contract will require separate contracts for transportation, insurance, and financing; these again have been omitted from the diagram to avoid confusion.

COMPENSATION CONTRACT CHECKLIST

1. Primary Sales Agreement
   a) parties

---

*Note that there will be a time lag before the Western firm's purchases can begin since the plant contemplated in the primary agreement first must be completed.

†The four subsequent contracts shown here are merely possible purchases of output that might be made during the life of the secondary agreement.

    b) recitals
    c) acknowledgment of obligation to purchase equipment/technology
    d) description of equipment/technology, specifications
    e) price, terms of payment
    f) method of payment, guarantee thereof
    g) time, terms and other details regarding delivery
    h) additional provisions related to specific aspects of agreement, such as performance of equipment/technology, use, improvements upon and transfer of technology, roles played by employees, consultants and technical advisors, and overall operation of equipment/technology
    i) packing
    j) shipping
    k) documents, documentary transfer
    l) guarantee of quality, quality control
    m) right to inspect
    n) right to neutral surveyor
    o) determination and settlement of claims
    p) penalties, remedies in the event of:
       —late delivery
       —delivery of nonconforming goods
       —failure to deliver
    q) force majeure
    r) arbitration
    s) choice of law
2. Protocol
3. Secondary Compensation Sales Agreement
    a) parties
    b) recitals
    c) acknowledgment of obligation to buy back goods
    d) quantity of counterpurchase
    e) price, terms of payment, guarantee thereof
    f) time period in which to fulfill obligation
    g) linkage
    h) marketing restrictions
    i) specifications, description, quality
    j) terms and other details regarding delivery
    k) packing
    l) shipping
    m) insurance
    n) documents, documentary transfer

    o) guarantee of quality, quality control
    p) right to inspect
    q) right to neutral surveyor
    r) determination and settlement of claims
    s) first party penalties, remedies
    t) second party penalties, remedies
    u) cancellation of primary sales agreement
    v) transferability of buy-back obligation
    w) force majeure
    x) arbitration
    y) choice of law

4. Formulation of joint committee to monitor agreement
5. Additional requirements concerning each individual purchase to be made from the list of available goods.

COMPENSATION CONTRACT

Primary Sales Agreement

The most immediate distinguishable feature of the primary sales agreement in a compensation transaction is that there is generally a much greater amount of money involved than in a counterpurchase transaction. This stems, again, from the fact that the Western firm is not simply selling goods to a foreign company, but is establishing a fully-operable plant or mine which requires a great deal of initial capital investment.

The compensation contract must include clear, detailed provisions establishing the rights and obligations of the parties regarding the construction and operation of the plant. These are important considerations in any turnkey-type arrangement but are particularly critical here since the Western firm has committed itself to purchase a certain amount of the facility's output. If the plant encounters operating difficulties some time in the future, the Western firm may face losses even if it has been paid in full for the materials used in building the plant.

Considerations to examine include the origin of the materials to be used in building the plant; performance of the equipment transferred; roles to be played by employees, consultants, and technical advisors; and operation of the plant after construction is finished. If technology is transferred, or goods involving patents or trademarks, the parties may want to examine restrictions on retransfer, marketing restrictions, or an obligation to improve the technology over time.

Secondary Sales Agreement

The buy-back obligation set forth in the secondary agreement is essentially similar to the counterpurchase obligation in a counterpurchase transaction. The concept of separate contracts is particularly important in a compensation arrangement because the parties will want to keep the large capital expenditures of the first agreement separate from the various difficulties that may occur over the life of the buy-back obligation.

There are several additional points which should be noted:

First, the contract may not include a list of available goods because the Western firm is presumably interested in purchasing only the goods produced in the plant it constructed. In fact, the Western firm may insist on a specific guarantee that all future shipments made pursuant to the buy-back obligation contain goods produced in that plant, and no other.

Second, the Western firm may seek additional guarantees of quality because it is obligated to purchase this particular product.

Third, the time period in which to fulfill the obligation will generally be longer than in a counterpurchase transaction. A period of at least five to ten years is common.

Fourth, linkage is probably not as important a concept here because the Western firm presumably intends to purchase goods only from the industry or company for which it built the plant.

Fifth, a pricing formula appropriate for the good to be produced must be established. The pricing formula must be flexible because it must retain viability over a fairly long period.

Finally, each party will be interested in negotiating marketing restrictions. The foreign country's main concern will be development of export markets for the portion of the output not sold under the buy-back arrangement. The Western firm will be interested in protecting its current market position and guarding against creating its own competition.

BIBLIOGRAPHY

Berman, J., International Commercial Transactions (1983) (supplement pt. III, folio 3 of *A Lawyer's Guide to International Business Transactions* [W. Surrey & D. Wallace eds. 1977]).

Dep't of Trade and Cooperatives, Republic of Indonesia, Guidelines for the Implementation of Linking Government Procurements from Imports with Indonesian Export Products Excluding Petroleum and Natural Gas (1982).

Gable, "Standby Letters of Credit: Nomenclature Has Confounded Analysis," *Law & Pol'y Int'l Bus* 12, 903 (1980).

Hoya & Stein, "Drafting Contracts in U.S.-Soviet Trade," *Law & Pol'y Int'l Bus* 7, 1057 (1975).

Marks, "Counselling U.S. Clients in Countertrade Transactions," in *Countertrade: International Trade Without Cash* 149 (Ehrenhaft, Chairman) (1983).

McVey, Contracts for Use in Barter and Countertrade Transactions (paper presented before the American Management Association, in New York, Dec. 4, 1980).

McVey, Countertrade and Barter: An Introductory Analysis (unpublished paper).

McVey, "Countertrade and Barter: Alternate Trade Financing by Third World Nations," *Int'l Trade LJ* 6, 197 (1980-1981).

McVey, "Countertrade: Commercial Practices, Legal Issues and Policy Dilemmas," *Law & Pol'y Int'l Bus* 16, 1 (1984).

Nelson, "Counselling U.S. Clients in Countertrade Transactions," in *Countertrade: International Trade Without Cash* 154 (Ehrenhaft, Chairman) (1983).

Note, "Bauxite for Butter: The U.S.-Jamaican Agreement and the Future of Barter in U.S. Trade Policy," *Law & Pol'y Int'l Bus* 16, 239 (1984).

Potter, "East-West Countertrade: Economic Injury and Dependence under U.S. Trade Law," *Law & Pol'y Int'l Bus* 13, 413 (1981).

Shillinglaw & Stein, "Doing Business in the Soviet Union," *Law & Pol'y Int'l Bus* 13, 1 (1981).

U.S. Int'l Trade Comm., Analysis of Recent Trends in U.S. Countertrade (1982) (USITC Publication 1237, prepared principally by Ronald J. DeMarines). USITC Publication 1237 contains an extensive bibliography at pages 52-62.

Verzariu, P., Countertrade Practices in East Europe, the Soviet Union and China: An Introductory Guide to Business (U.S. Dep't of Commerce, 1980).

Verzariu, "The Challenge of Countertrade," *Journal of Licensing Executives Society*, Dec. 1980, p. 262.

Vishny, P., *Guide to International Commerce Law* (1981).

Vogt, Jabara & Linse, Barter of Agriculture Commodities (1982) (Trade Policy Branch, International Economics Division (IED), Dep't of Agriculture, IED Staff Report).

PART TWO
BARTER SCENARIOS

4

COUNTERTRADE –
AS PRACTICED
IN EASTERN EUROPE

*Dr. Gerhart Vogt
and Heinrick Nowak*

INDIVIDUAL COUNTRY POLICIES AND PRACTICES

With most East European countries there is no published legislation or clearly defined set of guidelines governing countertrade. Trading House representatives in Vienna tend to dismiss the relevance of country-specific countertrade generalizations and underline that each countertrade deal has its own unique characteristics and has to be dealt with on that basis.

Still, it is relatively simple to distinguish general attitudes among the East European countries regarding countertrade. In this as in so many things economic, Eastern Europe is not a monolith, where the policies and practices of the Soviet Union can be taken to represent regional consensus.

Eastern European governments exercise their countertrade policies by full currency exchange controls and by a comprehensive import and export licensing system. In all cases these two levers of control place the government, through the Ministry of Foreign Trade and the National Bank/Ministry of Finance, in a primary coordination role, influencing Foreign Trade Organizations (FTOs) in their import decisions and ensuring, if appropriate, a requisite countertrade arrangement. It is common, though not always necessary, for representatives of the Ministry of Foreign Trade to participate directly in the negotiations of a countertrade contract. The Ministry will also serve as a type of brokerage operation in dealing with linkage questions or disputes about ratios, penalties, transfer clauses, and so on. (This "broker" activity is particularly undefined and inconsistently applied; the experience of Western exporters would tend to the view that they themselves have the difficult task of drawing together the many participants in the countertrade decision-making process for purposes of problem resolution.) It is possible that appeal to the Ministry of Foreign Trade can reduce the level of countertrade demanded or ensure earlier access to more acceptable countertrade products. However, it is generally true that the Ministry of Foreign Trade imposes countertrade requirements on the FTOs and enterprises having import/export authority and is an unlikely ally in any substantial disputes involving the need and type of countertrade demands.

Albania

Albania, with its limited and closely controlled contacts with foreign businessmen and its constitutional prohibition of official credit financing, relies on countertrade to generate balanced or surplus hard currency accounts. For significant capital equipment imports, Albanian FTOs require 100 percent countertrade. Chromium ore, often of an inferior grade, is the major countertrade commodity although other products are becoming available as Albania reorients itself from dependence on a few trade partners to a broader representation of the world's trading nations. With all FTOs reporting through the Ministry of Foreign Trade, coordination of countertrade arrangements across product sectors is possible. On a capital project it is likely that counterpurchase will be required during construction with a compensation deal becoming effective after plant start-up. This compounding of demands will put the aggregate countertrade ratio well in excess of 100 percent. However, as Albanian prices are low or at least market sensitive, the Western exporter can profit from an Albanian countertrade obligation. Also with the government's strict bilateral balance policy, the Western exporter may even find himself the beneficiary of a surplus in the Albanian favor, that is countertrade may be modest or removed altogether if Albanian exports are generating a positive cash flow.

Bulgaria

Bulgaria is one of the strongest proponents of countertrade in Eastern Europe, and has made industrial cooperation a key theme of its East-West economic relations. Major equipment and capital project imports face initial demands of 100 percent countertrade. A Canadian exporter has observed that a 40 percent obligation is the minimum countertrade ratio allowed. Bulgarian countertrade goods have a bad reputation on the basis of price, marketability, and availability. Linkage among FTOs is difficult although the Ministry of Foreign Trade can provide a coordinating service on priority transactions. Transportation and materials handling equipment are primary product categories that are featured in the Bulgarian drive for long-term cooperative arrangements using a countertrade lever.

Czechoslovakia

Czechoslovakian products are generally easy to market and the country has not been a major practitioner of countertrade. The more restricted recourse to countertrade results from Czechoslovakia's industrial tradition, relatively high level of development, established markets, and low foreign debt. However, with aging capital plants in many sectors, the Western recession and tight credit, Czechoslovak traders will be pressed to expand the low-level and relatively infrequent use of countertrade to maintain production and guard against increased debt. The Czechoslovak economic system is a very centralized one in which few market-type reforms have been introduced. With such an administered economy, countertrade will appear as an appropriate policy option to deal with the current economic downturn.

There is a reluctance by Czechoslovak authorities to agree to third-party intermediaries via a transfer clause in the countertrade contract. This reluctance is a function of the already developed export markets for Czechoslovak goods and the countertrade objective of opening up new markets. Distribution by intermediaries tends to blur the final destinations of countertrade goods.

A Canadian example of the Czechoslovak attitude towards countertrade was provided by the experience of H.A. Simons (Overseas) on the Ruzomberok pulp mill project. The Canadian contractor has the obligation to market 100,000 tons of pulp produced by the mill on an annual basis for ten years. Although a Czechoslovak Foreign Trade Organization (Ligna) took over the export contract on the pulp production the Canadian company still retains final responsibility for fulfillment of the multi-year 100,000 tons per annum obligation. Pricing on this and other countertrade commitments from Czechoslovakia is not a major problem. By the same token, penalty clauses have tended to be reasonable.

Although countertrade deals can be struck with many Czechoslovak FTOs, Transakta has been established as a go-between operating primarily in the consumer goods area. These are generally small countertrade packages, with Transakta drawing on the production from certain cooperatives and enterprises as well as the difficult-to-sell goods offered by various FTOs. Transakta has been an actor in the switch business as it is the clearing house for bilateral quantitative agreements between Czechoslovakia and selected Third World countries. This activity is diminishing as Czechoslovakia reduces the number of its non-Council of Mutual Economic Assistance (CMEA) bilateral agreements.

German Democratic Republic (GDR)

The GDR has always pursued countertrade arrangements with Western exporters, particularly under compensation terms for capital projects. This tendency has recently increased to the point where a large steel complex contracted with Voest-Alpine of Austria had provision for compensation and countertrade equivalent to 100 percent of the contract value plus the interest charges on the project financing. With a relatively burdensome hard currency debt and the prospect of economic retrenchment, countertrade ratios have approached 100 percent of all capital goods transactions.

GDR countertrade negotiations are regarded as being among the most straightforward of these negotiations in Eastern Europe. Technical goods are of a high quality and easily marketable by regional standards although there are reported problems with pricing. Penalty clauses have not been a particularly onerous part of the GDR countertrade contracts. The State Agency Transinter and the Ministry of Foreign Trade are important organizations within the GDR for the negotiation and fulfillment of countertrade contracts. It is not uncommon for the Western exporter to have to deal, on the countertrade part of his contract, with an intermediary within the GDR who tacks on a commission charge to the price of agreed countertrade goods.

Hungary

Hungary enjoys a unique position within Eastern Europe having come out publicly in opposition to certain forms of countertrade. In November 1979, the Ministry of Foreign Trade published a statement outlining the country's general orientation towards countertrade. This document was tabled in the GATT (part of document L/4633). It included the following references, among others:

Those forms of countertrade transactions—linkage of exports and imports—should be eliminated, where such products are imposed on the partners, which the enterprise itself is unable to sell, or it has no marketing organization for its proper distribution. . . .

Uneconomical, obsolete, not competitive products of inferior quality should not be offered as counteritems, because it is not desirable to conserve outdated production through countertrade.

It does seem that the Hungarian motivation for countertrade emanates more from a desire to develop the economy than from a rigid adherence to bilateral balancing to ensure markets for inferior but surplus production. A countertrade arrangement in heavy duty truck axles between Raba Works and International Harvester did develop into a mutually acceptable ongoing industrial cooperation. The Hungarian economy has had many "market" features introduced (that is, enterprise management, pricing, accounting, retained earnings, decentralization, indicative noncompulsory plans, export/import rights, among others) and it is only logical that the approach to countertrade would be affected from this general economic policy framework.

The Ministry of Foreign Trade retains its all-important licensing function and the Hungarian National Bank still has a monopoly on foreign exchange. There is an infrastructure that encourages buying as well as selling by the Western exporter and a tightening of the countertrade system would be a simple administrative adjustment. Hungary, alone in Eastern Europe, seems to have made attempts to incorporate goods exchanged on the intra-CMEA market into the countertrade goods available to Western exporters.

Poland

"All bets are off" in assessing the countertrade policies and practices in Poland. The chronic if undeclared bankruptcy of the last two years has constrained foreign trade to the level of priority items only, carefully monitored by Bank Handlowy. Unless a countertrade deal can be closed with almost simultaneous deliveries, few trading houses, or exporters seem prepared to test the Polish marketplace. Countertrade of 100 percent is thought to be the inflexible standard. In many respects commodities have to replace money as the medium of exchange. Poland must be regarded as a high-risk very complex market in which to carry out countertrade deals. Not only are there unusual problems of availability of suitable goods, delivery, pricing, and so on, these are compounded by a general uncertainty as to who is in control of foreign trade transactions.

One possibility for successful countertrade in the current circumstances is to operate through the Polish companies active offshore, like Dalimpex in Canada (part of the DAL International Trading Company, headquartered in Warsaw but with affiliates in several foreign countries). These companies can buy on their own account and may be of help in locating and delivering suitable Polish countertrade goods. The ratio is likely to remain at 100 percent as these companies can have limited buying possibilities from their own cash reserves.

Rumania

Rumania is the East European countertrade nation par excellence. It is the only country that has produced official decrees and legislations dictating strict adherence to countertrade practices and a regular balancing of the trade accounts by all FTOs. The Official Decree No. 276 of July 25, 1979, followed by an investment law, a foreign trade law effective January 1981, plus repeated exhortations of President Ceausescu place "contrapartida" at the center of Rumania's trade policy. The Rumanian Ministry of Foreign Trade is deeply involved in all countertrade transactions. Full countertrade coverage is expected of almost all imports and Rumania may have been the first country to seek countertrade obligations on imports of industrial raw materials and any other priority items. Rumanian goods offered for countertrade have a bad reputation for quality, pricing, and delivery. With Rumanian relative self-sufficiency in engineering there have been few capital turnkey projects supplied from offshore and therefore, few large compensation deals. Counterpurchase has been the form of countertrade most frequently used.

But Rumania remains a country with a tradition of haggling and everything is open to negotiation. It is in Rumania where Canadians, through the CANDU project, have had the greatest exposure to countertrade conditions, techniques, and negotiating tactics. What the CANDU countertrade negotiations proved was that Canadian companies, though loathe to undertake countertrade negotiations commitments, were able to conclude acceptable countertrade deals. There does not appear to have been any uniformity to these arrangements nor resemblance to the initial 100 percent countertrade requirement by Romenergo, the importer of record. The Organization of CANDU Industries attempted to establish countertrade limits through the negotiation of a protocol. While the conditions of this protocol may also bear little resemblance to the final signed countertrade contracts, the introduction it afforded to the concepts and negotiating pitfalls of countertrade appeared to benefit the major component suppliers.

Rumania has the most transparent countertrade system within Eastern Europe but, in many respects, it is the most confused, because it is the most bureaucratic. The Ministry of Foreign Trade, through its economic cooperation branch, maintains an organization expressly for coordinating, and advising on, countertrade deals. The FTO's Terra, Delta and Ilexim are each charged with assisting in the closing of countertrade arrangements. Despite the administrative overlay, the exporter remains charged with the primary responsibility for putting together his own countertrade deal. Once he has identified products and a contractural formula of which he is confident, he can then turn to the Ministry of Foreign Trade, the relevant sector Ministry, and the FTOs and others to seal the arrangements. Anything seems possible with countertrade in Rumania. Nothing is easily accomplished.

USSR

The Soviet Union has concentrated on the large-scale compensation deals, given the many major capital project opportunities in the country. For the Soviet economic authorities compensation is industrial cooperation. This concept has been enshrined in trade agreements and cooperation programs signed with several Western countries. Western companies have tended to be very receptive to these compensation deals, given the magnitude of the industrial projects and the marketability of the resultant products (chemical plants built to Western specifications, oil, gas, and other commodities).

As a result of this concentration on capital projects, counterpurchase deals affecting individual capital equipment sales have been modest or nonexistent. Priority commodity imports have not required countertrade obligations.

One reason posited for this low-level concern with counterpurchase has been the rigidity of the Soviet administrative system. Counterpurchase transactions cause the bureaucracy more trouble than they benefit the economy. Although Soviet counterpurchase goods suffer from the same quality, pricing, and marketing weaknesses of similar East European goods, they constitute only an insignificant amount of the Soviet Union's foreign trade and do not affect the country's balance of payments in any meaningful way. Like Canada, energy and resource exports figure largely in the Soviet Union's trade performance and will remain the mainstay of trade activity for that country.

The current credit restrictions and concern with foreign debt could lead the Soviet Union to become more preoccupied with counterpurchase transactions than it has traditionally. Since its performance on counterpurchase has been intermittent and cumbersome, a push in this direction would further complicate the exporter's attempts to sell on the Soviet market.

Yugoslavia

Yugoslavia is the most decentralized country in Eastern Europe, both politically and economically. Some would argue that Yugoslavia is not part of Eastern Europe and that business is conducted more on a Western format. For purposes of countertrade, Yugoslavia can be classified as East European; one could consider it a bundle of East European countries with its six republics and two autonomous provinces operating more or less independently. Experienced trading house officials consider Yugoslavia to be in some ways the most problematic of the East European countries because of decentralization.

Key organizations in the control of countertrade procedures in the various republics and two provinces are the "Self-Managing Interest Communities for Foreign Economic Relations" (SIZ). Each SIZ carries out monitoring operations of the regional trade in goods under the different import exchange categories. The SIZ grants authorizations for foreign currency which the importing enterprise takes to the Chamber of Economy of Yugoslavia to obtain a document that will free foreign exchange from a commercial bank. Before an import license and the requisite hard currency will be issued, the importing organization must present an export contract for an amount proportional to the planned import (now thought to be approaching 100 percent). The Federal Executive Council and Federal Trade Secretariat establish the countertrade ratios within the import exchange categories.

While Yugoslav countertrade goods are considered of better-than-average quality and there is a good deal of flexibility in what qualifies as countertrade, there are problems specific to Yugoslavia. The SIZ structure can constrain companies to work within one republic to fulfill the countertrade obligation. Inter-republic linkage is a particularly difficult arrangement to negotiate. The actual commitment to countertrade in many cases has to be finalized in a contract before the original import order can be ratified. Even if a suitable countertrade deal is agreed on, foreign currency constraints can still block the Western exporter's efforts.

Canada has had reasonable export success in Yugoslavia. It can be expected that Canadian exporters will meet with increasing pressure from Yugoslavia to balance or even exceed their sales with purchases given the country's high hard currency debt. The countertrade process in Yugoslavia, already complex and daunting to experienced Europeans, could be the source of even more difficult marketing problems for Western exporters in the current economic situation.

5

NORTH–SOUTH BARTER TRADE
Millicent H. Schwenk

INTRODUCTION

The current volume of barter transactions occurring between developed countries and less developed countries (LDCs), as well as between LDCs and other LDCs, is probably best understood in the context of the global recession and the scarcity of foreign exchange in many LDCs. Barter by these countries, however, is not a new phenomenon. One of the earliest instances of North-South barter dates back to colonial times when the American colonies traded European-manufactured goods for African slaves, which, in turn, were exchanged for molasses and rum in a triangular pattern. In a return to those practices of the eighteenth century, developing countries have increasingly used barter trade in promoting their foreign economic relations. For these countries, commercial relations usually have begun on a barter basis because of currency nonconvertibility. North-South barter trade, coupled with other countertrade transactions, is estimated to account for roughly 40 percent of total LDC trade.[1]

This chapter begins with a brief historical sketch and summary of barter negotiations to shed light on present trends. Then, since there is a paucity of material on international barter in developing countries, case studies of Indonesia and Malaysia are offered to provide a comparison of strategies for official promotion of countertrade. Finally, the concluding section describes those types of countertrade demands most likely to arise in the future.

HISTORICAL BARTER FLOWS

Extensive development of barter in the 20th century was first observed in Latin America during the 1920s and 1930s.[2] Nearly all trade in the area was on a barter basis, due to the lack of dollar and gold reserves. The most active traders at the time were Venezuela, Colombia, Ecuador, Chile, and Argentina. Up until the 1950s, almost 90 percent of total intraregional trade among these countries was attributed to this practice. Bilateral payments agreements encouraged this barter trade; the products involved included petroleum products, minerals, and agricultural commodities. By the end of the 1950s, however, bilateral arrangements with barter characteristics decreased in regional trade as a result of improvements in international payments methods and the establishment of the Latin American Free Trade Agreement ("LAFTA"), which promoted a multilateral clearing system and made cash transactions easier to execute.

Notwithstanding these developments, Mexico, Colombia, Argentina, Brazil, and Cuba began to develop barter exchanges with East European and Asian countries, primarily to dispose of agricultural surpluses. In relations with LDCs, Sino-Soviet bloc countries were especially persistent in insisting on barter forms of trade up through the 1970s.

Barter trade developed more slowly and on a smaller scale between countries in Africa and Asia after 1950. Efforts to accelerate economic development and demonstrate economic neutralism tended to foster bilateral trade by several developing countries in these regions. Gradually, this trade developed with the Sino-Soviet bloc rather than with OECD countries. The centrally planned, state-controlled economies of the Sino-Soviet bloc are particularly predisposed to enter barter arrangements. Burma, Sri Lanka, Indonesia, and India were among the first of the developing countries to establish countertrade relations with the Sino-Soviet bloc.[3] Of these countries, Indonesia has pioneered the most comprehensive countertrade policy. The remaining ASEAN member countries have only recently begun to explore new barter arrangements.

Often, LDC countertrade arrangements operate in the framework of more comprehensive bilateral agreements, particularly in trade with Sino-Soviet bloc countries and with other LDCs. Long-term arrangements, which are relatively rare, involve trade with the People's Republic of China, as well as agreements with other countries involving crude oil and related petroleum products. Among OECD countries, such agreements have been primarily initiated by Italy and Spain, whose foreign exchange earning capacity is relatively low compared to the more highly industrialized European countries. After the 1974 oil crisis, however, even France, West Germany, and the United Kingdom entered agreements with oil-producing countries. Some of these agreements were aimed at industrial cooperation, while oil for arms barter became increasingly significant as well.

Most of the countertrade activity generated today is largely ad hoc in nature. Although clearing arrangements are preferred by LDCs because they permit equilibrium in commercial exchanges, developed countries (with the exception of Greece and Spain, which have clearing arrangements with Brazil, Colombia, and Egypt) generally have opted for cash-based transactions. The Ivory Coast and Denmark, as well as Pakistan and Sweden, have established exchange relationships with payment through special accounts.

There are now approximately 28 countries that impose requirements to accept a certain percentage of payment for imports in locally produced goods. Although many governments prefer not to publicize this requirement, a 1979 OECD study reported that Pakistan, Colombia, Ecuador, Ghana, Iraq, and Egypt had officially endorsed and encouraged barter transactions. Their primary objective has been to dispose of surplus agricultural commodities in exchange for imports of investment goods, raw materials, and essential food products.

Similar motives can be ascribed to Sri Lanka, which has resorted to countertrade when prices for tea, rubber, and coconuts were depressed. Trade agreements have been signed at various times with Australia, Thailand, the Maldavian Republic, and Jordan to provide stable food imports and raw materials against payment, at least to some extent, with Sri Lankan exports.

As the following case studies of two other Asian nations, Indonesia and Malaysia, will show, economic imperatives, whether based on foreign exchange constraints, concentration of exports on a few vulnerable commodities, or the desire for export diversification, generally underlie official promotion of countertrade and barter transactions.

Since Indonesia adopted its controversial counterpurchase policy in January, 1982, other Southeast Asian countries, most notably, Malaysia, have awakened to the trade possibilities associated with barter-type arrangements. The Southeast Asian region subsequently has been identified as being in the forefront of the current world trend back to barter. Similar economic motivations, stemming from the global recession and the slump in commodity prices, have led the five member countries of ASEAN to become more active in promoting countertrade. Nevertheless, the approaches they have taken toward the role countertrade should play in trade policy have varied substantially. The cases of Indonesia and Malaysia are illustrative in this respect. Indonesia has instituted strict, mandatory counterpurchase regulations. Malaysia, by contrast, is presently developing an officially sanctioned, but more flexible, countertrade policy. An examination of the economic conditions in each of these two countries, the nature of their countertrade policies, and the types of deals they have concluded will provide an indication of the success of their approaches and a basis for assessing future trends in North-South barter arrangements.

INDONESIAN CASE STUDY

In the 1950s, Indonesia had bilateral agreements with all of the Sino-Soviet bloc countries except Albania and Bulgaria. It tended, however, to be a net creditor and the transactions ultimately proved to be disadvantageous when translated into comparable world prices. When these agreements expired in 1956, Indonesia seized the opportunity to eliminate those provisions which tied its trade too closely with Sino-Soviet exports.

Indonesia developed its countertrade program in part to spur exports hard hit by recent events.[4] Indonesia, an oil exporter, rode the wave of the petroboom during the decade preceding the 1982 oil glut. It was thus particularly hard hit by the more recent OPEC price and production cuts. The impact on Indonesia's current account has been dramatic. In 1982, for example, the World Bank pointed out that, although the country's trade balance had been expected to stay in surplus until the mid-1980s, the current account for 1981-82 went into deficit by $2.5 billion. For the year ending March, 1983, the Bank predicted a current account deficit of about $4.5 billion.

Falling prices for nonoil exports have aggravated the deficit. The value of exports of tin, rubber, and coffee, for example, decreased by even larger percentages than oil exports. In contrast, imports to Indonesia have been steadily rising. During the first three months of 1982, for example, imports increased approximately 32 percent to $3.96 billion from $2.98 billion in the same period of 1981.[5]

In the future the current account could also be adversely affected if the impact of drought conditions on rice production necessitates increased food imports. Eventually, Indonesia's ability to keep external borrowing within its debt-servicing capacity may be questioned. Persistent current account deficits and increased borrowing could substantially increase the debt burden.

These concerns led the Indonesian government to introduce a trade development program in January, 1982. This program liberalized export financing by extending payments terms, streamlining customs procedures, and introducing countertrade rules.[6] The countertrade policy is much stricter than practices common in Eastern Europe and elsewhere in the world because of the range of procurements covered, penalties for noncompliance, and "additionality" requirements. The countertrade provisions apply to all purchases by government departments and state entities, including state companies, of foreign goods in excess of Rps 500 million (U.S. $735,000). Essentially, foreign suppliers must agree to a 100 percent counter purchase of nonoil and gas products against the value of the imports brought into Indonesia.

The policy, however, does not apply to private sector transactions. Moreover, it does not cover foreign direct investment in Indonesia. Other exemptions from the policy include: (1) procurements financed through concessional bilateral loans or credits from the World Bank, the Asian Development Bank, the Islamic Development Bank, and other national development agencies; (2) expenditures for domestically produced components, including service components and applicable taxes and duties; (3) professional services provided by foreign accountants, lawyers, surveyors, and consultants, as well as the purchase of technology and patents; and (4) purchases from imports in the framework of joint ventures between state enterprises and foreign companies. Even with these exceptions, the policy covers much of Indonesia's external trade.

The exports linked to government procurement are primarily agricultural commodities, but some industrial goods such as steel pipes, tires, cement, glass, processed woods, and textile products are included on the periodic lists of eligible export commodities drawn up by the Department of Trade and Cooperatives. Values of the Indonesian exports and of the procurement contracts are to be determined on an FOB basis using the prevailing prices at the time of the contract signing.

An important aspect of the policy is the fostering of "additionality." Generally, exports associated with the fulfillment of countertrade obligations are to be sold or used in addition to transactions normally concluded with the country concerned. Diversion to a third country will only be permitted if that country has not already served as a market for the export commodity. Finally, upon completion of the procurement contract, the supplier will be liable for a 50 percent cash penalty against any unfulfilled export obligations.

The Indonesian countertrade policy has met with stiff resistance from overseas suppliers. Notwithstanding that resistance, Indonesian trade officials have pursued the policy. In their view, LDCs like Indonesia must use countertrade to maintain trade at appropriate levels.

It was only in August, 1982, several months after the guidelines were introduced, that the first agreement, involving Indonesia's annual fertilizer tender, was concluded. Five companies that had bid to supply some of the fertilizer were excluded from consideration for refusal to sign a counterpurchase commitment letter.[7] At the time of this writing, it was unclear whether the contract terms had been successfully satisfied as claimed.

The finalized transaction is expected to involve approximately $152 million worth of fertilizer (1 million metric tons) exchanged by ten foreign suppliers for various Indonesian products of equal value. The companies that agreed to supply the fertilizer are: International Commodities Export Company (ICEC), United States; Amitrex Corp. of the United States; Sagita International Ltd., United States; Fred Leker and Co., West Germany; Kuok (Singapore) Ltd.; Danubiana, Rumania; Harttindo Enterprise (Pte.) Ltd., Singapore; Kali Bergbau, East Germany; Woodward and Dickerson (Singapore) Pte. Ltd.; and Mitsubishi Corporation, Japan.

To provide an idea of the complexity of this deal, one has only to look at the transactions associated with ICEC's share of the arrangement. ICEC is a division of ACLI International, Inc., one of the largest independent exporters of fertilizer and fertilizer raw materials. It operates in over 60 countries and also deals in industrial chemicals and minerals, feedstuffs, and equipment and machinery ranging from construction to the electronics field. In the Indonesian deal, ICEC contributed the largest portion of the fertilizer supplied, approximately $58 million FOB. This value represents approximately 289 thousand metric tons of fertilizer, consisting of (1) 60,000 metric tons of bagged Iranian urea; (2) 10,000 metric tons of ammonium sulfate from West Germany; (3) 76,000 metric tons of potassium chloride from Saskatchewan, Canada; and (4) 143,000 metric tons of triple superphosphate from Tunisia and Turkey. In exchange, ICEC reportedly received $58 million worth of Indonesian rubber, coffee, cocoa, and cement.[8]

In assessing the significance of the fertilizer tender, foreign business executives and U.S. government officials have disputed the Indonesian government's position that this case was a sound test of the country's ability to impose its countertrade policy. They argue that with a glut on the world fertilizer market, competitive pressures forced the suppliers to be more flexible. Furthermore, settlement of the annual fertilizer tender proved cumbersome with the counterpurchase stipulations. Whereas the process usually takes two months, in 1982 over five months were required to conclude the agreement. As a result, cargo delivery dates were forced back at least two or three months, possibly jeopardizing Indonesia's ambitious program to increase its rice and plantation crops.

Beyond delays in the annual fertilizer shipments, the counterpurchase requirements have caused a drastic slowdown in the number of major contracts the Indonesian government has put out to bid. The reduction in tender activity may well reflect a recognition by Indonesian officials that they must slow government spending in light of oil revenue shortfalls. The countertrade policy has been an effective means of doing so. In reducing tender activity, the Indonesians may also be trying to reduce opportunities for bidders to demonstrate their dislike for this important aspect of Indonesian trade policy.

Since the fertilizer procurement, there has been only one additional major counterpurchase agreement. That deal involved a $1 billion oil refinery project bid won by Japanese companies, requiring a complementary counterpurchase over a period of several years. Given the enormous size of this agreement, Japanese officials have continued to meet with Indonesian officials in an attempt to negotiate revisions to or the elimination of the counterpurchase requirement.

There have been a number of small deals as well. Approximately 20 companies have pledged counterpurchase of some $350 million in all. This compares with total annual nonoil and gas exports of $4-6 billion over the past several years.[9] Half of these counterpurchase obligations are accounted for by the fertilizer and oil refinery deals.

Thus, even with the counterpurchase law, the government found it necessary to postpone indefinitely as of May 9, 1983 the country's four largest industrial projects, totaling $5.05 billion. The cuts are supposed to narrow the current account deficit by $4 billion in 1984, a sum comparable to the expected reduction in oil revenues following the recent decrease in the OPEC benchmark price. Significantly, the oil refinery project, to be built on Sumatra by the Japan Gas Co. and a group of Japanese trading companies, including C. Itoh & Co. and Nissho-Iwai Corp., was one of the four cancelled projects.[10]

Government expectations that the counterpurchase policy would boost export earnings by $2 billion a year have proved to be overly optimistic in light of resistance to the law's rigid provisions by most of Indonesia's non-ASEAN trading partners. Evidently, the National Planning Board overestimated the extent to which the recessionary buyer's market would mollify opposition to countertrade requirements.

Until the Mitsubishi Corp. took part in the fertilizer sale, Japanese business and government officials had been among the strongest opponents of the Indonesian policy. Taking into account Indonesia's worsening balance-of-payments position, these officials decided that, rather than outrightly reject the counterpurchase policy, they would go along with a 20 percent counterpurchase obligation and a maximum cash penalty of 5 percent. They also objected to the additionality requirements. Indonesian officials initially rejected these terms. There is now speculation that the Indonesian government is seeking a face-saving way to soften its counterpurchase regulations to accommodate partners like the Japanese. Nevertheless, the only concession Mitsubishi received for participating in the fertilizer tender was a short clause providing for review if the counterpurchase requirements could not be met due to difficulties on the part of the Indonesians.[11]

In spite of the opposition of its trading partners, Indonesia has continued to expand its counterpurchase requirements. For example, in February, 1983, Indonesia extended the policy to cover imports of kerosene and oil from Singapore by Pertamina, the state-owned oil company. Remuneration will be with a surplus low-sulphur waxy residue Pertamina has had difficulty marketing. Indonesia has also proved hard-nosed in granting countertrade exemptions. It currently makes those exemptions available only in those purchases explicitly financed on concessional terms. For example, a dispute has arisen with Canada concerning the purchase of Canadian equipment worth $160 million for the Bukit Asam coal mine project. Approximately $38 million of the equipment was financed on concessional terms by the Canadian International Development Agency (CIDA). Prime Minister Pierre Trudeau argued that since the CIDA portion was significant, additional financing by the Export Development Corporation on export-credit terms should be considered as part of one exempt package. The Indonesian authorities continue to maintain that the EDC portion is subject to the countertrade policy.

In retrospect, the Indonesian countertrade policy has not proved to be a very effective technique to promote exports. One must recognize, however, that it was enacted in response to a rapidly deteriorating economic situation. As long as the world continues suffering through a recession, LDCs like Indonesia may not be able to sell their principal commodities at favorable prices and will be tempted to pursue a countertrade policy. As for the future of the countertrade policy, Indonesia's past history of countertrade with the Sino-Soviet bloc would appear to indicate that once the economy begins to turn around, the present policy will be repealed or revised.[12]

Since Indonesia exports world-market products such as tea, coffee, rubber, and tin, and imports a wide variety of manufactured goods, the nature of its trade favors multilateral cash-based transactions. Indonesia's traditional trade pattern is, thus, heavily oriented toward Western industrial nations. When trade is active and commodity prices strong, it stands to gain little from strictly adhering to countertrade. Yet, when world demand falls, as the present situation illustrates, it can prove difficult to shift marketing to bilateral countertrade arrangements, especially when a strict policy is adopted. Moreover, recession is forcing ASEAN countries to be more competitive in vying for exports and direct investment than a few years ago. Governments therefore are showing an increased willingness to negotiate on all aspects of a project. Further drops in oil prices may ultimately serve to undercut nationalistic policies like the Indonesian countertrade requirement, especially since, within Indonesia itself, a consensus on the value of the countertrade policy is lacking.

MALAYSIAN CASE STUDY

In contrast to Indonesia's unilateral imposition of a demanding countertrade policy, Malaysian authorities have adopted a more pragmatic wait-and-see approach toward defining the role countertrade will play in their country's trade strategy.[13] Although there are as yet no formal laws, the Ministry of Trade and Industry has committed itself to creating a special countertrade unit in its International Trade Division. No reports have been issued from this unit thus far, but it is authorized to examine potential countertrade markets and products as well as to draw up guidelines for private business.

Countertrade first attracted serious attention in Malaysia during 1982. Unlike many other developing countries, Malaysia had traditionally insisted on hard currency payments from the Eastern bloc countries as well as convertible currency payments from other developing regions. With rising exports and large trade surpluses throughout the 1970s, there was no incentive or need to resort to barter.

A change of attitude occurred, however, in response to recent international economic developments. Malaysia's exploration of opportunities offered by countertrade basically stems from three major developments. First, shortages of foreign currency and restrictions on currency transactions made it difficult for Malaysia to maintain sales in East bloc countries, most notably, Rumania, the USSR, and Yugoslavia, and in new markets in South America. Second, the terms of trade on Malaysia's traditional commodity exports worsened. Third, Malaysia witnessed a decline in its ability to pay for imports with hard currency. The country's external reserves sank in the first eight months of 1982 to such a low level that only approximately ten weeks' worth of imports could be financed. The trade deficit simultaneously widened to $396.5 million.

The first indication that a change of attitude had indeed occurred followed a February, 1982 visit by the North Korean Premier, Li Jong Ok. The Malaysian Prime Minister, Mahathir Mohamad, apparently promised to investigate the possibilities of bartering palm oil, rubber, and natural gas for coal, fertilizers, metals, and construction equipment. The decision to create the countertrade unit in the Ministry of Trade and Industry confirms this decision to explore countertrade options.

Malaysian trade officials stress, however, that the current emphasis on countertrade is not so much a result of Malaysia's present economic situation, but rather a reflection of the desire to aggressively promote exports. Countertrade is viewed as one way of promoting trade with those countries. In July, 1982, the prime minister publicly espoused countertrading with Eastern European countries, in particular those with foreign exchange shortages. Since his speech, missions by Malaysian ministers and visits by foreign dignitaries to Malaysia have included discussions on countertrade.

The director of the Trade and Industry Ministry's international trade division, Asmat Kamaluddin, has also indicated that Malaysia would actively pursue countertrade with Pakistan, Burma, and Bangladesh, all experienced countertraders with whom Malaysia runs a significant surplus on its merchandise trade account. Malaysian trade officials also have indicated that they are seeking to promote countertrade with Thailand and Australia, two countries with whom Malaysia's trade has traditionally be in deficit. The current approach to countertrade thus indicates an attempt to even out surpluses and deficits.

There are still a number of ambiguities in the Malaysian stance toward countertrade. For example, there are many countries with which Malaysia has large trade deficits, such as the United States and various Middle Eastern countries, that have been viewed as unwilling to countertrade. Apparently yielding to this unwillingness, Malaysian trade officials have indicated that the government will not seek to impose countertrade obligations on U.S. exporters.

Malaysian trade officials have also pointed out that Malaysia would like to use countertrade in carrying out large-scale construction projects, particularly in the transportation infrastructure area. They have expressed a desire to import other basic products including sugar, wheat, grains, chemicals, and heavy machinery through countertrade too. However, likely partners for such transactions may be hard to find. Potential countertrade partners in capital goods and transport equipment from Eastern Europe have met consumer resistance in the past, at any rate, and Malaysian officials want to diversify their supply sources for certain of these manufactured items. Countries such as India, Pakistan, and Egypt, which could supply small-scale manufactured items and light armaments, offer only limited outlets for Malaysia's industrial raw materials such as rubber and tin. Palm oil, however, a major Malaysian agricultural commodity, is in high demand in India and Pakistan, thus suggesting the possibility of a deal involving that commodity. Indeed, the governments of Malaysia and Pakistan have pursued lengthy negotiations involving exchanging palm oil for wheat, cotton, rice, and railway equipment. Malaysian officials have also discussed bartering rubber and petroleum for two South Korean ships. In addition, it appears that there exist numerous possible countertrade opportunities involving these commodities with both Western Europe and the United States. Notwithstanding the reluctance of the U.S. government, one possible transaction, for example, might involve exchanging U.S. wheat for Malaysian rubber.

Much of the scope of future Malaysian countertrade depends on the initiatives of the new trading companies modeled after the *sogo sosha* of Japan. The government is presently trying to lay the groundwork for these quasi-governmental organizations which currently often buy for the government account. The five major companies are as follows: (1) Nastra, established in December, 1981 and owned in equal shares by Malaysia Mining Corp., the Federal Land Development Authority, the Kuok brothers group, and the state oil company, Petronas; (2) Mattra, or the Malaysian Transnational Trading Corp., a joint venture between Palmco Holdings, United Motor Works, the Selangor state government, and a state-owned food industry conglomerate, Kumpulan Fima; (3) PAM, formed by the Sabah-based Kim Chuan Seng Holdings group, the National Youth Cooperative, units of the Sarawak and Sabah state governments, and the Sabah Associated Chamber of Commerce and Industry; (4) Multipurpose Holdings, created in December, 1982 through the restructuring of a Singapore-incorporated subsidiary, Guthrie Bhd., along with the purchase of a half-share in ITM International by Guthrie and a sister company; and (5) Sime Darby Pernas Trading Corp., owned 60 percent by Sime Darby, a private trading company, and 40 percent by Perbadanan Nasional, or Pernas, a state trading company.

So far only Sime Darby has made it clear that, in addition to promoting trade and investment, it is being structured to take advantage of countertrade trends in the long-term. Each office will consist of a core of traders skilled in various barter trade methods and at trade in nontraditional commodities.

Malaysia's pragmatic approach to countertrade appears directed toward a more permanent, but flexible institutionalization of countertrade policy than in Indonesia. One must recognize, however, that Malaysia does not face economic problems as severe as Indonesia's.[14] It is likely that Malaysia will use countertrade more selectively than will Indonesia, primarily to take advantage of market opportunities that would otherwise be unexploitable. The Malaysians claim that they have not in any way been influenced by Indonesian policy and, indeed, it is more likely that their manner of organizing for countertrade will allow them more effectively to use countertrade for profitable purposes.

COUNTERTRADE IN OTHER COUNTRIES

Like Indonesia and Malaysia, Thailand and the Philippines export primarily agricultural commodities, which recently have been subject to declining terms of trade.[15] In response, both countries have institutionally organized for countertrade. Of the two, the Philippines has more aggressively explored the countertrade option, probably because of previous experience in the mid-1970s. Drawing on a 1959 law, detailed rules were at that time adopted to govern countertrade transactions. Exports suitable for countertrading were defined as those which could not be sold on the market for convertible currency. The Soviet Union and Rumania were natural trading partners.

A new state trading organization, the Philippine Trading Centre, was set up as the marketing arm of the Ministry of Trade and Industry. It has not yet signed a deal, but Philippine authorities have been exploring trade possibilities. The West Germans recently turned down a deal to exchange coconut oil for equipment because of marketing difficulties, but a deal was under negotiation with the Trade Development Corp. at the time of this writing. As a result of pressure from the International Monetary Fund, however, the Philippine government may avoid countertrade to the extent possible.

Thailand also has a government committee in charge of regulating barter trade. Under the November, 1982 approval of the Council of Economic Ministers, the committee was authorized to exchange Thai farm products for agricultural production materials and capital goods. As with the Indonesian law, though, exports have been restricted by additionality requirements and a stipulation against re-export to third countries. Thus far, new barter deals have been negotiated with only three countries—the Soviet Union, Rumania, and South Korea—supplying fertilizer in exchange for Thai maize and tapioca chips. Barter probably will have little impact on Thai exports in the near term, but there is scope for expansion.

In addition to countertrade demands in traditional export sectors, a distinguishing feature of new trends in countertrade outside ASEAN countries is the diversity of products involved. Although large-scale projects in oil-exporting developing countries like Mexico, Venezuela, and Algeria have been financed by oil exports, today newly industrialized countries such as Brazil, Mexico, and India are more aggressively encouraging countertrade exports of manufactured items.

Mexico, for example, has a national development plan which targets for self-sufficiency the electronics and automobile sectors. An official decree permits foreign equity ownership in the manufacturing of selected components in the electronics industry only if certain compensation requirements amounting to the export of at least 75 percent of output are met. Similarly, an earlier 1977 decree requires that each plant involved in automobile assembly or automotive parts manufacturing prepare an annual foreign exchange budget in which company imports are balanced by exports. Such requirements tend to foster compensation and counterpurchase arrangements.[16]

Brazil has stiffer and broader export requirements than Mexico because they apply to all industries. Since the December, 1982 debt crisis, officials have been more actively promoting countertrade, especially with countries which have accumulated debts with Brazil.

Countries such as Mexico, Angola, Nigeria, Chile, Argentina, Bolivia, Rumania, and Poland have debts outstanding to Brazil of some $4 billion, roughly half the 1983 petroleum import bill. American firms looking to dispose of countertrade goods from Brazil should be aware of Brazilian trade activity in these third markets and possibilities for triangular trade.

Brazilian countertrade with debtor countries brings up a third possible use of countertrade as a mechanism for the settlement of debt arrears. Although some banks are advising their clients on this use of countertrade, its potential as a means to ensure repayment of new and outstanding loans has not been fully explored. The Turkish government proved that this approach is useful in settling suppliers' credit arrears in 1979, following its debt rescheduling.

In January, 1980, Turkey announced a plan to settle some $2 billion in nonofficially guaranteed commercial arrearages involving approximately 100,000 transactions and 25,000 claimants. The arrearages arose from the Central Bank's inability to make foreign exchange transfers at the end of 1979. The settlement plan presented foreign suppliers with two options. They could accept payment either in Turkish lira or in one of five foreign currencies with extended payment terms. If a creditor accepted payment in lira, the payment had to be used to increase the working capital of an existing investment, serve as equity in a new investment, invest in fasconnage production or shipbuilding, extend payment to Turkish importers, make freight payments to Turkish transporters, or cover touristic expenses.

The Turkish government also attempted to use *façonnage* to its benefit. *Façonnage* entails job order production in which the contractor provides inputs or the cost in foreign exchange and takes a manufactured product in return. The Turkish government tried to promote this use of the lira payments as well as investment by applying more favorable currency translation rates.[17]

FUTURE TRENDS

In the future, official requirements for countertrade by LDC governments will be used for three major purposes. First, as has been illustrated in the case of ASEAN countries, countertrade will be used to promote exports of surplus commodities in order to counter widening trade deficits. As long as the volume of trade and prices of primary products exports remains low, the current account of the LDCs will tend to remain negative. As a result, as Table 5.1 suggests, most

Table 5.1 Current Account Balances (in U.S. $ billion)

	1979	1980	1981
LDCs	-41.8	-72.8	-109.7
Oil importers	-46.9	-71.1	- 10.1
Low income	- 8.7	-14.6	- 80.4
Middle income	-38.2	-56.5	- 70.3
Oil exporters	5.1	- 1.7	- 29.3

Source: World Development Report, 1982.

countertrade demands will come from the middle-income oil-importing countries.

If one additionally looks at GNP growth rates, the dramatic decrease of growth rates in Latin America presages a revival of countertrade there, especially since a number of the Latin American countries exhibit the highest debt service ratios in the world. Between the debt service payments and payments for oil imports, hard currency reserves are largely committed for many of these countries. It is from countries in similar adverse economic straits that countertrade requirements can be expected to be officially instituted.

The International Trade Commission forecasts a rise in compensation deals—deals involving transfer of production technology and capital equipment in exchange for a specific quantity of the plant's output—because the primary activity of multinationals in LDCs is in the mineral extraction area. Such projects are ideal for compensation arrangements in tight credit markets because they demand financing for large projects. Since exporters have been unable to form cartels for zinc, iron ore, bauxite, and copper, compensation agreements can also help regulate fluctuating demand for raw material exports and compensate for declining terms of trade. Moreover, with Western firms moving away from equity mining projects due to the risks of expropriation and other related risks, management contracts and compensation agreements can provide substitutes for direct foreign investment.

Several LDCs have official "development-for-import" programs that provide subsidized loans and credits to their mining companies to develop foreign sources of minerals. These programs are carried out through compensation or counterpurchase arrangements to secure long-term guaranteed supplies of strategic raw and process materials.[18]

If *façonnage* became a more widespread practice, it would permit repayment to creditors while stimulating employment and productive growth in the debtor country. Moreover, an assured outlet for production would alleviate some of the marketing problems that arise when numerous LDC trading partners are simultaneously undergoing austerity programs, cutting imports, and stimulating exports.

An expanded role for barter and countertrade transactions in North-South trade would benefit developed countries, too. For example, excess agricultural commodities could be exchanged for minerals from developing countries. In the United States, for example, the minerals then could be sold to the National Defense Stockpile. The National Defense Stockpile currently holds some $7.64 billion worth of strategic and critical materials against their possible need in event of a national emergency. In addition, the Stockpile has unfilled goals for a list of other materials representing future acquistion outlays of some $12.5 billion. The General Services Administration (GSA) makes purchases of needed stockpile materials on behalf of the U.S. government, with the aim of not unduly disrupting the usual markets in those materials. The current soft markets in some materials represent an opportunity for barter for minerals which are not otherwise readily saleable by the LDCs and which GSA could acquire at a currently favorable price without disrupting the market.

A possible scenario in this area would involve, for example, the barter of rice for cobalt from Zaire. Zaire is short of cash but has a bountiful supply of cobalt and other minerals. Cobalt, in particular, is a strategic material which is on the priority list for acquisition for the Stockpile. In fiscal years 1979-1983, GSA purchased some $114 million worth of cobalt from Zaire and Zambia for the Stockpile, leaving a deficit in the Stockpile goal of over $850 million.

A barter arrangement involving agricultural commodities and cobalt would entail two separate contracts and three parties: the bartering company, Zaire, and GSA. The private company holding the commodity, for example, could enter into one contract with Zaire to exchange the rice for cobalt, and into a second contract with GSA to sell the cobalt to the Stockpile. The barter agreement, although ultimately expressed in terms of a ratio of the two goods, could be negotiated by the parties with a view to "shadow prices" reflecting the parties' costs and current market prices. (An often unstated advantage to barter may be a "hidden" discount from official selling prices, made through the exchange ratio for the goods, without openly disturbing the official prices.) Notwithstanding its opposition to countertrade, the current administration could be expected to support an arrangement which would increase exports by the hard-pressed U.S. agricultural sector while fulfilling our national defense goals for the Stockpile.

Similar North-South deals organized on the same model as the Stockpile deal described above might involve bartering excess agricultural products for fuel to build up the Strategic Petroleum Reserve administered by the Department of Energy (DOE). The secretary of Energy has broad, discretionary authority to acquire oil for the Strategic Petroleum Reserve "by purchase, exchange, or otherwise," consonant with the objectives, among others, of minimizing the cost of the Reserve and reducing the vulnerability of the United States to a "severe energy supply interruption." This broad authority would allow DOE to enter a barter agreement to exchange rice for oil on a short-term or continuing basis.

One likely candidate for a "food for fuel" barter agreement would be Nigeria. Nigeria is an oil producer which is nevertheless suffering a hard currency shortage because of the current soft market in crude oil. In addition, Nigeria is a major consumer of rice.

Acting under his statutory authority, the secretary could enter an agreement to exchange rice for oil from Nigeria. The agreement could run for 12 months, with options to renew the agreement in succeeding years. DOE would then enter agreements with either the Commodity Credit Corporation (CCC) or private companies for the purchase of rice stocks. The agreement would benefit the administration by aiding agricultural producers without increasing the budget, while assuring a supply of oil to the Reserve.

Alternatively, DOE could rely on a private party acting essentially as a broker between the oil-producing country and DOE. The private company owning rice, for example, would enter into two contracts, one with Nigeria for the exchange of rice for oil and one with DOE for the purchase of oil. A protocol with DOE would be necessary to link the deliveries of oil to the Reserve with receipt of the oil from Nigeria.

CONCLUSION

Although controversial, countertrade will continue to be one form of trading used by LDCs. LDCs in all regions have utilized and are presently utilizing countertrade, predominantly among themselves and the Sino-Soviet bloc, but also increasingly with the industrialized countries. Although the Europeans, with their long-term commercial ties with former colonies in Africa, Asia, and Latin America, have traditionally been more active in countertrade, large American exporters, such as GM, Sears, PhibroSalomon, and General Electric, have become more active in these areas in order to maintain their market share. Other, smaller independent trading companies, like Cicatrade, an affiliate of the Brazilian trading company of the same name, are finding opportunities in countries just beginning to impose countertrade requirements. Cicatrade, for example, has a flourishing business and is involved in deals with Argentina, Chile, Paraguay, Uruguay, Nigeria, and Togo.

Countertrade is not a new phenomenon in LDCs, but its present uprise has two distinguishing characteristics. Both the number of countries involved and the variety of commodities exchanged are greater than ever. Although LDCs have traditionally bartered agricultural and mineral commodities with the north for capital goods, transport equipment, industrial plants and, more rarely, food, semi-industrial countries are now offering manufactured goods, as well as services, in countertrade. Thus, it appears that although countertrade has most often been resorted to because of foreign exchange constraints, as in the case of Indonesia, in the future it may also be used more frequently, as in Malaysia, as a device for promoting diversification of exports.

APPENDIX

Basic Provisions of the Linkage of Government Procurements from Imports with the Export of Indonesian Products Excluding Oil and Natural Gas

1. Government procurements from imports which are linked with the export of Indonesian products other than oil and natural gas are those procurements which are financed from the State Budget and from export credits.
2. The compulsory linkage of Government procurements with exports relates to purchases done by Governments, Non-Departmental Government Institutions, and State Enterprises which are coordinated under Presidential Decree No.: 10, 1980 (KEPPRES NO.: 10, 1980).
3. Exempt from such linkage are:
   a. Procurements financed through concessional bilateral loans and credits from the World Bank, the Asian Development Bank, and the Islamic Development Bank.

    b. Expenditures for domestically manufactured components which are included in the contract of the foreign supplier, which include among others: service components, goods, taxes, and duties.

    c. Services which are used by various Government agencies, including those provided by foreign accountants, lawyers, surveyors, consultants, as well as the purchase of technology, patents, etc.

    d. Purchases from imports in the framework of joint venture between state enterprises and foreign companies.

4. Export commodities linked to procurements are agricultural commodities, industrial goods, and other goods excluding oil and natural gas. The Department of Trade and Cooperatives will periodically draw up a list of the export commodities that are eligible for meeting linkage requirements for various countries or groups of countries. These lists will include the names of the exporters/ commodity associations.

5. The foreign supplier is to purchase or arrange the purchase of the Indonesian export commodities through one or several companies that are affiliated or otherwise have a relationship with the foreign supplier. A company of a third party in another country acceptable to the Government may also become the executing agency thereof.

6. Foreign importers fulfilling linkage undertakings may select one or several commodities to be imported from Indonesia. The export value of the Indonesian linked commodities must be equal in value to the Government procurement from abroad, taking into account the exceptions stated in point 3 above.

7. The value of the Indonesian export commodities and the value of the contract for the Government procurement are to be stated on the FOB basis. The price used in the calculation will be the price of the export commodity concerned at the time of signing the contract.

8. Foreign importers and Indonesian exporters will conduct negotiations directly and sign their trade agreement in conformity with normal practices, but inserting one additional clause concerning linkage undertakings. Copies of such contracts are to be sent to the Department of Trade and Cooperatives, to the attention of the Directorate General of Foreign Trade, as well as to the Department or Government Institution making the procurement.

9. Purchases by foreign importers have to be in addition to the total export transactions normally concluded with the country concerned. The Department of Trade and Cooperatives in cooperation with the commodity associations will monitor the implementation thereof.

10. Commodities exporters' unfulfillment of linkage undertakings must be sold or used in the supplier's country of origin. In the case of Government procurements from overseas supplied from several countries, the linkage undertaking is to be effected with either the country that has won the tender and/or the country of origin of the procured goods.

11. Export to a third country can only be permitted if the third country has not yet become a market for the Indonesian export commodity concerned or by special permit of the Department of Trade and Cooperatives.

12. Export transactions are to be made in United States dollars or other convertible foreign currency, as long as such currency is used by the supplier of the goods purchased by the Government.

13. Contracts concluded between the Indonesian exporters and the foreign importers are not to constitute a "future" buying arrangement designed to safeguard or "hedge" the position of the importer or the exporter against price fluctuations.

14. Indonesian export undertakings must be effected in stages during the contract period for the Government procurement and be completed prior to the termination date of the procurement contract.

15. The foreign supplier is responsible for the implementation of the contract for the export of the Indonesian commodity or commodities. The supplier will be liable to a penalty amounting to 50 percent of the value of any unfilled export undertakings upon completion of a procurement contract.

Letter of Undertaking

Each Tenderer should note that, as part of its Tender, it will be required to submit a Letter of Undertaking in the form contained in these Tender Documents. Copies of the "List of Indonesian Export Commodities available for Additional Exports" and of the "List of Indonesian Commodity Associations and Exporters" referred to in the Letter of Undertaking are available from the Department of Trade and Cooperatives upon request.

After the Tenders have been evaluated, one of the Tenderers will be notified that it has been selected for contract negotiations, which, if successful, will lead to contract award. Prior to, and as a condition of, contract award, such Tenderer (or any affiliate thereof or other third party acceptable to the Department of Trade and Cooperatives) will be expected to enter into arrangements with one or more Indonesian exporter, designed to satisfy its obligations under the Letter of Undertaking and otherwise satisfactory to the Department of Trade Cooperatives.

Each Tenderer is urged to initiate discussions with such Indonesian exporters promptly after the submission of its Tender Documents in order not to delay contract award should it be selected for contract negotiations.

[LETTERHEAD OF TENDERER]*

_____, 1982

Department of Trade and Cooperatives
Republic of Indonesia
Directorate General for Foreign Trade
Jalan Abdul Muis 87
Jakarta
INDONESIA

c/o [Insert name of Department, Agency or
    Corporation issuing Tender]

Dear Sirs:

We refer to [describe subject matter of tender and tender number] issued on _____, 198_ by [insert name of Indonesian Department, Agency, or Corporation issuing tender] and to our tender document no. _____ submitted on _____, 198_ in response thereto.

We hereby irrevocably undertake during the period from the date of award of the contract relating to such tender until final acceptance (or equivalent) of our work and services thereunder or until completion of deliveries thereunder, as the case may be:

---

*This letter should be signed and submitted by the Tenderer. If the Tenderer is a foreign contractor/supplier, this letter should be signed by the foreign contractor/supplier and not by its Indonesian agent, partner or representative, if any.

1. to purchase, or to cause to be purchased by one or more of our affiliated companies in the country or countries† to be confirmed by the Department of Trade and Cooperatives in a letter in the form of Annex A hereto or by third parties located in any other country or countries acceptable to you, agricultural and/or industrial products contained in Books A.1 and A.2, each entitled "List of Indonesian Export Commodities Available for Additional Exports in 1982," published in January 1982 and March 1982, respectively, by the Department of Trade and Cooperatives, and/or such other Indonesian products as you may approve in writing (hereinafter, collectively, the "Products"), from one or more of the commodity associations or exporters named in Books B.1 and B.2, each entitled "List of Indonesian Commodity Associations and Exporters", published in January 1982 and March 1982, respectively, by the Department of Trade and Cooperatives, and/or from other duly licensed Indonesian exporters (hereinafter, collectively, the "Exporters"), in an amount at least equal to the foreign currency value of all equipment, materials, and products to be supplied by us from non-Indonesian sources pursuant to the terms of the above-described contract, such value to be agreed with the Department of Trade and Cooperatives and confirmed in a letter in the form of Annex A hereto;

2. to use the Products, or to resell the Products for use, or to cause the Products to be used or resold, in the country or countries to be confirmed as aforesaid, unless with your specific authorization we are permitted to use the Products, or to resell the Products for use, or to cause the Products to be used or resold, in any other country or countries.

3. to purchase the Products, or to cause the Products to be purchased, before the end of the term of the contract relating to the above-described tender and, in any event, to purchase or to cause to be purchased, at least twenty percent (20%) of the total value of the Products to be purchased hereunder within six (6) months after the date of award of such contract; and

4. to submit, or to cause to be submitted, to the Department of Trade and Cooperatives the relevant PEB Form and such other evidence of the shipment of Products purchased pursuant to this undertaking as will permit the Department of Trade and Cooperatives to monitor compliance herewith.

---

†The Department of Trade and Cooperatives will normally only confirm the country of nationality of the contractor/supplier. However, depending upon the circumstances of any given contract, other countries may be confirmed by the Department.

In connection with our irrevocable undertaking contained herein, this will confirm our understanding that:

a. the commercial terms, including those related to price and delivery, in respect of each purchase of Products from an Exporter shall be negotiated by us or by other purchasers thereof at the time of actual purchase;

b. the amount of each such purchase to be applied towards our obligation hereunder shall be equal to the invoiced purchase price of the Products purchased, excluding, however, any shipping costs included in such invoice and any taxes or customs duties charged in connection therewith;

c. the amount of each such purchase (if measured in a currency other than the currency in which our obligation hereunder is measured) shall be applied against our obligation hereunder at exchange rates (as quoted by Bank Indonesia) prevailing at the date of the Exporters' invoice issued in respect of such purchase;

d. if we or our affiliated companies in the country or countries to be confirmed as aforesaid have traditionally purchased Products from Indonesian exporters, our undertaking contained herein shall be viewed as representing a commitment over and above such traditional level of purchases, it being the spirit and intention of such undertaking that purchases of Products hereunder shall be in addition to such traditional level of purchases;

e. if the contract relating to the above-described tender should be prematurely terminated, our undertaking contained herein shall also terminate without further obligation on our part; and

f. if, during the course of performance of our obligations contained herein, we should be of the view that sufficient Products are either not available in Indonesia or are not of suitable export quality or internationally competitive in price, you shall, at our request, review with us the actual circumstances at the time and shall consider, but without obligation, modifying the requirements contained herein (including, without limitation, and extension of the time during which our obligations contained herein must be satisfied).

If we fail to comply with our undertaking contained herein, we hereby agree to pay to you as liquidated damages an amount equal to 50% of the difference between the total value of Products actually purchased pursuant to this undertaking and the foreign currency amount to be confirmed as aforesaid.

In connection with our undertaking contained herein, we hereby represent and warrant to you that (i) we have full power and authority and legal right to enter into this undertaking and to perform and observe the terms and provisions hereof, (ii) we have taken all necessary legal action to authorize, execute, and deliver this undertaking, (iii) this undertaking constitutes our legal, valid, and binding obligation, and (iv) no law, rule or regulation, or contractual or other obligation binding on us is or will be contravened by reason of our execution and delivery of this undertaking or by our performance and observance of the terms and provisions hereof.

This undertaking shall be binding upon our successors.

Very truly yours
[NAME OF TENDER]

By _____
Name:
Title :

[LETTERHEAD OF DEPARTMENT OF TRADE AND COOPERATIVES]

_____, 198_

[Address of Tenderer]

Dear Sirs:

We refer to _____ Tender No. _____ issued on _____, 198_ by [insert name of Indonesian Department, Agency or Corporation issuing tender] (the "Tender") and to your tender document submitted in response thereto.

We acknowledge receipt of your Letter of Undertaking of _____, 198_ a copy of which is attached hereto and initialled for identification by the Department of Trade and Cooperatives.

In accordance with the provisions of paragraph number 1 of such Letter of Undertaking, we confirm the following:

1. The foreign currency value of all equipment, materials, and products to be supplied by you from non-Indonesian sources pursuant to the terms of the contract relating to the Tender shall be _____;

2. The country [countries] referred to in such paragraph shall be, _____.

Your signature in the space marked "Agreed" below shall be conclusive evidence of your agreement to be bound by the terms of your Letter of Undertaking of _____, 198_, as supplemented by the provisions hereof.

Very truly yours,
DEPARTMENT OF TRADE
AND COOPERATIVES

By _____

AGREED:
[TENDERER]

By _____

NOTES

1. In considering North-South barter scenarios, one should bear in mind that the United Nations General Assembly defines LDCs—the "South"—as those oil-importing countries with a per capita gross national product of $1,895 or less. This definition includes countries in Africa, East Asia and the Pacific, Latin America and the Caribbean, the Middle East, and Southeast Asia. In this paper, a broader definition is utilized since many of the countertrade demands come from a group of semi-industrialized countries sometimes referred to as newly industrialized countries (NICs), including Brazil, Mexico, Chile, Argentina, Uruguay, Iran, Iraq, and Venezuela, which have per capita incomes ranging from $2,050 to $3,630. The "North" is considered to include all West European countries, the United States, and Canada. Interestingly, Canada and some of the European countries, for example, Sweden, are more active countertraders than many of the NICs or LDCs.

2. See generally Ingelies Outters-Jaeger, *The Development Impact of Barter in Developing Countries* (1979).

3. See Behrman, "State Trading by Underdeveloped Countries," *Law & Contemp Probs* 24 (1959) p. 454.

4. See generally "Indonesian Official Explains Linkage Policy, U.S. Government in Opposition," *U.S. Import Weekly* 9 (Oct. 26, 1983) pp. 160-61.

5. First Countertrade Agreements Concluded, *Indonesian Development News* 5, (1982) p. 8.

6. See chapter appendix. For a further explanation of the program, see Maynard, *Indonesia's Countertrade Experience* (American Indonesian Chamber of Commerce, 1983).

7. Mangemo, "Indonesia Wins Its First Counterpurchase Contract," *Asian Wall St J*, Aug. 9, 1982, p. 8.

8. "Indonesia Signs Up Fertilizer Makers Under Its New Trade Development Plan," *Chem Marketing Rep* (Aug. 1982).

9. Awanohara, "Indonesia Is Sticking to Its Guns-for-Butter Principles," *Far E Econ Rev* (Jan. 27, 1983), pp. 49-50.

10. "Indonesia Halts Four Projects with $5.05 Billion Cost," *Wall St J*, May 9, 1983, p. 34.

11. Awanohara, "Indonesia Is Sticking to Its Guns . . .," pp. 49-50.

12. See Behrman, "State Trading. . .," pp. 467-72.

13. This case study is based on interviews with Malaysian trade officials and Segal, "Malaysia Changes Its Tune on Swap-Shopping Deals," *Far E Econ Rev* (Jan. 27, 1983), pp. 50-52.

14. For example, in contrast to the projected negative 3 percent growth of GDP for Indonesia, forecasts suggested a 4 percent growth rate for Malaysia in 1983. If export markets experience a recovery also, this would improve Malaysia's external payments position. The government was projecting a trade surplus of M$100 million (U.S. $230 million) in 1983 with an overall balance of payments surplus of the same amount. This is in contrast to a payments deficit of M$750 million and a trade deficit of M$2.5 billion in 1982.

15. See generally Sricharatcnanya, "There's Room for More Deals down on the Farm," *Far E Econ Rev* (Jan. 27, 1983), 52-53.

16. See U.S. Int'l Trade Comm'n, Analysis of Recent Trends in U.S. Countertrade 22 (ITC No. 1237) March, 1982. It is interesting to note that up until the 1970s, Mexico was an active countertrader as far as surplus commodities and nontraditional industrial products are concerned. Deals were carried out largely on a private basis with imports including wines from France and Spain, whiskey from Canada, viscose from West Germany and Italy, nylon from the United States, and pharmaceuticals from Switzerland.

17. Although some suppliers chose to litigate in order to recover arrears, the program generally was well received. By December 31, 1981, 90 percent of the outstanding suppliers' credits were covered by the program. A number of those initially electing the foreign exchange option switched over to lira payments, even with the attendant restrictions.

The most popular of the lira payment uses included the extension of credits to Turkish importers, increased investment in Turkey, and payment for fasconnage. Most importantly, the program served to help stem the outflow of foreign capital from the country. Net foreign investment, the majority in blocked lira, equaled $44 million in 1981 and $58 million in 1980 in comparison to a net outflow of $6.4 million in 1979.

18. See J.E. Tilton, *The Future of Nonfuel Minerals* (1979), p. 50.

6
BARTER OF AGRICULTURE COMMODITIES AMONG DEVELOPING COUNTRIES
Donna U. Vogt

INTRODUCTION

Characteristics of Barter Trade

Before money there was barter. As growth in international trade increased, countries used money or foreign exchange to transact trade. Recently, various nations have experienced a liquidity squeeze—not enough foreign exchange earnings in convertible currencies to pay for purchases of imports. Traders have returned in growing numbers to a version of this ancient trading tool of barter—currently known as countertrade or barter-type arrangements.

In this chapter barter arrangements mean linked transactions of goods and services in which a country or firm is compensated in whole or in part with goods or services rather than cash or credit. Frequently the exchanged goods are totally unrelated products, ranging from sophisticated technology to raw primary materials. The exchanges are not necessarily bilateral exchanges. One trading company could accept payments in kind of one load of corn and, in transit, switch it for a load of shrimp of equal value, thus involving a third party. Most of these switches are so-called "underground transactions."

A version of this chapter was presented at Metal Bulletin's meeting on International Barter: "To Trade or Countertrade," in New York City at the World Trade Center, Sept. 1-2, 1983. The views expressed in this paper are the author's and should not be attributed to the Congressional Research Service or the Library of Congress.

Barter trade lacks the transparency often associated with international tender or bidding arrangements, that is, it is difficult to find out exactly what is being traded, for how much, when, and through whom or whether the whole transaction is actually increasing world trade. The countries involved in barter deals avoid discussing the terms because they have, when the circumstances demanded, given discounts on the value of their exported goods. If these discount arrangements become known, future trading partners would be sure to insist upon the same treatment. It is possible that barter is maintaining trade at current levels, or actually diminishing trade to bilateral levels of the smallest exporter and locking in trade relationships that will diminish world trade over time. If so, this is worrisome.

The Rationale for Barter Transactions

Barter trade is characteristically residual, involving trade of goods that are not saleable at the price countries originally sought. Moving these residual goods through barter-type arrangements generally involves using unconventional financing, assuming countries want to maintain the fiction of competing on world markets.

This residual trade reflects the same cycles of commercial cash sales. When prices of commodities or goods are low, a country may try to export goods or services in a barter transaction at greater value than they could sell for the same goods for cash—in other words, make a "good business deal." At other times, perhaps as part of a marketing strategy, exporting countries may offer goods or services in barter deals at a discount from the cash price they might otherwise command. Thus, barter arrangements may disguise the real market value of goods or services by adding an artificial value to a product whose price for domestic purposes is determined by supply and demand or through discounts. Barter has also been used to get around some administrative restrictions—especially those which are instituted to prevent an outflow of foreign exchange for imports.

Few countries or firms wanting to export or import seek to barter in the first instance. They are usually directed toward such arrangements because their foreign exchange earnings or their own currency value would not be accepted on the international market. This "liquidity squeeze" is temporary among most developing countries. Of course, Eastern European countries—Rumania in particular—have been notorious champions of barter-type arrangements for the last two decades. Typically, these countries, even though they cannot obtain hard currency in a transaction in the international market place, want to obtain comparable value for their exports in some useful form. For them negotiations through the barter process are a good alternative. Countries use barter-type arrangements to maintain export volumes at times of worldwide recession. Countries often weigh the opportunity cost of producing or not producing for export when prices are low and find that export policies bring higher returns than import substitution policies.

World Bank studies have linked trade and export promotion policies to stimulation of economic growth and the creation of jobs in many developing countries. In a speech at the opening session of the UNCTAD meetings in Yugoslavia in June 1983, IMF Director Jacques de Larosiere underscored this link between sustained export volumes and national economic health. He stated that during the 1970s many nonoil developing countries kept exchange rates too high. This resulted in an erosion of competitiveness—exports were too highly priced and were discouraged while imports were promoted. The domestic currency could buy goods cheaper overseas for import. Capital flowed out to purchase such imports. Subsequently, when countries no longer had liquidity or enough foreign exchange, imports could not be financed so governments have had to restrict both foreign exchange use and imports. Consequently, trade flows slowed, growth programs were frustrated, and many countries turned to countertrade or barter.

WHY WOULD A COUNTRY BARTER AGRICULTURAL COMMODITIES?

Advantages

In addition to the advantages described above that are generally attendant upon barter transactions, many countries have come to appreciate the special advantages of agricultural barter.

Ensure Access to Supplies

If a country imports most or all of an essential commodity, for example, petroleum or food, and officials perceive that supplies are tight, governments may choose to barter in order to guarantee supplies of a commodity for a specified time period. A likely partner would be another government that foresees similar shortages of supply in a commodity that the first country produces in abundance. The reciprocal nature of barter agreements permits both parties to guarantee a supply of a commodity in a single agreement.

Excess Supply of Agricultural Commodities

Countries that offer producer price supports often acquire surplus commodities. Such countries frequently use barter to reduce excess supplies—especially when world prices are low.

Declining Terms of Trade

Interest in barter-type arrangements also arises when demand for a particular principal export declines. Declining export prices and quantities vis-à-vis import costs has been an incentive for developing countries in the past to enter into reciprocal agreements in order to offset fluctuating sales in multilateral markets. Although many barter exchanges take place, in effect, at world market prices, some developing countries have used barter agreements to increase the purchasing power of their exports vis-à-vis imports. Developing countries at times accept lower prices for their export products under barter arrangements in order temporarily to augment the market for their primary products during periods of declining demand.

Market Development

Countries may want to lessen their dependence on main suppliers (often former colonial powers) by diversifying their trading patterns to include new trading partners. Developing countries have also used barter agreements to expand exports of nontraditional items. Barter arrangements for these purposes are similar to many bilateral trade agreements whose purpose is to get a foot in the door, establish marketing relations, collect information about the nature of the trading partner's demand for exports, and, over time, graduate the barter arrangements to commercial cash sales. This is especially true among developing countries trying to maintain trade relationships with other developing countries when none of the parties has much foreign exchange.

Information

Barter transactions between countries give one country information about the needs of another country. This valuable information is similar to the information the countries might have exchanged in a bilateral arrangement to ensure supplies of commodities, here exchanged on a more informal basis. Barter negotiations to determine which and how much of various commodities might be included in a barter arrangement gives each party a notion of its partner's production, stocks, and the value the country places on its commodities. Also, in the course of the negotiations, bureaucrats or government representatives as well as industry representatives gain experience and expertise in the process. Personnel representing completely unrelated sectors learn about each other, and these relationships help maintain market channels and foster new opportunities for barter or cash deals.

Political Ties

Some countries establish barter agreements for strategic security reasons or to show political support for the leaders or political philosophy of a country. These agreements typically involve technical know-how or capital good exchanges for agricultural commodities. Such agreements are often statements of political support at the highest levels of governments.

Disadvantages

There are several reasons why countries would prefer to arrange sales on a cash basis instead of barter. These reasons are largely related to inefficiencies of formulating barter contracts and include:

Double-coincidence of Wants

Parties interested in a barter arrangement must find a partner that has a commodity for which they are willing to trade.

Government Involvement

Many barter agreements are negotiated on a government-to-government basis, often between state trading organizations. Countries in the European Community, the United States, and many non-European countries do not have marketing boards or state trading organizations to handle export sales. Because governments in these countries are often unwilling or unable to overcome resistance on the part of their citizens to have their export markets handled through government agencies, these countries have not been as actively involved in barter negotiations as have those governments represented by state trading organizations.

Lengthy Negotiations

Barter takes a great deal of negotiating time to work out, much more than an ordinary commercial sale in which a commodity is valued at an international market price and is purchased by anyone that has the currency to pay for it. Barter negotiations involve agreement on prices as well as quantities (values) to be traded. Although many agreements provide for sales at world market prices, negotiated prices in some agreements provide for discounts or premiums over equivalent world prices. For instance, an oil-exporting country could decide to barter petroleum for feedgrains at a value less than OPEC-set prices, thereby increasing the exchange value of the feedgrain. Since world prices change rapidly, lengthy barter negotiations could cause a loss or gain to one of the bartering parties. This would result in a windfall gain or loss to one of the parties.

Assessing Quality

All trade agreements specify the exact quality of the commodity to be delivered. Each commodity has different quality standards that have different prices. Because the barter arrangement involves a two-way exchange, it is more complicated than a normal sales agreement to guarantee the delivery of goods of quality agreed upon in the negotiations. One party's refusal to accept the offered commodity means a concomitant loss of a market for the other country. Therefore, the simple "refusal to pay" as in a commercial agreement becomes more complicated in a barter arrangement, especially because of the "residual" notion described above: goods that are bartered are ones that could not be sold at the price originally demanded. This gives rise to an initial expectation on the part of some trading partners that they will be receiving inferior quality goods to begin with, perhaps making them more cautious in accepting goods without scrutinizing inspection.

Tied Sales

For one reason or another, barter may be more useful to one side of the exchange than to the other. For example, when Brazil's debt service problem recently ballooned, the Brazilian State Company, Interbras, asked Mexico's Pemex to accept commodities instead of cash. Brazil had already received the petroleum and made arrangements to ship sunflower seeds and soybeans to Mexico in lieu of cash. Eastern European countries often demand that their commercial trading partners agree in advance to receive payment in goods in lieu of promised cash. When these arrangements are made at the insistence of one trading partner, the goods received in payment generally are not easily used or sold, but the commercial trading firm or country may be eager to pursue the agreement anyway, lured by the guarantee of an additional market for its wares.

Countries that insist on these undertakings often fail to appreciate the down-the-road consequences of their insistence. Although the recipient-party may not have the proper marketing channels for the products, it may sell them to a "switch house" at a substantially discounted price and the product may subsequently compete in the initial seller's market thereby displacing other valuable cash markets.

Another problem that could arise is that normal trade purchasing patterns are broken because the exporter suddenly received material normally purchased from other suppliers. Barter can therefore change normal buying routines and benefits. Third-country trading partners can also be affected to the extent the barter exchange disrupts customary trade flows.

Bureaucratic Rivalries

Negotiations within governments among agencies for control over and participation in barter agreements may be as elaborate as those between countries. Few ministries are willing to release control over supplies of one commodity in order to allow another ministry to receive a good that might unduly enhance the other's power, budget, status, or responsibility.

VOLUME OF BARTER-TYPE TRANSACTIONS AND SAMPLE TRANSACTIONS

Estimates of Amount Traded in Barter Arrangements

Total world trade amounted to approximately $2 trillion in 1982, according to General Agreement on Tariffs and Trade (GATT) estimates. Barter or countertrade transactions are estimated in news reports to be in the range of $200 billion to $800 billion, or 10 to 40 percent of world trade, but it is likely that there are numerous barter-type arrangements not being recorded as barter or countertrade. Thus, the underground aspect of some of the trade becomes apparent. Only with reliable information as to what is being countertraded, how the goods or services are valued, and how many times they change hands or are switched can an accurate estimate of total volume of barter-type arrangements be estimated.

Sample Barter Arrangements

In the samples collected in the appendix following this chapter, no attempt was made to estimate the percent of barter within total agricultural trade because of the difficulties in obtaining comprehensive information on all such agreements and actual annual trade flows.

In recent months, newspapers, magazine, journals, and State Department cables have reported many barter agreements. Listed here in Appendix Table 6.1 are 27 of these arrangements that have been entered into in recent months. The sample involves developing countries, many of which trade through state trading organizations. It is emphasized that this is an unstructured sample, not a survey, and no particular weight should be placed on the numbers and rankings as reflections of total barter trade.

The agricultural commodities offered in exchange both with each other and for other goods including petroleum are listed in the order of the frequency with which they occur in the sample:

rice 5	cotton 1
coffee 3	citrus 1
sugar 3	soybeans 1
wheat 3	frozen lamb 1
cocoa 2	palm oil 1
rubber 2	tobacco 1
bananas 2	jute 1
corn 2	

Every listed country exports these commodities on a cash basis, but is willing to use these commodities to avoid spending foreign exchange on imports. The other, nonagricultural bulk commodities were coal, bauxite, cement, copper, and nickel.

The countries involved in this sample are countries in which governments appear either to have mandated a policy favoring barter or countertrade or in which there is a specific product desired by many other countries, for example, oil. The USSR leads the sample with Iran, Indonesia, and Thailand following in that frequency. The other countries fall easily into regional blocs. The Latin America bloc includes Brazil, Mexico, Ecuador, Cuba, Jamaica, and Costa Rica. The Middle East and Southeast Asia blocs include Bangladesh and Pakistan. In Asia, South Korea, Malaysia, Japan, Vietnam, and New Zealand each have established at least one known arrangement. In Africa, South Africa has two, while Tanzania, Nigeria, and Zambia each have one arrangement. The sample also shows agreements made by private firms in the industrialized United States, Canada, France, and Sweden as well as some samples from the centrally planned economies of Poland, Rumania, and Bulgaria.

There are also regional arrangements, entered into specifically to help out a neighbor for "political solidarity" reasons. Brazil and Mexico are exchanging oil and oil-related products for sunflower seeds and soybeans. Other arrangements maintain political and economic contact. Japan and USSR have been exchanging synthetic fibers for raw cotton for some time, with both sides scrupulously maintaining a balance in the running accounts. Another example is that Zambia is using a type of payment-in-kind program under the guise of barter to repay Tanzania for use of the railway.

DEVELOPING COUNTRY POLICIES TOWARDS BARTER

Strong Advocate Countries

Indonesia

On January 1, 1982, the Indonesian government declared that all government procurements financed by the state budget (APEN) and by export credits of a value of U.S. $750 million must provide for counterpurchases of Indonesian goods valued at 100 percent of the goods Indonesia purchases.* After the bidding and award process normally preliminary to contracts with the government, the winning bidder must draw up a "letter of understanding" which sets forth what Indonesian products will be purchased and gives a time table. These counterpurchases must be made before the final delivery time of the cash contract or the contractor will be subject to a 50 percent penalty calculated on the amount of the nonfulfilled value. Conditions have been modified over time. Percent agreements have included clauses stating that if Indonesia does not offer competitively priced products or goods of sufficient quality, these contracts can be re-negotiated. Still, numerous problems remain. Indonesia reserves the right to refuse to negotiate. Primary commodity prices are volatile. The quality of commodities varies; they may be either inferior in quality or have the reputation of being so.

Uruguay

It has been reported recently that Uruguay has a policy giving preference to foreign suppliers of capital goods that undertake the counterpurchase of Uruguayan commodities such as wool, meat, and rice.

---

*For a further description of the Indonesian government's initiative, see Millicent H. Schwenk, *North-South Barter Trade* (Chapter 5 of this book).

Ecuador

The Government has decreed that any imports of alcoholic beverages would be paid for with exports of bananas.

Slightly Interested Countries

Malaysia

Because of declining exports, the Malaysian Government has begun looking into barter arrangements for a variety of reasons.* First, they seem to imply a degree of implicit price augmentation. Malaysia has entered a barter agreement only if the implicit price that is obtained through a barter price agreement would be above the market value. The government also wants to ensure that long-term contracts with current trading partners are continued. Such barter arrangements could help convince Malaysian farmers that the government is acting in their best interests. Barter arrangements could enable palm oil-producing countries to penetrate into non-traditional markets such as India, Pakistan, Egypt, and Jordan when they have periodic foreign exchange shortfalls. None of these reasons has been translated into an active policy such as that pursued by Indonesia.

Guyana

The present government has set up a committee which is looking into countertrade arrangements. It already has exchanged rice for soybeans with Jamaica. It is also seeking to export rice, timber, bauxite for cement, steel, and machinery, and may turn to barter arrangements as a way of entering these new export markets.

Governments Responding to Outside Pressure for Barter

South Korea

The government has set up an interministry barter trade committee to negotiate with 30 countries pressuring South Korea for barter deals. The committee has been dealing with problems such as the exchange of Korean fertilizer worth U.S. $29 million for Philippine bananas. The export letters of credit have not been approved because the South Korean government has banned banana imports and does not at this time want to initiate imports. It is feared that any sustained

---

*For a further description of the Malaysian government's initiative, see Millicent H. Schwenk, *North-South Barter Trade* (Chapter 5 of this book).

quantity of imports could create a tremendous internal demand that in later years would bring pressure to use foreign exchange to purchase bananas. Taiwan also has proposed to trade its bananas for Korean pears. Ecuador, Mexico, and Argentina have also expressed readiness to trade for Korean-made fire engines, textile fabrics, and steel products with their crude oil and canned beef.

Mexico

In January 1983 the government proclaimed that private Mexican companies unable to meet their foreign debt commitments might offer to repay the creditors with export merchandise. Italian creditors could be repaid using cotton, coffee, canned vegetables, auto parts, plumbing fixtures, diesel engines, and other manufactured goods. In the much publicized barter arrangement with Brazil described above, trade is being handled exclusively in pesos and cruzeiros with each country maintaining a bank account for the other country in its own currency. A similar kind of transaction has been used by Xerox de Mexico to do business with Xerox de Brazil for $6 million worth of goods.

Japan

In July, 1982 Iran proposed to Japanese trading houses that they barter for oil using a barter ratio of 1 for 0.5. In other words, Iran would buy Japanese products equivalent to half of its oil exports to Japan. Japanese trading companies in the past have not responded favorably to barter proposals—for example, they have dragged their feet on Indonesian proposals. They are interested, however, in Iran's proposal because it would involve Iran's purchase of an entire equipment production plant, which would be serviced in the future by the Japanese. In return, the Japanese would gain a tremendous growing market and large sales of entire plants and related services. The Japanese are carefully considering such barter transactions as a way of fostering good trading relations.

African Countries

Some African countries owe large sums to international airlines and have offered to pay off these debts in "in-kind" services such as repairs and goods. The airlines may be constrained to accept such proposals because, although they have large sums of money deposited in the national banks, they cannot easily convert it, and harsh refusal of such proposals may spur African governments to impede the airlines' access to their deposits.

CONCLUSION

The major problem with barter is that it is an inefficient mechanism for allocating resources because a barter arrangement cannot respond quickly to market forces. Locked into agreements, countries and companies may not be able to gain from an increase in market values after the time of the agreed exchange.

Another major conclusion is that there appears to be more talk about barter than there is action. For example, research regarding sample barter arrangements turned up not only 27 successfully executed transactions, but also 21 other planned arrangements that never took place. Many countries have proposed specific transactions only to be turned down by the opposite party because the arrangement was not perceived as beneficial to them. The difficulties of the arrangements should not be underestimated nor should the benefits be overestimated.

REFERENCES

Awanohara, Susumu, et al. "Asian trade back to barter," *Far Eastern Economic Review*, January 27, 1983: 49-56.

"Barter deals with communist nations to become popular, says UN official," *Business Day*, Philippines, January 5, 1983: 12.

Beardwood, Roger et al. "Back to barter," *ICC Business World*, Summer 1983.

Brevetti, Francine C. "Trading firm specializes in countertrade deals," *Journal of Commerce*, January 13, 1983: 1.

"Countertrade in Seoul," A broadcast of the official South Korean News Agency YONHAP, March 22, 1983.

Cowper, Richard "Indonesia stands fast despite problems," *Journal of Commerce*, January 1983.

Dizard, John "The explosion of international barter," *Fortune*, February 7, 1983.

Farrell, Paul V. "Countertrade: A special kind of buying and selling," *Purchasing World*, November 1979, Vol. 23, No. 11: 16-18.

Fleming, Louis B. "A worry for Washington countertrade," *Los Angeles Times*, July 5, 1983.

Goseco, Andres "Barter need not be primitive," *Far Eastern Economic Review*, May 5, 1983: 146-148.

Gray, Frank "Barter makes a comeback," *Bangkok Post*, February 6, 1983.

Gray, Frank "Why bad news for many is good news for some," *Financial Times*, March 1983.

Hakin, Jonathan "Cashing in on counter-trade," *The Economist Financial Report*, July 7, 1983: 2-3.

Manguro, Joseph P. "Indonesia wins its first counterpurchase agreement," *The Asian Wall Street Journal*, August 6, 1982: 1, 6.

Mardenberg, H. J. "Bartering aids poor nations," *New York Times*, January 17, 1983: D1, D8.

Murrell, Peter "Product quality, marketing signaling, and the development of East-West trade," *Economic Inquiry*, Vol. XX, October 1982.

"New restrictions on world trade," *Business Week*, No. 2748, July 19, 1982: 118-122.

Orme, William "Mexico suggests barter pacts to repay debts," *Journal of Commerce*, January 5, 1983: 30.

Orme, William "New Mexican policies provide trade impetus," *The Journal of Commerce*, June 27, 1983.

Rodota, Joseph D. "Back to barter," *Republican Report*, unpublished paper.

Sato, Masaaki "Exports to Iran begin recovering at far faster pace than hitherto," *The Japan Economic Journal*, April 19, 1983.

Vogt, Donna, Cathy Jabara, Dee Linse, *Barter of agriculture commodities*, USDA, ERS, IED staff Report, April 1982.

Whitley, Andrew "Brazil seeks to recover cost markets," *Journal of Commerce*, May 5, 1983: 6.

"Zambian–Tanzanian trade agreement signed," *The Citizen*, Johannesburg, December 6, 1982: 11.

APPENDIX A

Appendix Table 6.1 A Sample of Barter Agreements 1982-1983

Country		Export Commodity		Time Frame	Comment	Source
A	B	A	B			
Brazil	Mexico	Food stuff-soybeans (160,000 MT) and sunflower seeds petrochemicals oil products oil-drilling equipment total $3 billion	Oil at 80,000 barrels a day	3-month periods	This agreement was made to fulfill a previous cash sale of petroleum to Brazil. Brazil requested and got to repay in commodities rather than foreign exchange. The total transaction in U.S. $3 billion.	World Trade News *Financial Times* 5/25/83, p. 6
Ecuador	USSR	bananas	LADA cars NIVA cars SKM pickup trucks	1982 ongoing	Limited to $10 million annually or less. Engines may not be over 2000 cc in trucks and must have 1.5-3 tons carrying capacity. Must comply with historically set purchasing quotas from Ecuador before barter can take place.	Cable 00496 1/22/82

(**Appendix Table 6.1 continues**)

133

Appendix Table 6.1 (continued)

Country		Export Commodity		Time Frame	Comment	Source
A	B	A	B			
Ecuador	South Korea	bananas	Hyundai motor vehicles	1982 ongoing	Limited to $10 million annually or less Engines may not be over 2000 cc in trucks and must have 1.5-3 tons carrying capacity. Must comply with historically set purchasing quotas from Ecuador before barter can take place.	Cable 00496 1/22/82
Cuba	Bulgaria	sugar citrus	foods, toys, medicines, pesticides perfume camping equipment	1983 commercial accord	Value is approximately 315 million. Gives no U.S. $ equivalent.	Granma 2/19/83
Cuba	USSR	sugar nickel	food products petroleum and products fertilizers steel plates small tools equipment	1983 trade protocol	Total bilateral trade goal is 6,500 million rubles. Ninety two percent of contracts already are signed that make up this total. This transaction is part of the annual trade flows between the two.	Granma 2/16/82 State Department cable 01432 2/25/83

Cuba	Tanzania	computer system newsprint ceramics	coffee leather textiles	1983 once	The arrangement is a trade pact.	*Asian Wall Street Journal* 5/4/83, p. 18
Israel	Costa Rica	agrochemicals	coffee (440 tons)	4/12/83 one time transaction	Arrangement helps Costa Rica by reducing its coffee stocks outside global quota of International Coffee Organization. No drain on foreign exchange reserves. Chemicals will be sold to farmers by National Production Council at subsidized rates to carry out CR goal of making CR coffee more competitive.	UNCLAS San Jose 02552, 4/15/83
Brazil	Iran	goods and services	crude petroleum	1 year	Working well for a year.	*Financial Times* 5/25/83, p. 6
Brazil	USSR	soymeal beef frozen broilers	petroleum—increased from 20,000 b.a.d. to 30,000 b.a.d.	No time limit given announced in July 1983	Bank of Brazil made this announcement. It appears that this agreement is a continuation of present trade flows.	*Commodity News* 7/18/83
Jamaica	US—General Motors	bauxite	cars	1982		

(Appendix Table 6.1 continues)

Appendix Table 6.1 (continued)

Country		Export Commodity		Time Frame	Comment	Source
A	B	A	B			
Indonesia	International Commodities Export Co. ICEC	cement rubber cocoa coffee other products	fertilizer ($127 million)	1982 once	ICEC of U.S. is subsidiary of ACLI International, a privately owned U.S. company exporting agricultural chemicals. Conformed to Indonesian government regulations allowing a refusal of review of noncompliance or bad quality exports.	New York *Times* 1/17/83, p. D1 & 8
Indonesia	West Germany Japan U.S. supplies	cement rubber coffee cocoa	fertilizer ($127 million)	August 1982	First formal agreement cost of reselling commodities acquired was added to cost of original goods sold.	*Journal of Commerce* 11/18/82
Canada	Potash Corp. of Saskatchewan (PCS) (a provincial corporation)	76 MMT of potash (bulk of potassium chloride)	rubber coffee cocoa	1982 once	Seven million dollars handled through intermediary International Commodities Export Corporation of White Plains, New York. Reason given: sales had fallen 40% because were not willing to barter.	UNCLAS *Ottawa* 05492, 6/82

Bangla-desh	USSR	tobacco cigarettes copper wire coffee razor blades	kerosene oil	1983 annual trade protocol	Eighty four million dollars trade protocol, $800 million over 11 yrs. Increase by $9 million in last years.	Bangladesh *Post* 12/29/82
Bangla-desh	Thailand	jute	rice (possible 50,000 tons)	early in current rice season		*Business Day* 11/18/82 Reuters
Malaysia	Thailand	palm oil (30,000 tons)	rice (35,000 tons)		Result of pressure from Malaysia slowing imports.	Department of State telegram Kuala Lumpur 1/20/83
South Africa	USSR	corn (200,000 tons)	urea fertilizer	one time 1982	A study for ASSOCOM-South African Association Chambers of Commerce.	UNCLAS Pretoria 06205. 8/24/82
Rumania	South Africa	urea fertilizer (208,000 tons)	corn (200,000 tons)	May 1982 Dec. 1982	It is possible that this agreement is the same as the one described above.	State cable 03614 5/26/82
Nigeria	Thailand	crude oil (5 million barrels)	rice 5% (possible 500,000 tons)	part of regular shipments 1983	Proposed deal follow normal trade relations. Thailand would have to find a buyer for oil because already has a purchase agreement with Saudi Arabia.	*The National Review* 3/11/83, p. 13 UCN 3/14/83
USSR	Japan	raw cotton (10,000 tons)	synthetic fiber (4,000 & synthetic cotton; 6,000 & polyester short staple)	1982 and more 1983 several deals	Amounts are equal although accounts are settled separately.	*Nihon Keizai Shimbun*, 3/2/83 3/2/83 Daily Report of FBIS

(**Appendix Table 6.1 continues**)

Appendix Table 6.1 (continued)

Country A	Country B	Export Commodity A	Export Commodity B	Time Frame	Comment	Source
China	East Germany	rice canned fruit vegetables textiles chemicals machine tools	scientific instruments, printing machines, trucks, chemical fertilizers	1983 trade accord	The arrangement is called a bilateral barter trade accord and only gives volumes. The volume is supposed to increase 25% over 1982. The 1982 Sino-East German trade amounted to 580 M East German marks.	*Asia Research Bulletin*, 4/30/83 Vol. 12, No. 11 Dow Jones Publication Companies
Sweden	Iran	paper and pulp (U.S. $29 million), glass products (U.S. $22 million), Viscose (U.S. $6 million), general machinery	crude oil to be delivered before manufactured goods are exported	Oct. 19, 1982	Oil is to be delivered before Swedish goods sent. Value $64.8 million U.S. total covers more than 50% of Sweden's annual export to Iran. One of SUKAB largest deals.	*Dagens Industry* (Swedish Industrial Trade Magazine), 10/28/82, cable 04590 10/30/82
Pakistan	Iran	sugar (50,000 tons) wheat (130,000 tons) rice chemical fertilizer	crude oil	1983	Wheat would be 20% lower priced. State trading company of Iran. Total value $100 million.	*United Commodity News* 2/14/83
New Zealand	Iran	frozen lamb	crude oil	1982	Sold through independent broker, contract by the New Zealand Meat Board. Total amount was $200 million.	*Business Week* 7/19/82, p. 118

Malaysia	Pakistan	palm oil	50,000 tons of rice at $225 U.S. a ton	1 year	Not confirmed.	Department of State telegram Kuala Lumpur 00587 1/20/83
France	Poland	grain (160,000 tons —mostly wheat)	50,000 tons coal		Circumvents official French reluctance to sell Poland grain on credit.	FAS Report WR 2-83 weekly roundup of production & trade
France	Vietnam	fertilizer (400,000 MT), wheat and wheat flour annually (100,000 tons)	100,000 tons of rice, 500,000 tons of coal	5 years	One hundred million dollars (715 million French francs).	State telegram 10/6/82 UNCLAS Paris 34380

APPENDIX B

Appendix Table 6.2 Agricultural Commodities and Oil

Countries		Time Frame	Commodities Exported		Remarks	Source
A	B		A	B		
India	Iran	1980-81 1 yr	construction materials railway equipment rice wheat tea	crude oil raisins almonds	Trade was below expectations because Indian banks did not get good credit terms nor get paid promptly. Got oil from USSR and other sources.	*Economic Times of India*
Turkey	Iran	1980-81 1 yr	barley wheat horticultural items	crude oil	Worked well because of good border trade. Ports were out of service.	Foreign Broadcast Information Service
Brazil	Venezuela	1980	soybeans (200,000 mt.) sugar (360,000 mt.)	oil (80,000 b.p.d.)	Value B$400,000,000 or U.S. $93,500,000. Paid $732 for oil rather than $999.70, the world market price. The swap was incremental to another trade agreement.	*Unicon News* 2/24/80
Colombia	Algeria	1 yr 1980	coffee tobacco rice cocoa sugar	crude oil	The total value of this exchange on each side was $50 million.	Attaché Report CO-1016 4/7/81

Country	Partner	Duration/Date	Exports	Imports	Notes	Source
Brazil	USSR	5 yrs 1981	meat cotton bananas Soybeans (500,000t beans, 400,000t meal, 40,000 oil) Cocoa (10,000t of beans, 10,000t of liqueur) Corn (500,000t a year beginning in 1983)	petroleum 20,000 b.p.d. for 5 mo. (this to be between Aug. and Dec. 1981) Turbines for hydro-electric power	The Brazilian agricultural goods are valued at U.S. $300 million. USSR is restructuring its food import program.	ESS Agricultural highlights 7/20/81
Vietnam	USSR	5 yrs 1981-85	timber coffee tea spices vegetables fruits consumer goods	petroleum products (increased amounts) fertilizers cotton rolled steel motor vehicles construction mach. paper products	No quantities given. Trade will hopefully increase 90% in comparison with the 1976-80 period, according to news reports. Vietnam processes Soviet raw materials of cotton, wool, medical ingredients, and then ships textiles, carpets, and medicines back to USSR.	Cable 10865 Moscow 8/5/81
India	USSR	April 30 1981- June 30 1982	Rice (500,000t) barley (100,000t)	oil, crude (1 million mt.) petroleum products (350,000 mt.)	Third barter agreement. Value set at U.S. $750 million. First time agricultural commodities other than rice were included.	Cable 06698 New Delhi 12/3/81

(Appendix Table 6.2 continues)

141

Appendix Table 6.2 (continued)

Countries A	Countries B	Time Frame	Commodities Exported A	Commodities Exported B	Remarks	Source
		Follow on Agreement to 1979-80 and 1980-81	peanuts (20,000t) corn (200,000t) alumina (50,000t) sesame seeds (10,000t) semi-tanned goat skins (2 million pieces)		This exchange will benefit India's foreign exchange situation, particularly in offsetting imported petroleum. Largest and most diversified agreement with an LDC by USSR.	May 5, 1978 Latin American Economic Report
Brazil	Iraq	1976 5 years	sugar rice (164,000 mt.) soybeans Volkswagens (11,000) Iron ore (5.3 mt.)	crude oil		
Guyana	Venezuela	1976	bauxite and other minerals	crude oil (20,000 b.p.d.)	No quantities of value were listed.	"Have Barter, Will Travel," *The Economist* 1/24/76
Philippines	Indonesia	1981	rice	crude petroleum	The price of the rice in this arrangement was $232 mt.	*Asian Journal* 5/6/81

			compared with world market prices of $300 to $350 mt. The discounted price was bartered by the Philippines for priority in Indonesia's oil allocation.	
Argentina Iraq	1982	wheat (300,000 mt.) rice (40,000 mt.)	crude oil	No amount of oil was given but the Saudis have agreed to cover any Iraqi shortfall in shipping oil to Argentina.	Cable 12/28/81 No. 8123 Buenos Aires *Herald* 12/16/81' FAS Report

Key: b.p.d. = barrels per day.
Source: Vogt, Donna, Cathy Jabara, Dee Linse *Barter of Agricultural Commodities*. USDA, ERS, IED Staff Report, April 1982.

APPENDIX C

Appendix Table 6.3 People's Republic of China (PRC) Barter Agreements

Countries			Commodities Exported		Remarks	Source
A	B	Time Frame	A	B		
PRC	Brazil	3 yrs	Petroleum	Foodstuffs	Brazil sold $9 million. China got $3 million in trade per year. This is a trade understanding. No specific quantities mentioned.	Market Report International Commodities Export Comp. Report No. 851 3/1/78
PRC	Philippines	1979 1 yr	shengli oil worth U.S. $80 million approximately	copper concentrates (U.S. $11m to $22m) Coconut oil (U.S. $11m to $19.25m) Forest Products (U.S. $1m to $2m) PVC resins (U.S. $1.3 to $2.7m)	Sold oil at U.S. $9 a barrel whereas world market prices were U.S. $11.59 a barrel, so this is a discount price. This is their second agreement and a product of a joint trade committee meeting regularly.	China trade report Vol. 16 5/78
PRC	Sri Lanka	1952 every 5 yrs	Rice	rubber	Total trade is U.S. $60 million. China often sells its rice at below market price and buys rubber at a premium over the Singapore market price for rubber. Annual price adjustments are made so value ex-	"A Guide To The Barter In The China Trade" *The China Business Review* Vol. 6 No. 5 September/October 1979 pp. 10-16

144

change remains equal. Burma is involved in this barter arrangement, selling rice to China that will go to Sri Lanka.

PRC	Yugoslavia	1974 annually to 1978	petrol-coke foodstuffs frozen fish dried fruit honey & cocoa tin hides & skins bauxite	ships & ship engines artificial fertilizers steel goods-pig iron nonferrous metals electric machine building equipment	The agreement is called a trade cooperation. In 1974 worth $130 million; in 1976 worth $11 million.	Foreign Broadcast Information Service, 1/16/78
PRC	Bulgaria	1 year 1978	rice cotton wool & silk fabrics nonferrous metals chemicals consumer goods	electric & ice trucks computing equipment medical apparatus fertilizers	The agreement is called a trade and payments agreement.	Foreign Broadcast Information Service, 1/16/78
PRC	German Democratic Republic	1978	vegetable and animal raw mat. rice cotton textiles nonferrous metals	trucks diesel engines machine tools scientific apparatus	The agreement is called a trade and payments agreement	Foreign Broadcast Information Service, 1/20/78
PRC	Poland	1978	tea rice tungoil	machines & ind. equip. coal-mining machines	The agreement is called a trade and payments agreement.	*Tryburna Luda* No. 26

(Appendix Table 6.3 continues)

Appendix Table 6.3 (continued)

Countries A	B	Time Frame	Commodities Exported A	B	Remarks	Source
			bristles nonferrous metals consumer durables like: knitwear, carpets, silk, cotton	ships engines diesel eng. & parts machine tools steel products pharmaceuticals		
PRC	Thailand	1978	shengli-crude oil	tapioca flour (150,000 mt.) maize (5,000 mt.) beans (10,000 mt.) rubber (50,000 mt.) beans-mung (20,000) gunny sacks (12 mil.)	Total trade will equal $156 million. PRC supplies 3% of Thailand's energy needs.	ASEAN cable Hong Kong 04411, 4/10/78
PRC	Cuba	1972-75	rice (average 210,000 mt. a year)	sugar (average 319,000 mt. a year)	Annual exchange.	*Statistical Bulletin* International Sugar Organization 5/76
PRC	Peru	1976	rice (75,000 mt.)	fish meal (40,000 mt.)		*USDA News* 1057-76

PRC	Burma	1981 1 year	rice	rubber		Cable 043340-Peking (28) 2/20/81
PRC	Rumania	1976-80	cotton rice other foodstuffs machine tools prod. of chemical, textile, and food industry ferro-alloys metallurgical coke	machinery building industry goods drilling rigs lorries electric diesel locomotives wagons bearings and spare parts prod. of chemical metallurgical ind.		Foreign Broadcast Information Service, 5/76
PRC	Egypt	annual renewal	tobacco tea miscellaneous food	cotton-long staple	Approx. $100 million worth of trade.	Egyptian Gazette 12/81
PRC	India	1978-on annual renewal	petroleum tung tea antimony	tobacco cotton	Trade began in the late 1970s and reached substantial value in 1980 and 1981—trade protocol.	Attaché Report IN-1042 7/1/81
PRC	Albania	1961-80 annual renewal ceased in 1981	petroleum textiles	tobacco cigarettes sage	China was Albania's leading export market during some of 1970s and a major source of China's tobacco imports before the purchases in India and Zimbabwe in 1980-81.	Michael Kaser and Adi Schwytzer "Albania—A Uniquely Socialist Economy" East European Economies Post-Helsinki A

(Appendix Table 6.3 continues)

147

Appendix Table 6.3 (continued)

Countries		Time Frame	Commodities Exported		Remarks	Source
A	B		A	B		
						Compendium of Papers Submitted to Joint Economic Committee-Congress of US, Aug. 25, 1977 95th Cong/1st Session.
PRC	Thailand	1981	shengli crude oil (600 tmt. to 800 tmt.) diesel oil (100 tmt. to 200 tmt.) jet petrol (50 tmt.)	rice (100,000 mt.) maize (200,000 mt.) black matupe (40,000 mt.) rubber (30,000 mt.) tapioca flour (50,000 mt.) tobacco (2,500 mt.)	Trade protocol—but list of items very specific.	British Broadcasting Co., *Survey of World Broadcast*, Far East, WI1151, pp.A/B1

148

APPENDIX D

Appendix Table 6.4 Barter Exchanges of Agricultural Commodities Among Developing Countries

Countries		Time Frame	Commodities Exported		Remarks	Source
A	B		A	B		
Ethiopia	Algeria	3 yrs annual renewal	Coffee hides and skins oilseeds pulses spices and other Ag. products	industrial products	No specific quantity given. First trade agreement between these two countries. Signed at ministerial level.	Cable 01734 *Ethiopia Herald Newspaper*
Venezuela	Argentina	1976	iron ore (150,000 mt.)	200,000 mt. wheat 100,000 mt. grain sorghum, or corn	Prices to be established prior to each monthly shipment. Argentina will pay for the rest in cash. Shipments were delayed due to logistics problems.	"Have Barter will trade" *The Economist* 1/24/76
Peru	Argentina	1976-78	copper iron ore cotton	wheat, corn, beef, offal	Value equalled U.S. $150 million.	"
Peru	Hungary	1977-80	fishmeal cotton coffee minerals	wheat equipment	Value equals U.S. $40 million.	Foreign Agricultural Service, PR 6034 11/76

(Appendix Table 6.4 continues)

Appendix Table 6.4 (continued)

Countries		Time Frame	Commodities Exported		Remarks	Source
A	B		A	B		
Peru	Brazil	1977-80	minerals fishmeal	soybeans		Foreign Agricultural Service, PR 6012 4/76
Democratic Republic of Germany	Brazil	1981-83	soybeans and products	coal potash	Value on each side equals U.S. $100 million.	Foreign Agricultural Service, BB 0126 12/80
Mexico	USSR	Jan. 1981 started with no limit	coffee cocoa lettuce	petroleum extracting equipment textile industrial equipment agricultural tractors	This agreement may be a triangle trade pact: the agricultural commodities going to Cuba, and the USSR sending the equipment to Spain, and in the end swapping customers.	Telephone Conversation with Charles Reese, State Department 10/5/81
Egypt	USSR	1962-81 annual renewal	oranges, rice, Jasmine paste, wine, shoes, household items	paper, wood, metals, Industrial machinery	The commodity composition has changed as Egypt has shifted to cash markets for cotton, but substituting other items has prevented a slide in the value.	Rubinstein, Grigor "The African Developing Countries External Economic ties at the turn of the 1980s," *Foreign Trade*, No. 12, 1981 USSR

Thailand	USSR	12/17/81	corn (100,000 mt.)	fertilizer	Prices for corn are about $109 mt. and fertilizer $210 mt. Discussed bartering 300,000 mt. corn for 150,000 mt. fertilizer.	FAS incoming telegram 12/18/81 TH 1148
Thailand	Romania	12/25/81 March 1982 to June 1982	corn (200,000 mt.)	fertilizer (123,834 mt.)	Corn is priced at $109 mt. Composition 16-20-0 or 20-20-0 at $210 mt. To be delivered between March 5 and April 30, 1982.	TH 1358 FAS cable 12/30/80
Bangladesh	Bhutan	9/8/80	dried fish, newsprint, jute and jute products	forest products and stone boulders	Trade agreement. Signing had been delayed almost 2 years because of Indian displeasure over the agreement. Is of greater interest to Bhutan because country is eager to reduce dependence on India and it contributes to strengthening ties other small countries of the region.	Department of State telegram 10/10/80
Zambia	Zimbabwe	one time transaction Spring	Cottonseed (cottonseed cake) (10,000 mt.)	Cottonseed oil (2,500 mt.)	Barter agreement awaits purchase larger machinery for Zimbabwe. Zimbabwe will keep the cotton seed meal in payment for crushing the seeds	*Times of Zambia* Lusaka 11/4/81, p. 2

(Appendix Table 6.4 continues)

151

Appendix Table 6.4 (continued)

Countries		Time Frame	Commodities Exported		Remarks	Source
A	B		A	B		
	Uganda	2 yrs Nov. 81 Nov. 83	spices pepper cardamon oilcakes cotton	phosphates super-phosphates	and return the oil to Zambia. No foreign exchange involved. Each country will pay transport costs within its boundaries. Goods into both countries will be accorded most-favored-nation treatment. Simultaneously the two countries signed a memorandum of understanding providing for technical assistance in agriculture from India to Uganda.	Att. Report ND-1080 12/9/81
India						
Bangladesh Pakistan		2/8/82 March 1982 to May 1982	jute Agricultural goods	rice (100,000 mt.)	Over half of the rice has been paid for by Bangladesh exports; a small amount of cash may be involved in the end with no interest charge. Another source has stated agreement calls for Sindi rice 40 to 45% broken, in bags, $250 to $255 FOB Karachi.	*Foreign Agriculture Circular-Grains* 1/16/82

APPENDIX E

Appendix Table 6.5 Bangladesh Barter Agreements

Countries		Time	Commodities Exported		Remarks	Source
A	B		A	B		
Bangladesh	Czechoslovakia	9/21/77 1977-78 July-June)	jute, jute goods, tea, hides and skins, specialized textiles, electrical cables, telephone cables, glycerine, cellophane, newsprint and paper products, molasses, and ready-made garments	electrical equipment and accessories, ball and roller bearings, chemicals and dyes, sulphur, scientific hospital and laboratory equipment	Fourth Bangladesh-Czechoslovakia Barter Trade Protocol. Exchange of commodities $5.6 million each way. Exports from Bangladesh consist of 49% jute and jute goods and 51% nonjute products.	Department of State airgram No. A-126 10/17/77
Bangladesh	Poland	9/24/77 1977-78	jute, jute goods, tea, hides and skins, oil cake, oil bran, cables, specialized textiles, rayon yarn, crushed bone, molasses, handicraft paper, and paper products	corrugated iron sheets, dyes and chemicals, triple superphosphate, electrical equipment and accessories, tools and work shop equipment, and sulphur	Third Bangladesh-Poland Barter Trade Protocol. Exchange of commodities $12.9 million in each direction. Exports from Bangladesh consist of 46% jute and jute goods and 54% nonjute products.	Department of State airgram No. A-126 10/17/77
Bangladesh	North Korea	11/28/78 1 yr.	raw jute, jute goods, leather and leather products, newsprint, paper,	cement, pig iron, coal magnesia clinker, and mild steel billets	Second Bangladesh-North Korea Trade Protocol. Exchange of commodities	Department of State airgram A-86

(Appendix Table 6.5 continues)

Appendix Table 6.5 (continued)

Countries A	B	Time	Commodities Exported A	B	Remarks	Source
			sugar, soap and detergents, and enamelled copper wire		amounted to approximately $6,536,000 each way.	12/7/78
Bangladesh	PRC	12/10/79 1 yr.	jute, jute goods, sugar, newsprint, paper and pulp, leather, timber, particle board, hard board, rayon, and cellophane	cement, coal, mild steel billets, pig iron, light machinery, and tools	Third Bangladesh-China Barter Trade Protocol. Exchange of commodities $25 million each way.	Department of State airgram No. A-009 12/21/78
Bangladesh	Rumania	10/30/78 1978-79	raw jute, jute goods, tanned and semi-tanned leather, loose and packet tea, newsprint, viscose and rayon yarn, writing and printing paper, cottage industry products, towels, curtain cloth, handicrafts, coir fiber timber, tobacco, drugs, and medicine	mineral oils, soda ash, fertilizers, ball and roller bearings, diesel engines, spare parts for ambulances, tools and workshop equipment, and diesel garbage trucks	Fifth Bangladesh-Rumania Barter Trade Protocol. Exchange of commodities $7.5 million each way.	Department of State airgram No. A-80 11/1/78
Bangladesh	Bulgaria	8/20/79 FY 1980	raw jute, jute goods, leather and leather products, loose and packet tea, ready-made	pig iron, mild steel billets, iron sheets, hot and cold rolled steel	Seventh Bangladesh-Bulgaria Barter Trade Protocol. Exchange of commodities $10	Department of State airgram A-66

garments, specialized textiles, crushed bones, wires and cables, coir fibers, handicrafts, hard boards, particle boards, cutlery, rayon yarn, gib pipes, safety matches, and super enamelled copper wires

strips, electrical equipment, copper, zinc, tin plates, transmitters, forklift trucks, soda ash, pharmaceutical raw materials, medicines, and veterinary medicines

or $11 million each way.

9/6/79 and Department of State airgram A-47 5/21/80

155

7
DOMESTIC BARTER
James Higgiston

INTRODUCTION

Barter transactions have occupied a niche in the American economy from the earliest days. In 1626, while working for the Dutch West India Company, Peter Minuit traded $24 worth of cattle, trinkets, and blankets for Manhattan Island in what remains one of the most famous barter deals ever conducted.

With the development of the dollar as a universally accepted medium of exchange, the use of currency displaced the more cumbersome process of barter in most commercial transactions. Nevertheless, a residual level of bartering has endured, fluctuating in amount with changes in the economy. During World War II, American industries used barter to solve the problems of obtaining scarce and expensive materials. In one of the first reported examples of this type of industrial barter, the Cook County Electrical Contractors Association bartered essential electrical supplies and swapped surplus fixtures for materials and supplies it could not otherwise obtain.

Barter has been especially popular during periods of shortage or economic downturn. In 1933, during the Depression, the National Development Association in Salt Lake City had 5,000 members and swapped 15 different types of commodities and 103 lines of services, both skilled and unskilled. Once the economic crisis ended, however, the organization disappeared.[1]

The author gratefully acknowledges the assistance of Michael D. Esch in the preparation of this chapter. The views expressed herein are the authors and should not be attributed to the Department of Agriculture or the federal government.

Today, promoters of barter believe that barter can survive and flourish even during economically healthy periods. The motivations for engaging in barter that proponents most often cite are discussed first, followed by a survey of the three major varieties of barter: personal barter, barter clubs, and corporate barter.

MOTIVATION FOR BARTER

Barter clubs, the major public proponents of barter, offer their members several reasons for engaging in moneyless transactions. These incentives apply, to varying degrees, to corporate barter as well. Personal barter, on the other hand, has its own incentives, which are discussed separately.

Traditionally, the barter economy flourished during times of economic downturn. As tight money supplies and credit problems reduce the availability of cash, individuals have resorted to barter as a secondary alternative. Barter club officials are convinced, however, that barter can be worthwhile even during prosperous times, for several reasons.

First, barter may be used as a means to reduce excess inventory without having to sell the merchandise to a liquidator at less than wholesale prices. Such excess inventory may include slow-moving merchandise, over-production of a particular item, or an obsolete model. Not only may the manufacturer get a potentially better return in value through barter, but bartering may disguise any actual discounting of merchandise.

Second, purchasing departments of a number of commercial concerns are resorting to barter deals because they have found them useful in restraining vendor price increases in times of inflation and assuring adequate supplies of raw materials. Thus, long-term barter contracts, by expressing the "price" paid for the goods to be received in terms of a ratio of exchange for the goods to be delivered, may avoid the impact of price list increases made by a supplier. Likewise, a long-term contract may guarantee a supply of raw materials, while the accompanying arrangement to pay for those materials in kind reduces the cash flow exposure from such a long-term contract.

Third, barter may be used to supplement rather than supplant monetary transactions. By using the company's purchasing power as leverage, sales personnel may be able to develop new markets for a company's goods through barter. Particularly where a business may, through the additional barter transactions, expand production capacity to take advantage of economies of scale, bartering the additional output may provide greater returns on investment. Moreover, where barter is used as a marketing tool to gain entry to a new market, the company's marketing department may then be able to take over and develop that market on a longer-term, nonbarter basis.

PERSONAL BARTER

Personal barter generally involves individuals wishing to exchange services. The transactions generally occur on a more or less haphazard basis, stemming from personal contacts among friends and neighbors. A lawyer might, for example, exchange services for help on his or her tax return from an accountant, or in return for services from a neighborhood dentist. Because there is little or no hard "cost" for an additional hour of a professional's time, the individual may regard the bartered service as "cost-free." In return one receives a service for which one would otherwise pay cash. Such transactions are increasingly popular, in part because barter transactions make it possible for the participants to earn income that is easily concealed from the IRS. The growth of this underground economy is furthered by two factors: the increasing tax burden and the growth of transfer payments in the modern welfare state.

Prior to World War II there was little incentive to avoid tax payments; federal tax rates were only 4 percent on income up to $4000 (approximately $18,000 in 1978 dollars).[2] By the 1970s federal taxes and inflationary trends had forced people into higher and higher marginal tax brackets. Add to this the increase in Social Security payments and state and local taxes, and the incentive for middle class individuals to maximize their income by evading taxes becomes apparent.

Significant incentives to barter have also developed on the lower end of the income scale. Transfer payment programs, including welfare, social security, and other income-based aid, may operate as a stimulus for barter for many recipients. In an effort to avoid earning more income than allowed by a particular program, and thereby disqualifying themselves as recipients of aid, many persons may choose to work off-the-books in order to supplement their incomes. This tendency to avoid taxes and reductions in aid is not confined to the United States; in the United Kingdom and Sweden, two other countries with large welfare state programs, participation in the underground economy is even more common than in the United States.

Estimates on the size of the underground economy vary, but in 1976 the controversy exploded. In that year Peter M. Gutmann, a professor of finance and economics, estimated the size of the underground economy to be $176 billion or approximately 10 percent of the GNP.[3] While most researchers estimate that barter now represents between 1 and 3 percent of the United States GNP, or approximately $30 billion to $90 billion,[4] others have reported it to be as large as $700 billion, or almost 27 percent of the U.S. GNP.[5] Because of the considerable media attention given to these reports, the Internal Revenue Service (IRS) was compelled to investigate the situation to determine how much revenue was escaping federal taxation. In short, barter received more critical attention, particularly the growth in barter clubs and their operations.

BARTER CLUBS

A barter club has several functions. A trade barter club acts as a bank, controlling and supervising the deposit and withdrawal of credits for goods and services instead of cash. In addition, a club serves as a broker or sales agent, locating customers for members and their products. Many clubs also work in direct competition with their own members, obtaining and marketing their own merchandise within the system. They may also act as purchasing agents, finding equipment or acting as agents trading for media time or advertising space.

Numerous barter clubs operate in the United States. An estimated 400 clubs or individuals are now engaged in organized barter.[6] Approximately 75 percent of these clubs are sponsored by one of several major bartering companies: Exchange Enterprise International, of Salt Lake City, founded in 1970; Barter Systems Inc., of Oklahoma City, begun in 1976; Business Exchange International, of North Hollywood, California, organized in 1960; and the National Commerce Exchange in Springfield, Virginia. Atwood Richards, of New York City, is the oldest barter organization in the United States and one of the largest barter exchanges in terms of annual transactions. Founded in 1958, Atwood Richards did some $300 million in trading in 1981. The company trades a wide range of products, from jets to bat manure. Atwood Richards has well over 100 corporate clients, including B.F. Goodrich, Uniroyal, Olivetti, Lotus Motors, U.S. Borax, Shell Chemical Corp., and McGraw Edison.

Organization

Two keys to the success of a barter club are the ability to offer a range of goods and services to customers and the efficient dissemination of information about those offerings to the club's members. In many instances, barter clubs have developed the capacity to offer a wide range of goods and services by expanding through franchises. Most of the major barter clubs have offices or affiliated clubs throughout the nation. For example, Barter Exchange International has close to 65 offices. Barter Systems Inc. has 66, and the National Commerce Exchange, which has 30 offices at present, has plans to expand to 130 offices by 1985. Through these offices, the barter clubs offer a full line of goods and services from advertising of all types to boat charters to accounting, legal, and dental services. Moreover, barter clubs are constantly trying to expand the number and types of goods and services offered on the exchange. One barter official noted that they had contracted with over 1000 different types of businesses.

To disseminate information on their offerings, each organization publishes a periodic newsletter listing new items or services. The Full Circle Marketing Corporation, for example, publishes a 48 page tabloid called *Barter Communique* which includes a listing of goods and services available through the barter network. It is circulated to approximately 20,000 traders in the United States three times a year. Other organizations circulate newsletters on a monthly or quarterly basis.

An important component in barter's surge in recent years has been the advent of the computer, which has afforded barter club members easy access to information on the types of goods and services available. The computer can be used to match buyers and sellers, evaluate transactions, weigh the equivalence of deals, and determine the effect of a deal on the system as a whole, taking into account levels of supply and demand. Computers have also facilitated the record keeping necessitated by the establishment of lines of credit and debit, which are central to the development of fractional, nonsimultaneous, multilateral trading.

The barter organization, with the aid of the computer, can maintain internal balances within the barter network, ensuring that enough goods and services are available and that there does not exist any oversupply of one item or service. In addition, the club can keep close watch to ensure that members are not in excessive deficit or surplus, which might also result in imbalances.

Operations

Barter clubs allow members to obtain goods and services from other club members without paying cash. The clubs act as clearinghouses. All major barter clubs require an initial cash fee, to cover overhead, ranging from $100 to $500; some clubs require an additional annual membership fee. Some clubs offer discounts for two-year memberships or guarantee full refunds if the new member does not profit by at least the amount of the membership fee.

Having joined a club, a new member must build up a line of credit in the organization by agreeing to offer services or goods to other members in an amount up to a specified monthly dollar value. The barter organization issues to the member a card, similar to a credit card, or special checks which the member presents to other members when making "purchases."

A typical barter club transaction occurs as follows. A barter club member, in need of a watch, goes into another member's jewelry shop and "purchases" a $100 watch by tendering $100 in trade units or credits. To the extent that the owner's membership in the barter club brings in additional customers who would not otherwise patronize his store, the owner benefits by expanding total sales. The owner, who paid $50 wholesale for the watch, can now use the barter credits he receives from the customer to trade for $100 worth of some other goods or services offered by the club.

Most barter clubs stipulate a maximum percentage markup on merchandise, and require that services be offered at fair market value. Depending on the barter organization, either the buyer or the seller pays the barter club an 8 to 10 percent commission on each barter transaction. The commission may be paid in trade units, in which case it is debited to a member's account. Some barter exchanges, however, require that cash commissions be paid on transactions over a certain stated value.

Barter clubs have adopted a number of safeguards to ensure that members comply with the club's rules and that no product or service categories create an imbalance in the system:

- Any member wishing to spend trade units (which are usually pegged at the equivalent to one dollar) must contact the barter club prior to each purchase.
- Buyers must identify themselves to sellers as organization members prior to making a purchase.

- Clubs require that members submit signed and authorized invoices to the club within a certain time period (ten days in the case of the National Commerce Exchange, for example) following the transaction in order that accounts are maintained on a current basis.
- Barter clubs limit purchases of members to the amount of trade units in a member's account. Lines of credit may also be established with the barter club.
- All commitments must be made in writing.
- Barter clubs have the option to cancel the membership of any member engaging in unethical practices.

Criticism of Barter Clubs

Barter clubs have suffered periodically from bad press. The 1976 Gutmann report brought their operations to the public's attention. They then became the focus of government scrutiny. Representatives of the International Association of Trade Exchanges (IATE) contend that the IRS overreacted to reports about the underground economy.

The 97th Congress, in enacting sections 311(a) and 311(b) of the Tax Equity and Fiscal Responsibility Act of 1982, tightened up record-keeping requirements for barter clubs and consequently gave them a measure of legitimacy. Section 311(a) of the act requires more extensive record keeping and reporting by barter exchanges. Under the new regulations promulgated under the Act, barter clubs must submit accurate records of all transactions and the value of the club's trade credit in annual information returns to the IRS. Section 311(b) of the act recognizes barter exchanges as third-party record keepers under the Internal Revenue Code. As third-party record keepers, barter exchanges may refuse to turn over to the IRS members' records unless the taxpayer has been notified that his records are being sought for examination. This provides the taxpayer an opportunity to intervene and contest the IRS summons. The legislation, according to barter club representatives, will give them legitimacy and convince the public that barter clubs are not organized for the purpose of avoiding taxes.

Even with this mitigation of legal difficulties, several problems continue to plague barter clubs. First, some members have had trouble redeeming trade credits, as members drop out of clubs prior to rendering their services. Some transactions have involved damaged or inferior goods and inadequate follow-up service. Finally, some goods and services have proven to be more marketable than others. This arises in part from an imbalance observable in members' expectations. Middle-class professionals, such as podiatrists, accountants, and lawyers, wish to trade "soft" services, in other words, their time, which has little hard cost, and is a fleeting asset.[7] In return, they often seek "hard" goods such as video cassette recorders. The VCR retailer, however, has to expend cash to acquire his merchandise, making barter less attractive to him than a possible future cash sale which will allow him to recover his cash outlay.

Some critics also note that many, if not most, of the transactions engaged in by barter club members are not true barter transactions in the sense of goods being directly exchanged for other goods. Instead, the barter club sets up a parallel economy, with its own currency—the barter unit or credit—which is used to buy and sell goods. The advantage adhering to the barter club organization, however, is the capacity to overcome the problems of a liquidity shortage in the cash-based economy. The barter club can do this by creating a new, limited type of credit based on the individual member's offer of goods or services.

Indeed, it has been suggested by some proponents that barter might be a cure for our unemployment problems. The fact remains, however, that the people most in need of help are those with neither the skills nor the goods to participate. In addition, to the extent that barter club participation expands members' "sales" transactions by channeling members' purchases of goods or services to club members, thereby displacing purchases from nonmembers, no net gain to the overall economy can truly result.

CORPORATE BARTER

Method and Background

An estimated 65 percent of New York Stock Exchange-listed companies conduct at least part of their business through barter.[8] In contrast to barter clubs, however, which are quick to promote and advertise their services, corporate barterers prefer anonymity. Much attention has been focused on barter in the international arena, where many corporations have been forced, contrary to their inclination, to become involved in barter. Nevertheless, domestic corporate barter has become increasingly more common, taking place in three distinct forms.

Simple barter deals are usually referred to as straight barter transactions. Contracting parties agree on specific quantities of goods or services which are to be exchanged constituting full or partial payment. Some corporations present buyers with lists of goods for which they are willing to trade. Borg-Warner Corporation, for example, commonly trades chemicals for items in which it has shortages.

Reverse reciprocity represents a somewhat more complicated barter arrangement. A company will agree to trade goods if and only if the other company agrees to accept its products. The Federal Trade Commission (FTC) has been questioning the legality of such "tied" transactions, but there has been little or no attempt to stop them.

Finally, many corporations join barter clubs or use barter firms as a means of obtaining needed merchandise or for trading used or excess supplies. The barter club acts as a broker for the corporation and its supplies.

A number of large firms engage directly in barter. General Motors established its Motors Trading Company several years ago and it has carried out several domestic barter transactions. General Electric, Sears Roebuck, Rockwell International, and McDonnell Douglas all have established barter departments.

One of the major differences between straight corporate barter and barter clubs is the type of merchandise usually offered. Corporate barterers will usually barter the most modern equipment they produce. Motors Trading Company, for example, will deal only in the latest products. Barter clubs, by contrast, deal for the most part in excess supplies, obsolete models, and used, but serviceable merchandise.

Case Studies

A number of U.S. companies have been involved in barter transactions. The following cases illustrate the extensive possibilities which exist for companies in bartering.

- Xerox has bartered since 1981. During that time it has bartered for approximately $1 million worth of goods. In one deal, Xerox exchanged 170 copiers for about $500,000 of rented office space. The company expects barter business to grow by about 3 or 4 percent a year.
- The Climaco Corporation of Ohio found itself with a surplus of bubble bath at about the same time it began production of a new product, dungaree bleach. Climaco bartered its excess bubble bath for $300,000 worth of advertising to promote its Soft and Fade bleach.

- The University of Detroit joined the Michigan Trade Exchange in 1981. The school swaps sports tickets, seminar fees, part-time admissions, and even the entire cost of tuition for such needs as vehicles and air-conditioning services.
- A small town in Connecticut agreed to trade municipal services, such as parking, in exchange for office equipment from local businesses.
- Parker Pen Company traded $7 million worth of writing implements to Atwood Richards of New York in return for advertising time.
- Media barter has become a large industry. A TV station in need of a television control panel bartered $100,000 worth of media time to Atwood Richards in exchange for a control panel which cost $50,000. The total TV time was in turn traded by Atwood Richards to a watch manufacturer for its equivalent wholesale dollar value in wrist watches. Trading again, Atwood Richards received $85,000 worth of excess carpeting inventory. The company then gave the carpeting to a hotel chain remodeling its older units, taking in exchange $100,000 in room, meal, and meeting room credits. Atwood traded the space to an appliance manufacturer that wanted space for a national sales meeting in return for $125,000 in discontinued dishwashers and clothes dryers.
- William (Bill) Tanner of Memphis, Tennessee, was probably the largest individual barterer in the country in 1983, generating about $100 million in annual revenues by swapping TV time and products. In 1973, Tanner bartered for a modern 7-story office building worth $1 million, which now houses his offices. He took title of the building in exchange for a plot of undeveloped land he owned. At the same time, Tanner swapped his prize Stutz Blackhawk in a trade for $69,000 worth of broadcast time.[9]
- Tanner's company, Media General, Inc., has been involved in a number of lucrative deals. One of its larger deals involved its exclusive syndication rights to four college basketball conferences. Two hours of game time is provided along with 19 commercial spots used by nearly 100 television stations around the country, once a week during the basketball season. The stations give Tanner ten of the 19 spots to trade with his customers in lieu of cash.
- A manufacturer of appliances began the production of a new rotisserie model. Forty thousand unassembled units of an older model, however, were being stored in the company's warehouses. The company needed the warehouses and was almost forced to sell the older units below its own manufacturing cost, resulting in a partial loss.

The company was instead able to barter the obsolete wares for television and radio time and advertising space in a magazine.

- A sporting goods manufacturer had a surplus of long skis due to a sudden change in consumer tastes. The company's executives preferred not to discount the merchandise in order to preclude unwanted competition between its larger dealers and smaller outlets. The company instead decided to barter the skis for travel services, hotel convention space, and media time.
- Diversified Products, Inc., another sporting goods manufacturer, had an excess supply of inventory, including racquetball racquets, gloves, and other sporting goods equipment worth $4.4 million. The company turned to Atwood Richards and obtained $2 million worth of steel from United States Steel Corporation, rental car services from American International Rent-a-Car, a few dozen Great Dane truck trailers, thousands of hotel rooms for conventions, $80,000 in television and magazine advertising, and an assortment of printing and office equipment.
- Wilson Sporting Goods Company had a surplus of specialty golf balls worth $100,000. The company traded the golf balls in a barter deal for five forklift trucks.
- The Civil Aeronautics Board has ruled that airlines may provide transportation in exchange for goods and services. Northwest Airlines was granted permission for a one-year program in which it could trade airline seats for $4 million worth of television, radio, and print advertising. Continental, Western, and Frontier Airlines have also considered bartering for advertising time and space.

THE FUTURE

The bartering industry has burgeoned in recent years. In 1982, the dollar value of domestic bartering grew an estimated 10 to 15 percent. One sign that barter is becoming more attractive to the general population is its greater visibility. Credit cards for barter, and newsletters devoted to the promotion and expansion of barter, have appeared more frequently in recent years. Larger companies are still reluctant to become involved in barter transactions, preferring cash deals instead, but they are increasingly willing to discuss their barter transactions.

Barter's growth has been spurred to a significant degree by recent economic conditions. The 1981-82 recession lowered the demand for goods and left companies with large inventory surpluses, with significant associated carrying costs. But barter has expanded most significantly in goods or services on which value is based on time. As soon as a plane leaves the ground with an empty seat, for example, the revenue for it is gone forever. Air travel, hotel accomodations, and radio and television advertisement spots are prime candidates for barter.

The greatest potential for barter growth, however, lies abroad. With the expansion of our trade sector, many markets not previously considered important as suppliers or customers are now becoming vital. More recently, the international financial situation has hampered international trade. Suffering from foreign exchange shortage, countries often require companies to accept payment in local products. Yet bartering offers U.S. companies the chance to expand their markets, increase their profits, and locate new sources of supply. In this area, domestic bartering clubs have begun to expand overseas. Atwood Richards already has offices in Paris, London, and in Eastern Europe. Most experts in the barter industry believe that it is simply a matter of time before their domestic clubs expand overseas.

NOTES

1. Poe, "The Great American Barter Game," *Across the Board* (Jan. 1981): 17-18.

2. See Ross, "Why the Underground Economy Is Booming," *Fortune*, Oct. 9, 1978, p. 95.

3. Peter M. Gutmann, "The Subterranean Economy," *Financial Analysts Journal* 27 (Nov.-Dec. 1977).

4. Gruson, "Corporate Barter on the Upswing," New York *Times*, Feb. 20, 1983, p. F4.

5. Poe, "Great American Barter Game," p. 17.

6. Kaikati, "Marketing without Exchange of Money," *Harvard Business Review* 8 (Nov.-Dec. 1982).

7. Pfeister Barter in New York, for example, has found it necessary to limit the number of chiropractors and podiatrists that can join its organization. See Rohmann, "Cashing in on Cashless Swaps," *Forbes*, March 29, 1982, p. 120.

8. Kaikati, "Marketing without Exchange of Money," p. 8.

9. In 1984 William Tanner was indicted for income tax evasion. He has also been sued by Media General for misrepresenting the financial condition of his company when it was acquired by Media General. See F. Schwadel, "Ex-Chief of Media General Unit Pleads Guilty to Mail and Income-Tax Fraud," *Wall St. J.*, Jan. 31, 1985, p. 10.; M. Potts, "Media General Rebuilds Unit Hit by Scandal," *Wash. Post*, Jan. 28, 1985 Washington Business Section p. 1.

8
U.S. GOVERNMENT INTERNATIONAL BARTER

Donna U. Vogt

INTRODUCTION

Public barter by the U.S. government is a complicated way of doing business and is not an actively pursued goal at this time. The government had an ongoing barter program under the Department of Agriculture from 1950 to 1973, which disposed of surplus agricultural commodities, acquired strategic materials, and filled government needs overseas. It was suspended when there were no more large agricultural surpluses. Today, pressures are mounting in Congress and in the administration to reopen such a program.

This chapter gives a history of the suspended program, discusses current government policies, and examines the only barter agreements in the past 15 years—the 1982 U.S.-Jamaica Barter Agreements—which resulted in an exchange of bauxite for dairy products. The chapter then considers the major advantages and disadvantages to the whole concept of government barter. Current laws providing the authority to barter

A version of this chapter was published as part of *National Defense Stockpile Amendments of 1983: Hearings on H. R. 3544 before the Subcommittee on Seapower and Strategic and Critical Materials of the House Committee on Armed Services*, 98th Cong., 1st Sess. 187 (1983).

The author gratefully acknowledges the contributions of Elaine Deming, Nancy D. Montague, Scott Morse, and Robert B. Stack to this chapter.

The views expressed in this chapter are the author's and should not be attributed of the Congressional Research Service or the Library of Congress.

and the constraints in current law to any government barter program are also considered.

Barter has become an increasingly popular technique of conducting trade for many countries with severe foreign exchange problems. This chapter uses the word *barter* to mean all forms of barter and countertrade. Examples of this form of trade are shown in the context of possible trading partners for U.S. government barter, and scenarios that could be followed.

HISTORY OF THE U.S. BARTER PROGRAM

A U.S. government barter program operated from 1950 to 1973.[1] It satisfied three objectives: the disposal overseas of surplus agricultural commodities in U.S. government inventories, the acquisition of strategic materials from abroad that could be stockpiled and used by U.S. industries in times of national emergency, and the acquisition of goods and services "offshore" that were needed by U.S. development programs and for military purposes. The total value of agricultural commodities exported under the barter program was $6.65 billion in the 26-year period (see Table 8.1). The program began because farm programs encouraged the production of commodities in excess of domestic U.S. demand. However, because prices were supported above the market equilibrium level, large inventories, which were expensive to maintain, were acquired by the Commodity Credit Corporation (CCC) of the Department of Agriculture (USDA). At the same time, overseas nations were not capable of paying for large quantities of agricultural imports, which they needed to feed their populations.

Congress, intrigued by the idea of disposal and acquisition without tremendous costs, included barter provisions in the Commodity Credit Corporation Charter Act of 1949 and incorporated barter into the Agricultural Trade Development and Assistance Act of 1954 (Public Law 480). These two laws gave the secretary of Agriculture legal authority to reduce, through barter agreements, inventories of surplus agricultural commodities owned by the CCC. In return, the secretary could obtain strategic and critical materials for a national emergency stockpile or could obtain foreign-produced supplies and services for U.S. agencies operating abroad.

The strategic stockpile was owned, operated, and maintained by the General Services Administration (GSA). Another agency, the Office of Emergency Preparedness, performed the policy analysis for stockpile management decisions for the president.[2] The purpose of such a

Table 8.1 CCC Barter Program*: Value of Agricultural Commodities Exported under Strategic Material and Offshore Contracts, 1950-1975 (in $ U.S. thousands)

Fiscal Year	Strategic Contracts	Offshore Contracts	Total Program Exports
1950	7,782	–	7,782
1951	8,524	–	8,524
1952	42,818	–	42,818
1953	14,113	–	14,113
1954	34,398	–	34,398
1955	124,605	–	124,605
1956	298,387	–	298,387
1957	400,486	–	400,486
1958	99,830	–	99,830
1959	132,255	–	132,255
1960	149,190	–	149,190
1961	143,951	–	143,951
1962	198,369	–	198,369
1963	47,447	12,641	60,088
1964	43,458	68,715	112,173
1965	31,926	98,222	130,148
1966	32,074	196,745	228,819
1967	22,477	273,170	295,647
1968	6,339	295,948	302,287
1969	1,405	267,788	269,193
1970	–	467,836	467,836
1971	–	870,050	870,050
1972	–	875,894	875,894
1973	–	1,088,291	1,088,291
1974	–	293,758	293,758
1975	–	4,692	4,692
Total	1,839,834	4,813,750	6,653,584

– Indicates no contracts.
*Program suspended 6-30-73. Activity after that date reflected phasing out of open contracts.
Source: FAS/GSM/ED/PDD (P&E), January 28, 1982.

stockpile was, and is still today, to preclude dependence upon foreign sources for strategic materials in times of national emergency. GSA has authority to acquire strategic materials through the Strategic and Critical Material Stock Piling Act, as amended in 1979 (50 U.S.C. § 98 ff.).

There were three phases of the U.S. barter program. The first phase operated under the authority of the CCC Charter Act of 1949. Very little happened. The second phase gathered momentum under P.L. 480, and between 1954 and 1962 large quantities of CCC-owned agricultural commodities were exchanged for strategic materials. The third phase of barter activity began in 1963, when the acquisition of strategic materials through P.L. 480 was curtailed. The CCC Charter Act Authority was used to exchange surplus agricultural commodities for foreign-produced supplies and services used in construction projects for the Department of Defense (DOD) and in projects of the Agency for International Development (AID). The barter program was suspended in 1973, when CCC stocks were largely depleted, stockpile goals changed, and the strong foreign commercial export market no longer justified the need for a barter program.

Barter Logistics

Contracts for barter were signed between the CCC and private U.S. firms, rather than directly with foreign countries.[3] During the first and second phases of the program (1950-1962), the Office of Barter (OB) of the U.S. Department of Agriculture publicly announced and invited private U.S. firms to submit offers to export agricultural products held by the CCC and to import specific strategic materials. Exporters sold agricultural commodities released to them by the CCC at world market prices to specific countries, and imported strategic materials with the proceeds. Specialists at GSA and representatives of other government agencies reviewed the bids with respect to specifications and prices of strategic materials, and then negotiated contracts with these private firms.

Contractors imported the strategic materials to U.S. ports, where GSA would take title and transfer them to stockpile locations. In return, contractors would receive a specified quantity of agricultural commodities from CCC inventories and ship them abroad to countries in accordance with their contracts. The value of the commodities turned over to the contractors for resale abroad was usually slightly more than the value of the strategic materials. This additional value compensated the contractor for incurring special financing costs and for assuming risk in exporting commodities to USDA-restricted destinations. This extra amount was known as a "barter discount."

Most barter contracts for strategic materials took from one to three years to complete, and were valued at between $1 and $5 million.

In due course, CCC was reimbursed, either by the government agency receiving the materials, such as GSA, out of its annual budget, or from the annual USDA budget appropriation, which contained line items for this purpose. The CCC and the OB bore the administrative costs of the program.

Barter contracts were negotiated only with those countries where the USDA determined that regular U.S. commercial sales displacement would be at a minimum.[4] Barter was permitted in certain commodities because countries with poor balance-of-payments positions were not expected to become substantial cash markets for any of the commodities bartered at any time in the future. Each country was assigned a category depending on the trend of its imports of U.S. agricultural commodities. These categories were periodically reviewed and countries reclassified, according to their financial position, history of cash commodity imports, and projected future cash imports.

The barter review committee was conscious of not wanting to displace any possible commercial sale. The committee streamlined the program into a commodity-country system with four categories. The "A" designation meant that bilateral and multilateral transactions were permitted after the USDA determined that the export of the commodity would not unduly disrupt world prices or replace U.S. cash sales, but would add to normal sales. The "B" designation meant bilateral and multilateral transactions could take place with proof that the goods reached their final designation. The "C" category had no restrictions, and the "X" category meant that the commodity could not be traded. Some countries had three of the four categories. For example, in 1960, Guatemala was designated "A" for cotton, "B" for wheat, rice, and tobacco, and "C" for rye, corn, grain sorghum, barley, nonfat dry milk, and butter.

As CCC-held surpluses increased, the secretary of Agriculture received authority in 1956 to increase the barter program by expanding the list of agricultural products which the program could use to barter. When these commodities were bartered for whatever the secretary of Agriculture could get in exchange (often minerals and metals that were on the National Defense Stockpile list), the bartered material received would go into a supplemental stockpile. This supplemental stockpile did not have a national security value in a military sense, but it did include metals and minerals that were "nonrenewable." The CCC retained title to these stockpiled commodities when they were not needed by the strategic stockpile.

The Third Phase of the Barter Program

Until 1962, most barter transactions were confined to exchanges of CCC-owned commodities for strategic materials.[5] By 1962, changes in planning for wartime needs had reduced stockpile goals and, in many cases, inventories exceeded minimum requirements. Also, the CCC's agricultural inventories had been greatly reduced. Starting in 1963, more emphasis was placed on barter to procure foreign-produced supplies and services for overseas military installations and for projects of AID than to procure strategic materials. These transactions came to be known as "offshore contracts." Barter agreements during this time period increasingly relied upon authority in the CCC Charter Act, which allowed barter contractors to export private stock commodities (see Table 8.1).

Barter logistics under this third phase "offshore" program were similar to those described above. The Department of Agriculture invited barter offers from private firms to supply foreign-produced goods or services overseas at the request of government agencies. Depending upon the type of agreement, the contractor would use the funds generated by the sale of commodities abroad to purchase supplies and ship them overseas, or the contractor would transfer the funds directly to an overseas installation. If private stocks were used to generate these funds, the CCC paid an exchange value or a "commission" to the contractor. Financial coverage for agricultural commodities taken in advance of barter material deliveries was required in the form of cash deposits or irrevocable letters of credit in favor of the CCC. Most of the goods acquired during the 1960s were used by the military. Cement was often a bartered item, as was military housing abroad.

"Additionality"

Past discussions of the U.S. barter program have focused on three questions. Will the barter transactions displace cash sales or be in addition to other cash purchases? Will these exchanges disrupt world prices of agricultural commodities? And, what effect might they have on the U.S. balance of payments position? All of these questions are attempting to find out whether barter sales are in addition to normal commercial sales and have found new markets for U.S. farm exports—in other words, have provided "additionality" for U.S. exporters.

Additionality generally reflects a range of possibilities rather than a fixed percentage or category. It cannot be measured with precision. There are many variables present in every transaction, and it is difficult to determine with certainty whether the transaction will or will not result in a displacement of a cash sale. Nor is it possible to determine, if there is a displacement, whether it will be partial or complete. A barter transaction represents an actual, demonstrable disposal of an agricultural surplus. There is usually no way of determining with any degree of finality the value of cash sales that might have been made if a barter transaction had not been consummated. A barter transaction can benefit the U.S. balance of payments to the extent that the commodities are substituted for cash in the acquisition of materials when this overseas acquisition would have been made in the absence of barter.

The OB commodity-country review system, as well as an "additionality committee," constituted a watch system, albeit a slow and laborious one. The committee reviewed barter offers to cash markets, distributed information on the program, advised on barter policy, and determined whether there was any additionality problem. USDA felt this watch system prevented any claims of government interference in commercial sales.

Another useful perspective is the impact of barter on foreign economies of interest to the United States, a sort of reverse form of additionality. The strategic and critical materials acquired in exchange for the agricultural commodities would not otherwise be acquired by the U.S. government because money was not appropriated. The stockpile had no "transaction fund" (as today's revolving stockpile fund is called) with which to purchase materials. Supporters of barter claimed that barter created a market for foreign materials with the result that unemployment abroad was decreased, mining and processing facilities were more fully utilized, and the general economic situation of those countries was stimulated. Thus, U.S. farm product exports increased with the additional trade. However, while the mining sector was stimulated, the agricultural sector in these countries may have been undercut. There is a question about the general economic effect of barter because it is possible that cash purchases of foreign minerals might have had a stronger positive effect on their economies.

Assessment of the Barter Program under Public Law 480 and the CCC Charter Act

In the first decade, a major objective of the barter program was to export surplus agricultural commodities in order to reduce the cost of government-held inventories. As mentioned previously, the barter program shifted emphasis in 1963 to offset part of the dollar drain caused by U.S. spending abroad. Barter increased after that date under the CCC Charter Act, which permitted barter of privately held stocks of commodities.

The last barter contract for strategic materials was negotiated in 1967 when Australian rutile was exchanged for cotton and other commodities. The program was suspended on June 30, 1973, although exchanges of materials contracted prior to that time continued until 1975.

Detailed information on countries and commodities is available for barter contracts authorized under P.L. 480 and is provided in Tables 8.2-8.6. The total value of agricultural commodities exported from July 1954 to June 1976 through barter contracts under this authority was approximately $1.73 billion. The bulk of these contracts were negotiated prior to 1963 and receipts were largely confined to strategic

Table 8.2 Title III, Public Law 480: Agricultural Commodities Exported under Barter Contracts in Specified Periods*

Commodity	Unit	Cumulative, July 1, 1954 through June 30, 1975
		(thousand units)
Wheat[†]	Bu	368,471
Corn	Bu	239,422
Grain sorghums	Cwt	70,617
Barley	Bu	93,007
Oats	Bu	41,961
Tobacco	Lb	196,676
Cotton	Bale	2,513.1
Dry milk	Lb	129,340
Butter	Lb	23,183
Other[††]	MT	808.36
Total quantity (thousand metric tons)		23,327.25
Total value ($ million)		1,732.2

*Includes adjustments to previously reported exports. Exports after December 31, 1962, under contracts relying on authority other than Public Law 480 have been excluded.

[†] Includes 17,573 million bushels of wheat acquired from CCC shipped as wheat flour during 1958-62.

[††] Includes rye, soybeans, rice, wool, cheese, flaxseed, linseed oil, dry edible beans, cottonseed oil and meal, and peanuts.

Source: U.S. Department of Agriculture, Foreign Agricultural Service. *Food for Peace*, the 1975 Annual Report of Public Law 480, 1975.

Table 8.3 U.S. Agricultural Exports under Public Law 480 Barter Contracts by Region and Major Country, 1954-1975

Region/Major Country	Value Thousands of Dollars	Region Percentage of Total	Country Percentage of Region	Country Percentage of Total
Europe	1,053,386	60.8	100.0	
Belgium	118,447		11.2	6.9
Germany, West	147,635		14.0	8.5
Netherlands	143,298		13.6	8.3
United Kingdom	305,219		29.0	17.6
Other	338,787		32.2	19.6
Africa	55,163	3.2	100.0	
Canary Is.	14,020		25.4	0.8
S. Africa	13,315		24.1	0.8
Other	27,828		50.5	1.6
Near East & South Asia	185,752	10.7	100.0	
India	74,639		40.2	4.3
Israel	47,094		25.3	2.7
Turkey	17,585		9.5	1.0
Other	46,434		25.0	2.7
Far East & Pacific	263,808	15.2	100.0	
Japan	193,672		73.4	11.2
Philippines	15,760		6.0	0.9
Taiwan	16,042		6.1	0.9
Other	38,334		14.5	2.2
Latin America	170,593	9.9	100.0	
Brazil	63,446		37.2	3.7
Colombia	15,401		9.0	0.9
Mexico	19,659		11.5	1.2
Peru	32,968		19.3	1.9
Other	39,119		23.0	2.3
North America	3,484	0.2	100.0	
Other	13		100.0	
Total	1,732,199	100.0		100.0

Source: U.S. Department of Agriculture, Foreign Agricultural Service. *Food for Peace*, the 1975 Annual Report of Public Law 480, 1975.

materials. Wheat, corn and other feedgrains, tobacco, nonfat dry milk, butter, and cotton were the major commodities exported from CCC stocks (Table 8.2).

A total of 123 different countries received agricultural commodity exports from the United States under barter contracts authorized by Public Law 480. The bulk of the agricultural exports under early P.L. 480 barter arrangements—72 percent—went to the European countries and Japan. The Near East and South Asia received 11 percent; Latin America 10 percent; and Africa 3 percent (Table 8.3). The regional distribution of barter exports under both P.L. 480 and, later, the CCC Charter Act gradually changed. By 1968, developing countries were receiving 76 percent of agricultural exports under barter programs; during 1969-75, they received 61 percent (Table 8.4). Developing countries such as the Republic of Korea, Taiwan, Malaysia, the Philippines, and Hong Kong became major outlets for agricultural commodities during the 1963-1975 period when barter was used for offshore procurement of supplies and services.

Receipts of strategic materials, supplies, and services under the P.L. 480 barter program totaled $1.68 billion. Approximately 27 percent of barter imports were from Africa, 21 percent from Latin America, 19 percent from Europe, 14 percent from the Near East and South Asia, 10 percent from the Far East and Pacific, and 9 percent from North America (Table 8.5). Dollar values for imports of materials, supplies, and services and exports of agricultural products are not equal by country because transactions were not required to be exclusively bilateral until 1968. The inequality is especially notable with respect

Table 8.4 U.S. Barter Exports by Destination (in thousands U.S. $)

Destination	July 1954-June 1957	July 1957-December 1962	January 1963-June 1968	July 1969-June 1975
Western Europe and Japan	753,282	430,046	257,845*	1,510,050
Others	70,197	321,631	838,518	2,359,674
Total	823,479	751,677	1,096,363	3,869,724

*65 percent represents exports of commodities, particularly tobacco.

Source: Nollmeyer, Jean B., "USDA's Barter Program—How It's Changed, What It's Doing," *Foreign Agriculture* VI, no. 40, September 30, 1968, pp. 2-4; and unpublished data FAS/GSM/ED/PDD.

Table 8.5 Value of Materials, Equipment, and Services Received Under Public Law 480 Barter Contracts by Region and Major Country, 1954-1975

	Value Thousands of Dollars	Region Percentage of Total	Country Percentage of Region	Country Percentage of Total
Europe	324,062	19.3	100.0	
Belgium	24,012		7.4	1.4
France	91,914		28.4	5.5
Germany, West	56,168		17.3	3.4
Italy	24,766		7.6	1.5
Norway	13,863		4.3	0.8
United Kingdom	67,073		20.7	4.0
Yugoslavia	17,190		5.3	1.0
Other	29,096		9.0	1.7
Africa	452,328	26.9	100.0	
Ghana	20,220		4.5	1.2
Mozambique	21,783		4.8	1.3
Rhodesia	35,218		7.8	2.1
South Africa Rep.	176,131		38.9	10.5
Zaire	51,939		11.5	3.1
Other	147,037		32.5	8.8
Near East & South Asia	230,114	13.7	100.0	
India	125,238		54.4	7.5
Turkey	92,139		40.1	5.5
Other	12,737		5.5	0.8
Far East & Pacific	169,696	10.1	100.0	
Australia	34,365		20.2	2.1
Japan	94,151		55.5	5.6
Philippines	27,252		16.1	1.6
Other	13,928		8.2	0.8
North America	154,288	9.2	100.0	
Canada	141,797		91.9	8.4
Other	12,491		8.1	0.8
Latin America	348,342	20.7	100.0	
Brazil	84,239		24.2	5.0
Jamaica	94,773		27.2	5.6
Mexico	70,778		20.3	4.2
Surinam	30,931		8.9	1.8
Other	67,621		19.4	4.0
Other	1,698	0.1		
Total	1,680,528	100.0		100.0

Source: U.S. Department of Agriculture, Foreign Agricultural Service, *Food For Peace*, the 1975 Annual Report of Public Law 480, 1975.

to Africa. Barter contracts to deliver strategic materials, supplies, or services could be negotiated with one country, and agricultural exports could be delivered to another country, until that date.

A comparison between the value of materials and equipment received ($1.68 billion) in Table 8.5 with that of the U.S. agricultural products exported ($1.73 billion) in Table 8.3 shows a difference of $50 million. Although there are no clear records to account for this amount, a probable reason is that this figure covered the cost of bartering to private firms. This $50 million was probably the sum paid in brokerage fees, the so-called "barter discount," to the private U.S. companies handling these transactions.

Table 8.5 lists the major countries with which barter contracts for strategic materials, supplies, and services were executed from 1954 to 1975 under P.L. 480. The Republic of South Africa leads in percentage of barter contracts at 14 percent. Canada, India, Jamaica, and Turkey follow. These countries are of interest because they indicate a range of countries that could supply the United States with strategic materials in the event of a new barter program. Under these contracts, the United States was provided with a variety of strategic materials described in Table 8.6.

The P.L. 480 barter program was a secondary method for moving agricultural commodities into world markets in return for strategic materials and other supplies. The prices for agricultural commodities and materials were relatively low in the world market during this period. At the same time, there were several benefits from the program:

- To the extent that these bartered materials were additional sales, that is, they did not displace U.S. commercial sales, barter fostered the development of new markets in some countries;
- The program provided foreign countries with a method of receiving needed commodities in exchange for materials and other items that could not be sold on world markets to generate foreign exchange; and
- The program removed surplus commodities from costly U.S. government storage.

Problems with the barter program were clear from the beginning. Each contract became a complex, time-consuming, legal question. Negotiations took much more time than a normal sale. The question of additionality and displacement of cash sales constantly haunted the program. The specification of bilateral sales was only made in 1968, so that it was assumed, but never proved, that many commodities were resold and did displace commercial sales. The idea of subsidizing these exports also caused some concern.

Table 8.6 Title III, Public Law 480–Materials, Equipment, and Services Received under Barter Contracts, July 1, 1954, through June 30, 1975

Country and Area	Procurements for U.S. Government Agencies*	Stockpile materials†
Europe:		
Austria		Aluminum oxide (abrasive grain), diamond (stones).
Belgium	Supplies and services	Cadmium, cobalt metal, diamond (stones), farromanganese, lead, selenium, waterfowl feathers and down, zinc.
Denmark	Supplies and services	Copper billets.
France	French housing	Aluminum oxide (abrasive grain), aluminum oxide (crude), chronium metal (oxothermic), diamond dies, ferrochromium, ferromanganese, manganese ore (battery grade), palladium, silicon carbide, thorium nitrate, waterfowl feathers and down.
Germany, West	Caribbean cable, fertilizer, supplies and services	Aluminum oxide (abrasive grain), aluminum oxide (crude), bisouth, cadmium, chronium metal (exothermic), diamond (stones), ferrochromium, ferromanganese, fluorspar, lead, selenium, zinc.
Italy		Cadmium, ferrochromium, fluorspar, mercury, zinc.
Netherlands	Fertilizer	Chromium metal (exothermic), diamond (stones), palladium, platinum, waterfowl feathers and down, zinc.
Norway		Ferrochromium, ferromanganese, zinc.
Spain		Fluorspar, lead, mercury.
Sweden		Ferrochromium, lead, selenium.
Trieste	Fertilizer	
United Kingdom	Fertilizer	Antimony, bismuth, cadmium, celestite, chromium metal (exothermic), diamond (bort), diamond (stones), ferro-

Yugoslavia	Supplies and services	chromium, ferromanganese, lead, paladium, platinum, ruthenium, tin (pig).
Unspecified European countries	Supplies and services	Antimony, bismuth, ferrochromium, ferromanganese, lead, zinc.
Africa:		
Angola		Manganese ore (metallurgical), mica.
Botswana		Asbestos (chrysotile), manganese ore (metallurgical).
Ghana		Diamond (stones), ferromanganese, manganese ore (battery grade), manganese ore (metallurgical).
Malagasy Republic		Beryllium (copper master alloy), graphite, mica.
Malawi		Beryllium (copper master alloy).
Morocco		Manganese ore (battery grade), manganese ore (chemical).
Mosambique		Beryl ore, beryllium (copper master alloy), beryllium metal billets, ferrochromium, ferrochromium-silicon, zinc.
Nigeria		Columbite.
Rhodesia		Asbestos (chrysotile), beryllium (copper master alloy), beryllium metal billets, chromite (metallurgical), cobalt metal, copper, ferrochromium, ferrochromium-silicon, mica, zinc.
South Africa, Republic of		Antimony, asbestos (amosite), asbestos (chrysotile), asbestos (crocidolite), beryl ore, beryllium (copper master alloy), beryllium metal billets, chromite (chemical), diamond (stones), ferrochromium, ferrochromium-silicon, fluorspar, lead, manganese metal (electrolytic), manganese ore (metallurgical), palladium, platinum, rare earths, thorium nitrate.
Tanzania		Mica.

(Table 8.6 continues)

Table 8.6 continued

Country and Area	Procurements for U.S. Government Agencies*	Stockpile materials†
Uganda		Beryllium (copper master alloy).
Zaire, Republic of		Beryllium (copper master alloy), cadmium, diamond (bort), diamond (stones), manganese ore (metallurgical), tin (pig), zinc.
Unspecified African countries		Beryl ore, diamond (bort), diamond (stones), mica.
Near East and South Asia:		
Greece		Manganese ore (battery grade).
India		Beryl concentrates, beryl ore, beryllium (copper master alloy), beryllium metal billets, ferrochromium, ferrochromium-silicon, ferromanganese, manganese metal (electrolytic), manganese ore (metallurgical), mica, thorium nitrate.
Israel		Diamond (stones).
Pakistan		Beryllium (copper master alloy).
Sri Lanka		Graphite.
Turkey		Boron minerals, chromium metal (electrolytic), chromite (metallurgical), ferrochromium, ferrochromium-silicon.
Far East and Pacific:		
Australia		Asbestos (crocidolite), beryllium metal billets, lead, rutile, zinc.
Japan	Cotton yarn, fertilizer, raw silk, sirconium sponge	Cadmium, chromium metal (electrolytic), ferrochromium, ferromanganese, iodine (crude), raw silk, selenium, silk bisu and/or lap waste, titanium sponge, zinc.
Korea	Ordance, raw silk	Tungston carbide powder.
New Caledonia		Ferrochromium.
Philippines		Chromite (refractory), chromium metal (electrolytic), ferro-chromium, ferrochromium-silicon.

Taiwan	Waterfowl feathers and down.
Thailand	Tin (pig).
North America:	
Canada	Aluminum oxide (abrasive grain), aluminum oxide (crude), asbestos (chrysotile), cadmium, ferrochromium, ferromanganese, lead, palladium, platinum, selenium, silicon carbide, waterfowl feathers and down, zinc.
United States	Fertilizer, soybeans
Latin America:	
Argentina	Beryl ore, beryllium (copper master alloy), beryllium metal billets, mica.
Bolivia	Cadmium, lead, zinc.
Brazil	Beryl ore, beryllium (copper master alloy), beryllium metal billets, diamond (stones), ferromanganese, manganese ore (metallurgical), mica, quartz crystals.
Chile	Ferromanganese, iodine (crude), lead.
Colombia	Platinum.
Cuba	Chromite (refractory), ferrochromium-silicon.
Guyana	Bauxite.
Haiti	Bauxite.
Jamaica	Bauxite.
Mexico	Bauxite.
Peru	Antimony, bismuth, cadmium, celestite, fluorspar, lead, zinc.
Surinam	Bauxite.
Venezuela	Diamond (stones).
Unspecified sources	Beryllium metal billets.

*Materials, goods, equipment, and services procured for U.S. government agencies under contracts entered into prior to January 1, 1963.

†Materials required for the national and supplemental stockpiles.

Source: U.S. Department of Agriculture, Foreign Agricultural Service, Food For Peace, the 1975 Annual Report of Public Law 480, 1975.

CURRENT BARTER TRANSACTIONS AND POLICIES

A new U.S. government barter program could accomplish three goals. First, barter could acquire materials, goods, or services for the National Defense Stockpile, the Strategic Petroleum Reserve, military bases overseas, and for development projects. Second, in return for such acquisitions, the U.S. government could dispose of surplus goods and materials such as agricultural commodities, surplus military materials, or even surplus metals or minerals. Third, barter could generate political support for or enhance the strategic advantage of the United States by establishing a close economic relationship with other barter countries. Barter transactions are going on around the world in many different countries. The tables cover seventy-four known completed barter transactions within the last seven years (1976 to 1983). Each agreement includes agricultural commodities traded by at least one party. There are hundreds of additional agreements that have been talked about, explored, and abandoned because concluding such transactions would be too costly in terms of time, discounting of prices, and problems with the disposal of unwanted goods.[6]

Purpose of Barter for the United States

Any government barter transaction would have to match certain "needs." Economists call this mixture of filling needs a "double coincidence of wants." Two types of wants would necessarily be involved: the acquisition needs of the government would have to be matched with its disposal needs. Certain foreign and defense policy criteria would presumably have to be met before barter arrangements could take place.

The list of 61 strategic and critical materials listed in the National Defense Stockpile, as well as the oil needed in the Strategic Petroleum Reserve, could serve as a starting point for possible barter transactions. Appendix A contains a list of deficit stockpile materials, excluding oil, and the countries where these materials are found and exported. Appendix B explains the procedures necessary to make up this list in what is formally known as the Annual Materials Plan. The United States also has agricultural commodities that it could export.

Availability of CCC Commodities for Barter

Commodities in CCC inventory are acquired under the 1949 Agriculture Act, as amended. This Act gives the authority under which the government acquires so-called "nonperishable" price support commodities such as dairy products, peanuts, oils, cotton, and a variety of grains. These items accumulate because the legislated price support levels are above world market prices. Large inventories of certain products have accumulated at various times (especially dairy in recent years) because farmers benefited more by selling to the government than by selling on the open market.

Surplus U.S. commodities may or may not be controlled by the CCC. For example, much of the more than 1 to 2 billion bushels of wheat in storage earlier in 1983 actually were in the farmer-owned reserve or were being held as collateral pending repayment of loans made by CCC to producers, and thus were not under CCC's control. In addition, the Payment-in-Kind (PIK) Program has, for the present time, effectively committed most of the surplus grains that were under CCC control from the inventories in recent months, including rice, wheat, corn, and grain sorghum (see Table 8.7).

Any barter program of the United States using CCC agricultural commodities will have to operate under the rules for release of CCC-held stocks. Unless current laws are changed, the CCC cannot sell stocks

Table 8.7 *CCC COMMODITY INVENTORY*, September 9, 1983 (in million units)

Commodity	Committed	Uncommitted	Total
Wheat (bu)	153.6	—	153.6
Corn (bu)	631.7	—	631.7
Grain sorghum (cwt)	37.3	—	37.3
Rice (cwt)	22.5	—	22.5
Barley (bu)	2.7*	3.3	6.0
Oats (bu)	—	0.7	0.7
Rye (bu)	—	0.04	0.04
Soybeans (bu)	—	19.0	19.0
Honey (lb)	65-75.†	—	65-75.
Butter (lb)	106.8	414.6	521.4
Cheese (lb)	148.3	910.2	1,058.5
Nonfat Dry Milk (lb)	187.5	1,348.3	1,535.8

*Disaster reserve.

† Reserved for school lunch program.

Source: USDA, Agricultural Stabilization and Conservation Service, September, 9, 1983.

of wheat or feed grains at less than 110 percent of the acquisition price (normally the loan rate or so-called support price). The CCC minimum sales price for cotton cannot be less than 115 percent of the loan rate. These provisions for CCC release of commodities could potentially affect the types of commodities bartered and the countries interested in barter when release prices exceed world market levels. Dairy products, as well as rice, grain, sorghum, barley, rye, and honey, can be exported at not less than prevailing world market prices. Furthermore, bartered agricultural commodities may not disrupt world market prices (7 U.S.C. § 1727g) (1982).

Other statutory provisions, because of their budgetary effects, may affect CCC's willingness to engage in barter deals. Some statutes authorizing barter activity provide for reimbursement to CCC in an amount equivalent to the value of the agricultural commodities released. For example, the Commodity Credit Corporation (CCC) chartering statute authorizes the corporation "to accept strategic and critical materials produced abroad in exchange for agricultural commodities acquired by the Corporation" [15 U.S.C. § 714(h) (1982)]. The act further provides, however, that the CCC "shall be reimbursed for the strategic and critical materials so transferred to the stockpile from the funds made available for the purposes of the Strategic and Critical Materials Stock Piling Act, in an amount equal to the fair market value as determined by the Secretary of the Treasury." Other statutes governing CCC transfers, by contrast, do not require that the CCC receive reimbursement. [See, for example, U.S.C. § 1743(a) (4) (1982)].

Estimate of Possible Barter Trade for the United States Government

At least four government acquisition programs could directly benefit from a barter program. If each program's needs were completely filled with bartered goods and services, the estimated value would reach $27.25 billion.

	($ Billion)
National Defense Stockpile (unfilled inventories)	10.00
Strategic Petroleum Reserve (unfilled inventories)	14.00
AID overseas expenditures (annual)	1.25
DOD overseas expenditures (FY82 annual cost of military construction overseas)	2.00
Estimated total	27.25

(See Appendix E for the source of the figure for each program.)

U.S.-JAMAICA BARTER AGREEMENTS*

On February 25, 1982, two barter agreements were signed with the Bauxite and Alumina Trading Company, Ltd. (BATCO) of Jamaica for 1.6 million tons of bauxite. The first agreement, signed by the CCC for the United States, directed that 400,000 tons of bauxite be exchanged for 7,238 metric tons of nonfat dry milk and 1,905 metric tons of anhydrous milk fat (butter oil) from the CCC stockpile. The total value of the agricultural commodites bartered was estimated at $13 million. The second agreement, with GSA, acquired the remaining 1.2 million tons of bauxite through cash purchases and an exchange. The latter exchange meant the bartering of excess stockpile material (for example, tin and tungsten) in exchange for the bauxite.

Under the first agreement, delivery terms for U.S. bartered dairy products were free alongside ship (f.a.s.) U.S. Gulf ports; the delivery period for the dairy products was May 1982 through February 1983. Bauxite delivery was completed by September 30, 1982. The CCC is vested with the title to the bauxite, but the bauxite itself has been comingled with all the other U.S. stockpiled bauxite. It may not be sold by the USDA because title is only vested with the CCC until GSA appropriations pay for the bauxite, which is to occur no later than September 30, 1984. All transportation, handling, and storage costs for the bauxite were directed in this agreement to be paid for from the stockpile transaction fund under GSA fund management.[7]

This barter transaction, the first of its kind since 1967, was a success in several respects. First, the stockpile inventory for bauxite was in a deficit position. Second, USDA was able to barter dairy products that it would not have been able to sell. At the time the agreement was entered into, Jamaica was importing nonfat dry milk and anhydrous milk fat from Canada, France, and New Zealand. These countries were consulted prior to the signing of the agreements. Third, according to President Reagan, this agreement promoted American regional foreign policy goals. "While improving our own defense posture," he noted in his November 1981 announcement, "this program will contribute to Prime Minister Edward Seaga's strategy for Jamaica to rely to the maximum extent possible on production and exports to fuel its economic recovery. The stability and economic strength of Jamaica are important to our national security interests in the Caribbean."[8] The bauxite was delivered according to plan, and is being stored near an operating aluminum plant, on 22 acres leased to the federal government by the Reynolds Corporation for $1 per year.

---

*This section was prepared with the assistance of Robert B. Stack.

There were three primary problems in the arrangement for USDA. The first was the time spent finding a material or commodity at suitable prices that Jamaica would accept. Jamaica originally wanted U.S. wheat and corn, but federal restrictions on their sale priced the grains above the world market price and the price Jamaica could afford. Jamaica finally decided that it would accept the butter oil and dry milk, if they were less than three months old, put in a form acceptable for Jamaican consumption, and delivered in allotments on a timetable allowing immediate consumption without stockpiling. All these details involved time-consuming negotiations, especially the quantity of dairy products that could be consumed within Jamaica and not trans-shipped to some other country.

Another problem was the determination of the value of the bauxite. Most bauxite is traded vertically within a company; very little reaches the open market, and the assignment of value ($32.50 a ton) took time. The other problem was the lack of competitive market conditions in the negotiations. Jamaica knew that President Reagan had announced the exchange, and, therefore, Jamaica struck a hard bargain during negotiations.

A second U.S.-Jamaica barter agreement was signed on November 17, 1983, exchanging diary products for 1 million tons of bauxite for the National Defense Stockpile.

As noted above, the CCC Charter Act grants the CCC authorization to accept strategic and critical materials "produced abroad" in exchange for agricultural commodities acquired by the CCC. The act further provides that materials acquired by the CCC shall be transferred to the stockpile to the extent approved by the president, who has delegated this approval authority to FEMA. Upon transfer to the stockpile, the CCC is then reimbursed for the fair market value of the minerals it transfers.

Relying on these provisions, the Jamaican deal involved acquisition of $13 million worth of bauxite, and raised certain legal and practical consequences worth considering in the future. First, there is no requirement in the act that it use competitive bidding to find the best offer for the dairy products. Thus, in contrast to the sale component of the deals, this portion of the Jamaican barter/exchange/sale transaction required no waiver of the use of competitive bidding. Second, this part of the Jamaican deal had a significant budgetary impact on the GSA.

The absence of a competitive bidding requirement could have several consequences. First, it could upset other suppliers of raw materials who feel that they could offer the material at a better price. In this case, Brazil, Haiti, and the Dominican Republic are also suppliers of bauxite; they might have been able to provide better terms. Failing to require competitive bidding presents the possibility that the CCC could manipulate barter transactions by tailoring the package of excess commodities the CCC is seeking to dispose of. The CCC therefore may have engineered the deal so no other country except Jamaica wanted $13 million worth of dairy products. Thirteen million dollars of some other commodity, however, could be an attractive offer to another country. Because the CCC and the Agriculture Department can dictate the initial disposal from the agricultural reserves and because they are not required to bid competitively, they can thus do deals backwards—decide in advance what commodity to dispose of, the amount and fair market value of the commodity, *and then* hunt for a country that has a need for that commodity and which has some excess raw materials. Of course, the CCC also must be careful not to displace already existing American export markets. When a deal reaches the political level, such as the Jamaican deal, things get a bit more complicated in that a country that the United States wants to "help" may be preselected and the barter/exchange/sale transaction set up to meet the needs of that country. As a result of this flexibility, there is little to ensure that the best deal is struck.

The requirement that GSA reimburse the CCC at the fair market value, however, means that GSA bears the *cost* of any economic inefficiency. Competitive bidding might reduce that cost.

Second, the reimbursement requirement presents certain problems. The CCC statute does not make clear when the fair market value is to be determined for reimbursement purposes—this problem does not exist when a cash transaction takes place since the GSA pays the market price at the time of the transaction. This problem may be more apparent than real, however. The "risk" that the price of the acquired commodity will decline is no greater than it would have been had the GSA paid cash in year one only to discover a sharp decline in price in year two. The difference between barter deals and cash purchases can be minimized to the extent that GSA has input regarding the timing and valuation chosen in the barter transaction.

A final problem that arose in the bauxite deal was that the GSA did not have the funds in 1982 for the bauxite. Thus, it agreed to reimburse the CCC for the bauxite no later than at the end of fiscal year 1984. This $13 million expenditure will be a significant portion of the GSA's budget when it is paid. The 1982 budget was only $57 million and the 1983 budget is not expected to be much higher than that. This future repayment provision underscores two points about the use of barter. First, Congress probably will decline to appropriate additional money earmarked for the reimbursement. This means that the barter part of the transaction has had a significant effect on the careful planning that goes into estimating stockpile needs. Although it is unlikely that this would become the normal way of doing business at the stockpile, the barter transaction, in effect, overrode the decisions represented by the annual materials plan. Second, the lack of current appropriations may in the future be a reason given by the GSA for not participating in a barter transaction when a more routine, less dramatic, case comes along. FEMA's statutory authority to use its discretion whether to accept materials purchased by the CCC could restrict considerably the viability of any such barter program—as long as GSA's budget is as limited as it is.

The Stock Pile Act declares that the "[m]aterials in the stockpile, the disposition of which is authorized by law, shall be available for transfer at fair market value as payment for expenses of acquisitions of materials, or of refining, processing, or rotating materials under this subchapter" (50 U.S.C.A. § 98e(c)(2) (1982)). This exchange authority thus can be used to acquire needed materials by disposing of excess materials in the stockpile. Although Congress must authorize the disposal of the materials involved, these exchange transactions do not require the expenditure of appropriated funds. The exchange provision, therefore, even more than the barter provision, provides an attractive way for the GSA to obtain needed materials. The Jamaican deal, however, added a new twist to the standard exchange because it provided that the GSA would "pay for" $18 million worth of bauxite with excess minerals. But because Jamaica apparently had no need for these excess materials either, the agreement further provided that GSA would sell those excess materials "on behalf of Jamaica, receiving a two percent commission for its efforts."

The Stock Pile Report's language on this aspect of the transaction is curious and indicates an area of legal ambiguity. The report notes that the GSA will sell the excess materials "on behalf of Jamaica." The GSA must not have thought that it had carte blanche authority simply to sell excess materials and to use money so acquired for the purchase of excess materials. Were GSA to have read its authorizing statute as providing this authority, Congress would have been able to exert much less control over the stockpile through its appropriation authority. This is because GSA has a substantial excess of stockpile materials authorized for disposal and revenues generated by disposing of these materials that go into the "transaction fund." If GSA were free to spend that money, it could act substantially independently of congressional appropriation. In 1982-83, for example, the stockpile raised $148 million through sales of excess materials; yet, its appropriations budget was significantly less than this amount—$58 or $100 million. But, by agreeing to sell the materials on behalf of Jamaica, GSA appears to have arranged to do indirectly what it cannot do directly. For, recharacterized, the exchange portion of the Jamaican transaction was a purchase of $18 million worth of bauxite at a 2 percent discount paid for with money from the sale of excess stockpile materials. Were this transaction not carried out "on behalf of Jamaica" a strong argument could be made that it was an unauthorized and, therefore, illegal expenditure of monies received for sale of excess stockpile materials. Whether finding the purchasing country first and including the magic words "on behalf of" in an agreement should make any difference as to the legality of the expenditure is a question that may never be litigated.

This legal problem may be less troublesome than it initially appears. FEMA, in the Annual Materials Plan, reports annually to Congress its planned exchanges, barter deals, and purchases. Congress then implicitly approves the AMP when it appropriates a lump sum of money. Further, the GSA must inform Congress when it changes the plan in any way. This information control mechanism minimizes any danger that GSA will appropriate money to itself by keeping the returns from sales of excess materials—or by structuring multi-country "exchanges" that are little more than sales and purchases. To the extent that GSA does get involved in such transactions and to the extent that Congress knows about it, one would expect that other appropriations would be adjusted downward to reflect the "gain" from the exchange. Thus, as long as Congress is informed of proposed activities and does not object, it seems logical to assume that the GSA is acting within its authority in making the deals.

The sale portion of the Jamaican bauxite transaction yields little of note to discuss. It is remarkable to note, however, that $30 million out of a budget of $57 million for one year, in addition to the amount of money that will have to be reimbursed to the CCC, represents a rather large outlay of GSA stockpile money. It is also worth pointing out that the sale portion of the transaction contained numerous statutory requirements that were waived because of the special circumstances of a barter/exchange deal.

The Role of the President

The transaction described above depicts in textbook fashion the combination of methods available to carry out transactions with a cash-poor country to help the United States use up some of its excess farm supplies. The Jamaican bauxite deal, however, involved the president to a degree that he probably would not be involved in a routine barter transaction. The question then is whether, absent this degree of involvement, barter deals can become viable or even common alternatives to traditional cash deals.

According to the New York *Times,* for example, "President Reagan's express wish to transform Jamaica into an economic showplace of the Caribbean has prompted three federal agencies to waive laws and bend rules, thereby providing more than $100 million to bolster the Jamaican operations of leading American aluminum companies."[9] The *Times* went on to point out that the deal "illustrates the extent to which the Federal bureaucracy responds to Presidential directives, especially when the President has publicly and repeatedly voiced enthusiasm for such a project."

The president's direct involvement in the Jamaican transaction was marked in five ways including presidential waivers of procedures normally required in such a transaction. Contrary to the implication of the *Times* report, however, each of these waivers clearly was within the president's legal authority.

First, the president waived competitive bidding requirements. The statute permits such a waiver provided that the president, through the GSA, tells Congress that he is waiving the requirements and the reasons he is doing it. See 50 U.S.C. § 98(d) (1982). In the Jamaican case, the GSA informed Congress that the acquisition would not be competitive because the president had directed a government-to-government negotiation for "foreign policy" reasons. In its letter to the House Armed Services Committee, the GSA Federal Property Resource Service commissioner tied the waiver to more general practical concerns:

> We have determined that the use of competitive procedures of the acquisition of material is not feasible. The specifications of the material for stockpile purposes are such that the Jamaican type currently being procured in Jamaica is the best source for this material. Market analysis indicates a soft position in the sales of bauxite and it would be in the government's best interest to negotiate for this transaction .... It is not feasible nor in the government's best interest, to solicit competitive proposals from a single source of supply.[10]

Significantly, the statute does not require any particular reasons for waiving competitive bidding; it requires merely that Congress be notified of *some* reason for the waiver. Thus, it was probably unnecessary for the White House to brandish the "foreign policy" talisman. If this move establishes a precedent as to when competitive bidding can be waived, it could become a meaningless rationale incanted only as a matter of form in the future when other deals—less significant from a foreign policy perspective—are struck. Further, the waiver was only necessary in the straight sale part of the transaction; neither the CCC barter nor the exchange require competitive bidding procedures to be used.

The second example of presidential involvement was the waiver of the requirements of the Cargo Preference Act of 1954 (46 U.S.C. § 1241 (1982)), which requires federal agencies to use American vessels when available. The GSA ignored this requirement and instead let the Reynolds ships, registered in Panama, carry the shipment, explaining that, "other carriers did not qualify because their ships would not 'properly interface' with the unloading facilities at the Reynolds installation."[11]

The Act requires agencies to "take such steps as may be necessary and practicable to assure that at least 50 per centum of the gross tonnage of such equipment, materials or commodities . . . shall be transported on privately owned United States-flag commerical vessels, to the extent such vessels are available . . ." (46 U.S.C. § 1241 (1982)). Statutory exceptions are limited to cases in which Congress or the president or the secretary of Defense declares that an emergency exists "justifying a temporary waiver of the provisions" of the Act. In the Jamaican case, however, the government relied on the "availability" language to relieve itself of this requirement, arguing that suitable vessels were not available. The unusual circumstances giving rise to this waiver probably will not arise in most other "normal" barter transactions.

Another mark of the president's intervention was that FEMA was required to rearrange its priorities for stockpile purchases. According to GSA personnel and sources quoted in the New York *Times*, bauxite ranked only seventh or eighth on a list of 13 items set for purchase in 1982 in the Annual Materials Plan. In rearranging these priorities, FEMA has the requisite authority provided that it notifies the appropriate Congressional committees 30 days before any transaction (See 50 U.S.C. § 98d (1982)). Thus, here too, the President clearly acted within his authority in altering the AMP priorities—notwithstanding his perhaps misleading November, 1981 statement in which he declared that his bauxite acquisition program would fill a critical deficiency of 12 million tons of bauxite.[12] In fact, the stockpile was in deficit in many areas in which neither Congress nor the Executive branch has urged such immediate action to close the existing gap.

The Jamaican transaction was also characterized by a high degree of personal presidential involvement. The Rockefeller Committee enjoyed substantial government support in its efforts and ready access to the president.

Finally, the president intervened in certain decisions of the Overseas Private Investment Corporation (OPIC) pertaining to the Jamaican deal. OPIC ordinarily does not grant the amount of political risk insurance involved in the Jamaican deal, but the president prevailed upon OPIC to provide substantial loan guarantees and political risk insurance to aluminum companies involved in a Caribbean bauxite joint venture.

Whether barter deals of the future will require such extensive presidential involvement and political brokerage is unclear. This description of President Reagan's involvement in the Jamaican deal underscores the unique aspects of this transaction and thus raises legitimate questions as to whether such deals would work as a matter of bureaucratic routine.

ADVANTAGES AND DISADVANTAGES*

From the experience of the old barter program and the recent U.S.-Jamaica barter agreement, issues have arisen that may not, at first, be clear.

Advantages of Barter

Additional Resources for National Security

If DOD could acquire needed materials or services overseas through barter, then congressionally appropriated monies could be used for other resources, thereby enhancing national security or other national priorities.

Assure Access to Supplies

If the United States imports most of an essential commodity (for example, strategic and critical ores, metals, and petroleum) as assurance against peacetime and wartime dispruptions, the U.S. government may

_____

*This section was prepared with the assistance of Scott Morse.

barter in order to guarantee supplies of a specific commodity for a specified time period, if there appears to be an advantage to the government. The reciprocal nature of barter agreements permits both seller and buyer to guarantee a supply of a commodity in a single agreement. Both parties gain markets or could lose these same markets, so there is an added incentive with a barter agreement.

Disposal of Surplus Agricultural Commodities[13]

The U.S. government's agricultural price support system, under which it acquires surplus commodities, used barter to reduce excess supplies—at a time when world commodity prices were low. This is often referred to as a "surplus disposal method," and certainly was the major motivating factor in the previous barter program. The need to dispose of agricultural surplus is likely to spur further efforts to initiate barter transactions in the coming years if the value of the dollar remains relatively high, making U.S. exports unattractive to foreign buyers.

Circumvent Nontariff Barriers

Where a special trade restriction or marketing condition makes a United States commodity uncompetitive in a particular market, a barter arrangement through its long negotiating process and the reciprocal nature of the arrangement could seal the trade for the United States. Barter can meet "spot" opportunities to increase United States agricultural exports.

Storage Savings

In FY 1983, annual storage and handling costs alone for agricultural commodities in the CCC inventories was about $382 million (this excludes transportation and other costs also associated with such commodities). The cost of storing materials in the strategic stockpile, because of their nondeteriorating characteristics, is much less, but still significant. Barter can result in savings to the government because it moves deteriorating goods out of storage, particularly when the only feasible alternative is destruction or sustained storage without prospects of use.

Declining Terms of Trade

Interest in barter arrangements also rises when market demand for a particular principal export declines. In the past, declining export prices and quantities vis-à-vis import costs have been an incentive for developing countries to enter into reciprocal agreements in order to offset fluctuating sales in multilateral markets. Although many barter exchanges take place, in effect, at world market prices, some developing countries have used barter agreements to increase the purchasing power of their exports vis-à-vis imports. On the other hand, developing countries at times accept lower prices for their export products under barter arrangements in order to augment temporarily the market for their primary products during periods of declining demand, and avoid formally reducing posted prices.

Benefit to the U.S. Budget

Whenever a barter transaction replaces a cash purchase by a United States government agency, the total federal budget benefits. This is because the agricultural commodities used have already been paid for, so no new funds are needed to acquire the imported materials, thus reducing the CCC's borrowings from the Treasury. If the items acquired by barter are covered by an approved government program for which no appropriation has been made, there is a potential benefit to the United States Treasury.

Market Development

The United States government may want to lessen its dependence on main suppliers by diversifying to new trading partners. Developing countries have also used barter agreements to expand exports of nontraditional items. Barter arrangements for these purposes are similar to many bilateral trade agreements the purpose of which is to get a foot in the door, establish marketing relations, collect information about the nature of the trading partner's demand for exports, and over time graduate the barter arrangements to commercial cash sales. This is especially true between developing countries trying to maintain trade relationships when neither country has much foreign exchange.

Barter arrangements may also afford U.S. exporters an opportunity to penetrate less-developed-country markets where there is demand for luxury high value agricultural items such as oranges, strawberries, and raisins, but where currency restrictions prevent cash sales. Over time, there might arise a similar opportunity to graduate the country to cash sales.

Information

Barter transactions give one country information about the needs of another country. This information is similar to bilateral arrangements that ensure supplies of commodities. If market information is a closed and guarded secret, a list of sought for commodities to import in a barter arrangement could give the other country a notion of production, stocks, and value the first country places on its commodities. For the United States, this can be very valuable information about Soviet bloc countries. Also, in the course of the negotiations, government representatives, as well as industry representatives, gain experience and expertise. At times, completely unrelated sectors learn about each other, and an acquaintanceship develops among personnel, which helps maintain market channels. This same familiarity can spill over into other areas.

Political Ties

Some countries establish barter agreements for strategic security reasons or to show political support for the leaders or political philosophy of a country. These agreements involve technical know-how or capital goods exchanges for agricultural commodities. They may, in effect, be a politically advantageous form of foreign aid. Agreements made under this aegis are often statements of political support at the highest levels of governments. The Jamaican bauxite barter deal is an example of this kind of statement.

Disadvantages of Barter

Inconsistent Trade Policy

The United States was a founding member of the GATT and is a major adherent to the principle of nondiscriminatory treatment in international trade. This means that a trading country must treat all of its trading partners in the same manner. The United States signed both the Subsidies Code and the Government Procurement Code under the GATT. Use of CCC commodities in barter transactions at less than support prices would mean they were subsidized. Government procurements in barter agreements also lack the transparency generally agreed to under the Government Procurement Code. Nontransparency means that other nationals do not have the same opportunities to bid to fulfill the government contract because the government procurement request is not open and clear (transparent) to all countries.

Double-Coincidence of Wants

Sellers interested in a strictly barter arrangement must find a buyer that also has a commodity for which the seller is willing to trade. This can be difficult, and sometimes proves impossible. For example, dairy products are the only commodities in substantial surplus now owned by the CCC, so it would be necessary to find a barter partner that wants dairy products and at the same time has materials the United States considers a top priority for acquisition.

Government Involvement

Many negotiated barter agreements are on a government-to-government basis, basically between state trading organizations. Countries in the European Economic Community (EEC), the United States, and many non-EEC European countries do not have marketing boards or state trading organizations to handle export sales. In some nations, trade is a private sector function and is not within the domain of the state. Governments encounter strong resistance on the part of individuals to having their markets government-controlled in any way.

Complex Price and Quantity Negotiations

Barter usually takes a great deal of negotiation to work out—much more than an ordinary commercial sale, where a commodity is valued at an international market price and is purchased by anyone who has the currency to pay for it. Barter negotiations involve agreement on prices, as well as quantities (values) to be traded. Although many agreements provide for exchange effectively at world market prices, negotiated prices in some agreements provide for discounts or premiums over equivalent world prices. For instance, an oil-exporting country could decide to barter petroleum for feedgrains at a price lower than Organization of Petroleum Exporting Countries (OPEC)-set prices, thereby increasing the exchange value of the feedgrain. Since world prices change rapidly, lengthy barter negotiations can cause a loss or gain to one of the bartering parties, as prices fluctuate during the negotiations. This could result in a windfall gain or loss to one of the partners.

Assessing Quality

All trade agreements specify the exact quality of the commodity to be delivered. Each commodity has different quality standards. Since the barter arrangement involves a two-way exchange, it is more complicated than in a normal goods-for-currency sales agreement to guarantee the delivery of the quality agreed upon in the negotiations. Moreover, refusal to accept the delivered commodity means a corresponding loss of a market for the barter partner. Therefore, the simple exercise of refusal to pay, as in a commercial agreement, becomes more complicated in a barter arrangement. Finally, since there is a notion that goods are bartered precisely because they cannot be sold for cash in international markets, there is an expectation on the part of some partners that they will be receiving inferior quality goods.

Tied Sales

For one reason or another, barter may be more useful to one side of the exchange than to the other. For example, when Brazil's debt service problem became so large, the Brazilian state company, Interbras, asked Mexico's Pemex to accept commodities as payment instead of cash to repay the agreed amount. Brazil had already received the petroleum, and requested Mexico to accept sunflower seeds and soybeans in lieu of cash. Eastern European countries often demand agreement from their commercial trading partners to receive payment in goods. When these arrangements are made at the insistence of one trading partner, the goods received in payment may not be easily used or sold, but the guarantee of an additional market provides the incentive for the other commercial trading firm or country to pursue the agreement.

Another aspect of these tied sales is that the recipient may not have the proper marketing channels for the acquired products (if not, they can be sold to a switch house at a large discounted price), and the product may subsequently compete in the initial seller's market, thereby replacing other valuable cash markets. This is known as "displacement of cash sales."

Another problem that can arise is that normal trade-purchasing patterns are broken because the exporter suddenly receives material normally purchased from other suppliers. Barter can therefore change normal buying routines with a loss of the benefits from the normal routine. Third-country trading partners can also be affected to the extent that the barter exchange disrupts customary trade flows.

Circumvention of International Monetary Fund Conditionality

When the International Monetary Fund (IMF) requires a country to incorporate certain austerity measures into its import policy as a condition for receiving further funds, it generally has acted on a judgment that the situation is grave and that the government must be made to confront difficult but important policy questions. Restricting imports of luxury or high value goods may be a politically unpopular move, but may be, in the IMF's judgment, the only way of conserving enough hard currency to rescue the country's failing financial structure. Barter transactions, because they involve no hard currency, provide a way of avoiding those difficult choices and may undermine the IMF's rescue package. The transactions may do that in two ways. First, barter transactions that allow some segments of the population to obtain luxury goods even in times of so-called austerity may make the IMF conditions seem superfluous, and may generate sentiment for ignoring them. Second, attention is diverted from import substitution and self-sufficiency efforts to efforts to produce the items to be offered in exchange for the luxury goods. Thus, even though barter transactions use no hard currency and therefore technically do not contravene IMF conditions, they may undermine those conditions indirectly.

Bureaucratic Rivalries

Negotiations among agencies within a government for barter agreements may be as elaborate as those between countries. Few ministries or departments are willing to release control over supplies of one commodity in order to allow another ministry to receive a good that might competitively enhance the other's power, budget, status, or responsibility. In addition, the purposes of the department may be at odds. For example, USDA's purpose is to support agricultural exports on a commercial basis, while DOD's goal is to enhance national security at the lowest cost. Even if bartered commodities displaced 1 percent of such cash sales, the USDA might feel that it would be in conflict with the U.S. foreign trade policy of maximizing free international trade in agricultural commodities. In addition, any depression of commodity prices resulting from barter would be harmful to farmers and thus violate the USDA's goals of stabilizing and supporting commodity prices and farm income.

Higher Transaction Costs

Because of the cumbersome nature of barter transactions, they are costly to negotiate. The time alone is more lengthy because many traders are not familiar with the characteristics or peculiarities of the commodities they are trading. Brokerage fees range from ½ percent to 3 percent of the value of the whole transaction, while in a normal cash trading transaction they would not be more than 2 percent of the total value. In a government-to-government barter, the necessary expertise needed in trading has not been developed over time in the United States, and, therefore, must be acquired at cost by the government. There is also a chance that if barter practice is expanded, a whole separate institution would need to be established, which would run counter to the Reagan administration's "less government" philosophy.

There seems to be no consensus of how a barter program would be incorporated into the proposed Department of International Trade.

LEGISLATION

There are several statutes already in place that give authority to the Executive Branch to barter. These include the Strategic and Critical Materials Stock Piling Act (as amended in 1979), the CCC Charter Act of 1949, Public Law 480, and section 416 of the Agricultural Act of 1949.

The Strategic and Critical Materials Stock Piling Act, 50 U.S.C. § 98ff. (1982), contains the legislative authority for the National Defense Stockpile. It encourages the use of barter in the acquisition or disposal of stockpiled materials "when acquisition or disposal by barter is authorized by law and is practical and in the best interest of the United States." The Act further provides that "to the extent otherwise authorized by law, property owned by the United States may be bartered for materials for the stockpile."

The Charter of the Commodity Credit Corporation, 15 U.S.C. § 714b(h) (1982), as amended, authorizes the secretary of Agriculture to exchange agricultural commodities for strategic materials, and authorizes their transfer to the stockpile to the extent that the president approves the transfer. The title to the strategic materials remains under CCC authority until reimbursed, whereby if the CCC is not reimbursed "in an amount equal to the fair market value" as determined by the secretary of Treasury, the CCC can dispose of such quantity as it deems proper to carry out the CCC function and protect its assets.

The Agricultural Trade Development and Assistance Act (P.L. 480), (7 U.S.C. § 1727g) (1982), provides that:

> The Secretary [of Agriculture] shall, whenever he determines that such action is in the best interest of the United States, and to the maximum extent practicable, barter or exchange agricultural commodities owned by the Commodity Credit Corporation for . . . such strategic or other materials of which the United States does not domestically produce its requirements . . . . He is directed to use every practicable means, in cooperation of other Government agencies, to arrange and make, through private channels, such barters or exchanges or to utilize the authority conferred on him by Section 714b(h) of Title 15 to make such barters or exchanges.

In the Agricultural Act of 1949, as amended, in section 416 (7 U.S.C. § 1431) (1982) authority is given to the Commodity Credit

Corporation "in order to prevent the waste of commodities . . . to barter or exchange such commodities for strategic or other materials as authorized by law." The barter authority in section 416 is not currently being used.

LEGISLATED CONSTRAINTS TO A BARTER PROGRAM

There are at least seven major constraints in current law and in international agreements that could hinder a barter program from operating successfully in today's world markets. They were placed there either by Congress to ensure that any barter program would not hinder commercial sales or by the fact of U.S. membership in the "multilateral" trading system under GATT.

Reimbursement

Amendments to the CCC Charter Act require that the CCC be reimbursed at "fair market value" for the commodities it releases for barter trade. Since GSA is currently not receiving appropriations from Congress to pay for the filling of the stockpile goals, it will take several years before CCC is reimbursed from the first United States-Jamaica Barter Agreement. The law states that the CCC must be reimbursed in a way that will protect CCC assets.

The problem of reimbursement could be solved through direct appropriation by Congress, by negating the reimbursement provision in the law, or by setting up a separate agency that would receive title to the CCC commodities without having to reimburse the CCC. This separate agency would contract barter agreements with private contractors. Another solution to the problem would be through the process of memoranda of understanding between government agencies, in which the value of the commodities could be negotiated to a level where a trading partner country, which exported strategic materials, oil, or other goods, would be attracted to such a barter arrangement.

Limitation on Release Prices

There is a legislated minimum on the valuation of agricultural products before they can be released for export in a barter arrangement.

Wheat and feedgrains	110 percent of the release price
Cotton	115 percent of the loan rate
Rice	Price set by the CCC
Dairy products	Price set by the CCC at no lower than the current market price. In addition, dairy

products may be "donated through foreign government and public and nonprofit humanitarian organizations for the assistance of needy persons outside the United States," under section 416 of the Agriculture Act of 1949, as amended. The donation may be in addition to the assistance programmed under P.L. 480.

These minimum requirements make the price of the CCC inventory commodities much more expensive than competing country products. Unless such constraints are removed, there would be little chance that any barter arrangement could be made.

Proof of Additionality to Trade

The current barter authority requires that barter trade be in addition to cash sales; it cannot replace dollar sales, and all barter negotiations must "take reasonable precautions to safeguard usual marketings of the United States." This criterion is extremely difficult to justify. The old barter program had an Executive Stockpile Committee examine additionality, and it concluded that the evidence in the end was based on subjective judgment.

Displacement of Competitors' Markets

Under the P.L. 480 legislation, there is the requirement that the barter transaction "assure that barter or exchange will not unduly disrupt world prices of agricultural commodities." Also, such transactions must "endeavor to cooperate with other exporting countries in preserving normal patterns of commercial trade with respect to commodities covered by formal multilateral international marketing agreements to which the United States is a party." With the recent worldwide recession, and the liquidity squeeze around the world, United States exports are competing with many other countries for a smaller amount of trade. Barter trade could be useful in these competitive markets for United States exports. However, such trade is likely to affect and may well displace trading partner markets.

Limitation to Bilateral Deals

The CCC-owned stocks can only be bartered under P.L. 480 on a bilateral basis. The foreign nation must guarantee that there will be no resale or transshipment of the surplus agricultural commodities to other countries. This regulation was made to prevent displacement of other U.S. commercial sales. Open-ended barter, as was done under CCC authority, would not put such restrictions on the final use of the bartered commodity.

An opposite approach, sometimes called "multilateral barter," is to permit third parties to purchase the commodity—paying cash or more useful goods in lieu of the bartered commodity. These arrangements are called "switch" in international trade. Both open-ended and multilateral barter hold open the possibility of the developing country acquiring cash to pay off creditors.

Cargo Preference

If a United States agency accepts direct responsibility for handling and transportation, the 50-50 requirement under the Cargo Preference Act of 1954, 46 U.S.C. § 1241b (1982), would have to be met. This requirement would also apply, even if private contractors made the shipments. Under P.L. 480, the USDA pays the additional handling and transport costs, but such costs under a barter arrangement could be reimbursed by other government agencies.

The barter partner could also be asked to provide the strategic material or oil at a United States port or at a negotiated price that included the cost of transportation. Payment of such costs could be negotiated before an agreement was signed.

Use of Private Stocks

If the USDA chose to use private stocks under the authority of the CCC Charter Act, it could seek bids from private contractors to obtain the desired agricultural commodities on the open market. The commodities could be obtained at market prices, eliminating the restrictions applying to CCC-owned stocks, and make it unnecessary to ship in U.S. flag carriers.

Trading Rules of the GATT Agreement on Government Procurement

The United States is a signatory to the Government Procurement Code, which essentially requires that national treatment and nondiscriminating treatment be applied to the procurement of products by entities under the direct or substantial control of signatory governments from suppliers in other signatories. The point of the code was to secure greater international competition in the purchases done primarily by governments. With barter agreements, since the negotiations are bilateral, these transactions are discriminatory—especially the price at which the traded commodities are valued. Usually, such prices are not made public for this very reason; participating countries do not want to have to extend discount prices to other trading partners.

THE REAGAN ADMINISTRATION'S RESPONSE TO BARTER

The Reagan administration established an interagency Working Group on Barter in January, 1984 to respond to proposals to barter with the U.S. government. In the past, the U.S. government has bartered agricultural surpluses mainly for strategic materials. The question now arises as to the possibility of barter arrangements of U.S. nonagricultural goods. Barter proposals will now be reviewed on a case-by-case basis by the Emergency Mobilization Preparedness Board (EMPB), a group charged by the president with emergency mobilization for national security. This group, chaired by the national security advisor includes representatives from 23 executive branch organizations. Its operational activities are carried out by working groups. A Working Group on Barter, mandated through an Executive order in January 1984, is charged with determining whether or not a particular barter arrangement will be in the "best interests of the country."

The Working Group on Barter met for the first organizational meeting on April 13, 1984. Since most of the 23 member agencies were represented at this meeting, many felt that the size of the group was unwieldy. The chairman, the under secretary for International Programs and Commodity Affairs of the U.S. Department of Agriculture (USDA), recommended that a task force of representatives from five core agencies first do the initial review and analysis of any formal barter proposals, and then report back to the Working Group. This core group will consist of representatives from USDA, the General Services Administration (GSA), the Federal Emergency Management Agency (FEMA), the Council of Economic Advisors (CEA), and the Office of Management and Budget (OMB). The actual size of the group will vary depending on the material in the barter proposals (for example, the Department of Energy, if petroleum is involved). If a barter agreement is anticipated to have an effect on U.S. trade relations, then the core group will bring in representatives from some or all of the trade policy agencies, including State, Treasury, Commerce, and the Office of the U.S. Trade Representative for their additional review of the proposal.

Once this core group has reviewed the barter proposals, recommendations will be forwarded to the larger Working Group on Barter. This group will make a collective recommendation to the EMPB which in turn will review the proposal. The National Security Advisor will then present the EMPB recommendations to the president.

Recent increases in agricultural surpluses combined with concerns about levels of strategic and critical materials in the National Defense Stockpile and inadequate funds to fill the national security stockpile goals has prompted increased congressional interest in barter. This growing interest is evidenced by the introduction of approximately 20 barter bills in the 98th Congress alone. Hearings, bills, amendments, and letters from members of Congress have intensified the pressure on the administration to barter. Part of the mission of the new Working Group on Barter will be to review barter proposals on a case-by-case basis.

The Working Group on Barter is seen by some analysts as representing a more systematic and formal approach to barter on the part of the Reagan administration. Prior to this Group's establishment, the administration dealt with proposals to barter on an ad hoc basis. Although many feel this Working Group's establishment represents the administration's recognition of the importance and potential of barter, others argue that the case-by-case review process of the Group reflects the administration's lack of a coherent and comprehensive barter policy. In fact some feel that the group's establishment may simply be a stalling device, particularly if no positive decision on any barter arrangements is made. Still others have adopted a wait-and-see attitude, reserving judgment until the Working Group actually begins to review and make decisions on specific barter proposals.

Administration officials have been struggling with the issue of formalizing a barter policy for several years. Two separate executive branch groups have debated a U.S. government policy on barter. The Senior Interdepartment Group-International Economic Policy (SIG-IEP), made up of senior government officials, was asked by the president to make recommendations on a U.S. policy on barter. A second interagency group known as the Inter-Agency Group on Countertrade and Barter, chaired by the Office of the U.S. Trade Representative, also considered policy options on barter for the U.S. government. Both groups' recommendations remain confidential, but reportedly both agreed that U.S. government involvement in barter should only occur when the government is one party to the transaction. They did not attempt to formulate specific regulations or directives for private U.S. companies involved in barter. However, this is not to say there is no federal interest in private barter or countertrade transactions. For example, over the last few years, the Commerce Department has given normal market intelligence, trade policy information, and support services to private companies or foreign governments interested in countertrade.

Reportedly, the major concern that surfaced in these groups' discussions on barter is that some barter transactions may in fact be considered to be export subsidies, and perhaps, contrary to U.S. obligations under the General Agreement on Tariffs and Trade (GATT). Those viewing barter as involving considerable federal subsidies cite the fact that some barter arrangements contain a valuation of exchanged goods that is less than production or acquisition costs. If such sales are determined to cause market displacement of another country's exports, then a complaint would likely be lodged against the United States in the GATT. Increased use of barter resulting in repeated and publicized complaints would weaken the U.S. position in the GATT, which has been to argue forcefully and loudly against other countries' use of export subsidies.

This particular issue has already surfaced with regard to the recent barter sales between the U.S. government and Jamaica. The dairy products used in all three barter agreements were priced by the U.S. government at world prices, but were actually acquired by the USDA at higher than world prices because of the dairy price program. Three countries—the European Community, Australia, and New Zealand—have all formally complained in working groups of the GATT against these barter sales.

In addition, these sales also prompted extensive discussions over the question of reimbursement among the federal agencies, USDA and GSA, involved in the transactions over the question of reimbursement. Since one department, USDA, was releasing resources, and the other, GSA, was acquiring resources, the matter of settling accounts needed to be resolved. This reimbursement issue was settled through a memorandum of understanding between GSA and USDA. GSA will pay USDA for its commodities over a three-year period beginning in 1988.

In addition to bartering dairy products, congressional pressure is growing to include a wider range of goods, or property, such as surplus government-owned materials, and excess and surplus defense industrial property in exchange for strategic materials. Such an expansion in the types of materials available for barter may make it possible to expand the use of barter by the U.S. government.

Given the likelihood of continued agricultural surpluses and the lack of adequate funding for the National Defense Stockpile, barter can be expected to remain a topic of congressional debate over the next few years. It is too early to assess the impact of the Working Group, but it is possible that Members of Congress will continue to pressure the administration to use barter to help reduce price-depressing agricultural surpluses and to meet the goals of the strategic stockpile.

CONCLUSION

A U.S. government barter program is one technique the U.S. Department of Agriculture could use to dispose of surplus agricultural commodities. Other government agencies could also rid themselves of surplus goods. The stockpile could acquire updated critical materials, and the petroleum reserve could gain oil. There has been some concern expressed that large stockpiles of minerals and metals will have a price-depressing effect on world markets for such items. The same idea holds true for the petroleum reserve. It seems less likely that agricultural commodities will be bartered for military uses through the Department of Defense because the military has its own developed supply system. Because the purpose of foreign assistance under AID is to develop the capacity of developing nations to produce goods and services for themselves and for export, barter is often not totally consistent with AID goals. Certainly, some small amount of barter is possible, but most developing nations have few items to export for foreign exchange. Strategic materials are some of the export items that will bring in hard currency. Thus, it is unlikely that developing nations in need of hard currency would normally forego the cash sale of strategic materials to accept bartered dairy products.

A major reason for the U.S. government to barter would be to acquire materials for the stockpile, oil for the reserve, and in circumstances where savings could be realized or advantages accrued in a politically acceptable form such as aid or in reductions of costly surpluses. Pending legislation has demonstrated that some members of Congress want this to happen. The administration is still studying the issues, and will soon be formulating and reporting a policy. Barter could also help to dispose of surplus agricultural commodities that have accumulated in CCC inventory, particularly dairy products. A critic might validly point out that the successful barter of dairy products would reduce the pressure to revise the dairy subsidy program. However, the currently large dairy product inventory is unlikely to be substantially reduced by even the most successful barter effort.

APPENDIX A

Appendix Table 8.8 Stockpile Materials in Deficit as of April 28, 1983; Country Import Sources, and CCC Commodities

Commodity Unit[1]	Deficit[1]	U.S. Import Sources[2]	Potential Barter CCC Commodities[3]
Bauxite			
Abrasive metal grade (LCT)	699,229	Jamaica	wheat, corn, cheese
Jamaica type (LDT)	10,541,656	Guinea	nonfat dry milk
Surinam type	800,403	Australia	cheese
Refractory grade	1,200,074		
Cadmium	5,371,191	Korea	wheat, corn, nonfat dry milk
Columbium concentrate (IBCB)	2,645,827	Brazil	wheat, nonfat dry milk, corn
		Canada	cheese, nonfat dry milk, corn
		Thailand	wheat, nonfat dry milk
Copper (ST)	870,952	Chile	corn, wheat
		Canada	cheese, nonfat dry milk, corn
		Zambia	corn
		Peru	cotton, ex. linters, wheat, grain sorghum, corn, nonfat dry milk
Fluorspar (SDT)			
Acid grade (SDT)	504,017	Mexico	cotton, ex. linters, grain sorghum, corn, wheat, barley, nonfat dry milk
		Republic of South Africa	corn, sorghum, nonfat dry milk, cheese
		Spain	barley
		Italy	barley, corn
Metallurgical Grade (SDT)	1,288,262	Mexico	cotton, ex. linters, grain sorghum, corn, wheat, barley, nonfat dry milk

Appendix Table 8.8 (continued)

Commodity Unit[1]	Deficit[1]	U.S. Import Sources[2]	Potential Barter CCC Commodities[3]
Iron ore*		Canada	cheese, nonfat dry milk, corn
		Venezuela	wheat, corn, grain sorghum, cheese
		Brazil	wheat, nonfat dry milk, corn
		Liberia	wheat, corn, cheese
Lead (ST)	498,968	Honduras	wheat, corn, nonfat dry milk
		Peru	grain sorghum, cotton, ex. linters, corn, nonfat dry milk
		Australia	cheese
Manganese			
Battery: syn. dioxide (SDT)	21,989	Brazil	wheat, nonfat dry milk, corn
Nickel (ST)	167,791	Canada	cheese, nonfat dry milk, corn
		Norway	wheat, grain sorghum, corn, wheat
		Dominican Republic	wheat
Platinum group			
Iridium (TROZ)	74,410	Republic of South Africa	corn, sorghum, nonfat dry milk, cheese
		USSR	wheat, barley, corn
		United Kingdom	wheat, corn, sorghum
Palladium (TROZ)	1,744,988	Republic of South Africa	corn, sorghum, nonfat dry milk, cheese
		USSR	wheat, barley, corn
		United Kingdom	wheat, corn, sorghum
Rubber (LT)	731,428	Indonesia	wheat, corn, nonfat dry milk, cheese
		Malaysia	wheat, corn, cheese
		Liberia	wheat, corn, cheese
Tantalum minerals (LBTA)	5,544,616	Thailand	wheat, nonfat dry milk
		Canada	cheese, nonfat dry milk, wheat, rice
		Malaysia	wheat, corn, cheese

		Other Nonferrous Metals	
Titanium sponge (ST)	162,669	Japan	corn, wheat
		USSR	wheat, barley, corn
		United Kingdom	wheat, corn, sorghum
		China (PRC)	corn, wheat
Zinc (ST)	1,046,684	Canada	cheese, nonfat dry milk, corn
		Honduras	wheat, corn, nonfat dry milk
		Peru	cotton, ex. linters, sorghum, nonfat dry milk
Antimony (thou. short tons of metal)	(excess 4,708)	China (PRC)	corn
		Mexico	cotton, ex. linters, grain, sorghum, corn, wheat, barley
		Republic of South Africa	corn, sorghum, nonfat dry milk, cheese
Cadmium (thou. metric tons of metal)	5,371,191	Canada	cheese, nonfat dry milk, cheese
		Australia	cheese
Chromium (thou. short tons gross weight)	1,243,176		
Chromite:			
Metallurgical-grade		Republic of South Africa	corn, sorghum, nonfat dry milk, cheese
Chemical-grade		Philippines	corn, wheat
Refractory-grade		USSR	wheat, barley, corn

(Appendix Table 8.8 continues)

Appendix Table 8.8 (continued)

Commodity Unit[1]	Deficit[1]	U.S. Import Sources[2]	Potential Barter CCC Commodities[3]
Chromium ferroalloys Chromium metal		Turkey	
Cobalt			
(thou. short tons of metal)	41,607,769	Zaire Belgium	wheat, nonfat dry milk corn
Mercury (176-pound flasks of metal)	(excess 173,815)	Spain Algeria Italy Yugoslavia	barley barley corn, barley barley, corn, sorghum

*Not listed as an official stockpile material.

Sources:

[1] General Services Administration. Federal Property Resources Service Monthly Report on the Inventory of Stockpile Materials, April 30, 1983.

[2] Bureau of Mines. Mineral Commodity Summaries 1983. United States Department of the Interior.

[3] Foreign Agriculture Service Data Base and Agricultural Stabilization and Conservation Service, CCC Commodity Inventory Activity Report. Unpublished data.

APPENDIX B: ACQUISITION AND DISPOSAL OF MATERIAL UNDER THE STOCKPILE ACT: THE ANNUAL MATERIALS PLAN*

This appendix will explain the acquisition and disposal functions of the General Services Administration and the acquisition policies of the Strategic Petroleum Reserve. It also will explain current barter authority possessed by each and the statutory interaction between these statutes and other agency statutes that authorize barter for strategic materials or oil.

Materials are acquired for the stockpile according to provisions made in the Annual Materials Plan (AMP) prepared for Congress by FEMA. The AMP is a list of stockpile materials proposals for both acquisitions to and disposals from the stockpile; it is developed annually through an interagency committee chaired by FEMA. An official at GSA pointed out that the AMP breaks out the proposed transactions for the year by type of transaction: barter, exchange, or sale. Thus the committee can consider the effect of barter, for example, on appropriations and material selection. The Departments of Defense, Commerce, Interior, Energy, Agriculture, State, and Treasury, along with the CIA, GSA, and OMB are each represented on the AMP Steering Committee.

The process begins when FEMA develops a proposed list of materials for purchase and/or sale. This process involves making difficult choices because mineral deficits are so large (roughly $10 billion worth of materials at current prices) and the acquisitions budget is relatively low ($57 million for fiscal year 1982). FEMA's initial list is passed on to GSA which assesses market conditions, and determines the amounts of minerals and materials that could be bought and sold without undue market disruption. After GSA indicates market constraints various subcommittees review the list to determine the impact of the proposal on defense requirements, international trade commodity markets, and to study the revenue and cost projections of the proposal.

After the various recommendations of these subcommittees are incorporated, the AMP is reviewed by all member agencies. FEMA then submits the plan to the National Security Council (NSC) and to OMB. Any further revisions are made jointly by the NSC, OMB and FEMA.

This latter provision concerning revisions is important because, although Congress requires that such a plan be submitted to it each

---

*This appendix was prepared by Robert B. Stack.

year in order for Congress to appropriate funds, it also allows revision of such a plan if the appropriate committees of Congress are notified of the change.

NOTES

1. See Vogt, Jabara & Linse, *Barter of Agricultural Commodities* 13-20 (USDA, ERS, IED Staff Report AGES820413, April 1982).

2. Today the determination of the quantity and quality of materials to be held in the stockpile is performed by the Federal Emergency Management Agency (FEMA).

3. Conversations with Jean Nollmeyer, Sid Constantinos, Rose Zammichielli, and William Randolph of the U.S. Department of Agriculture.

4. In addition, barter contracts required that (1) proof of export from and import into the designated countries be submitted by the contract; (2) barter commodities could not be re-exported; (3) financial coverage in cash or letters of credit be provided if agricultural commodities were acquired before materials were delivered; (4) materials delivered meet prescribed specifications; and (5) where ocean transport was necessary for delivery of materials, at least 50 percent be shipped on privately owned U.S. flag vessels, if they were available at fair and reasonable rates.

5. See Vogt, et al., *Barter of Agricultural Commodities*, p. 14.

6. See Dizard, "The Explosion of International Barter," *Fortune*, Feb. 7, 1983, pp. 88-95; Beardwood, "Back to Barter," *ICC Business World* (Summer 1983), pp. 6-10.

7. Conversations with Paul Ballou of the General Services Administration.

8. U.S. Executive Office of the President, Office of the Press Secretary, press release (Dec. 9, 1981).

9. New York *Times*, April 28, 1982, p. A1, col. 3.

10. Letter to the House Armed Services Committee from GSA, reprinted in House Committee on Armed Services, Full Committee Consideration of H. Res. 287, General Services Administration Proposed Acquisition of Metallurgical Grade Bauxite, 97th Cong., 1st Sess. 13-14 (1981).

11. New York *Times*, April 28, 1982, p. D4, col. 1.

12. Statement of President Reagan, Nov. 24, 1981, reprinted in House Committee on Armed Services, Full Committee Consideration of H. Res. 287, General Services Administration Proposed Acquisition of Metallurgical Grade Bauxite, 97th Cong., 1st Sess. (1981).

13. For a discussion on the related topic of advantages and disadvantages of barter of agricultural commodities among developing countries, see Chapter 6.

PART THREE
PROBLEMS WITH BARTER

9
LEGAL IMPLICATIONS
OF BARTER AND
COUNTERTRADE TRANSACTIONS
Kathleen M. Harte

INTRODUCTION

Consider the following hypothetical: negotiations between an American soft-drink manufacturer and the Rumanian government's trade ministry have been going smoothly. The manufacturer's representatives feel sure they will reach an agreement to sell the American company's "secret formula" syrup at terms agreeable and fair to all concerned.[1] In the final stretch, however, the Rumanians balk. They are uncomfortable with the large one-way cash outflows contemplated in this deal. Perhaps the Americans could help neutralize the currency effect of the sales, they suggest, by agreeing to buy a quantity of, say, Rumanian wine, the value of which would represent a specified percentage of the value of the syrup that the Rumanians will buy. The Americans hesitate. The proposed countertrade transaction treads upon unfamiliar territory that may contain legal pitfalls for the unwary. The American company is particularly concerned about tax liability arising from the transaction (or transactions) and about whether the contract may raise antitrust concerns. Such liabilities may lead to unforeseen costs that may make the deal far less profit-

Prepared with the assistance of Peggy Mevs and Thomas B. McVey. Ms. Harte currently serves as law clerk to the Honorable Pauline Newman, United States Circuit Judge for the Federal Circuit. The views expressed herein are those of Ms. Harte and should not be attributed to Judge Newman, the court, or the federal government.

able than the simpler form of the deal originally contemplated—or may make it altogether unprofitable.

Similar concerns arise in barter transactions in which the foreign buyer, perhaps a Third World or Eastern bloc country, makes clear from the outset that it will not pay cash for the American company's goods. Instead, it offers some quantity of a raw material readily available in the country, or manufactured goods overstocked domestically. How should the American company compute its tax liability when it receives goods in lieu of cash? If the contract involves the foreign buyer's supplying raw materials to the American company for a few years in payment for the American goods, will the "supply" contract be vulnerable under American antitrust laws? Uncertainty over these issues likely has caused more than a few would-be barterers and countertraders to opt for the "simpler" cash transaction whenever possible —and to walk away from potentially profitable, market-opening deals when it was not possible to insist on cash.

This chapter discusses the tax and antitrust implications of barter and countertrade transactions. A brief background section introduces key concepts and terminology for readers unfamiliar with the tax code. The chapter then contrasts direct barter transactions with the operations of a barter or countertrade exchange so that the reader will have in mind a picture of how a barter or countertrade transaction might actually occur. Next, the chapter explains and applies the theoretical principles that would govern the taxation of a barter or countertrade transaction and discusses the Internal Revenue Service's enforcement position. The chapter briefly discusses like kind exchange treatment, an exception to the general principles governing taxation that may—but in most cases probably will not—provide favorable tax treatment for barter and countertrade transactions. Finally, the chapter presents hypothetical barter and countertrade transactions and explains how these transactions would be taxed under the present code.

Moving to a discussion of potential antitrust implications in barter and countertrade deals, the chapter discusses three elements that may surface in barter and countertrade contracts—reciprocity, tying, and exclusivity—that may give rise to liability under the antitrust laws of the United States or the European Community. The discussion focuses principally on countertrade deals which are more likely than barter deals to prove problematic. The chapter next compares and contrasts the state of the law on these issues in the United States and the European Community and suggests certain "safe harbor" approaches least likely to lead to difficulty under the two legal systems.

TAX IMPLICATIONS

Background: Key Concepts and Terminology

Both sales and exchanges of goods and services are "taxable events" under the tax code. When they occur, the parties involved in the sale or exchange must take into account the gain or loss realized on the transaction. An individual who purchases a pair of snowshoes for $100 and sells them the following year for $125 has realized a gain of $25 on the transaction. He will be taxed not on the $125 in cash that he put into his pocket when he sold the snowshoes, but only on his profit on the deal. Similarly, an individual who buys stock today for $25 per share and sells a year from now for only $20 per share will be permitted to recognize a loss of $5 per share which he may use to offset certain other kinds of income.

Generally, taxpayers compute the amount that they have gained or lost on a transaction by subtracting from the amount realized (i.e., the amount actually put into pocket) the basis of the item sold. Basis is usually equated with the article's cost at the time of purchase. An item's basis may be adjusted, however, to reflect, for example, a decline in its value due to depreciation. Numerous provisions of the tax code provide for adjustments to basis to reflect the operation of tax rules that allow for deferral—but not forgiveness—of tax liability in circumstances in which policymakers have deemed such deferral desirable. Adjusting basis in these circumstances ensures that the tax eventually will be paid.

Equally important as how much tax is paid is *when* tax is to be paid. IRS regulations recognize two broad classes of accounting systems: cash method and accrual method.[2] Most individuals and some businesses without inventories are cash method taxpayers; they are required to take into income whatever they receive whenever they receive it. Likewise, under the cash method, deductions "count" only when the deductible expense is actually paid. For economic and financial reasons, taxpayers generally seek to postpone payment of taxes, and thus may prefer in certain cases to receive income later than sooner.

An accrual method taxpayer, by contrast, is required to recognize income as soon as he possesses the right to collect it. An accrual method taxpayer who sends out bills on December 1, 1983 bearing the legend "due within 15 days of billing date" probably has income to report on his 1983 return even if his laggard customers do not send payment until January 1, 1984. Unlike a cash method taxpayer, moreover, an accrual method taxpayer may be entitled to deduct expenses before he actually takes the money out of the till to pay the expense. Expenses for September, 1983 advertising probably are deductible on the taxpayer's 1983 return even if the advertising manager does not send the check until January, 1984.

Taxpayers are not entirely free to choose between these accounting systems. A business with an inventory, for example, must elect the accrual method. And regardless of which method the taxpayer chooses, the IRS may challenge his choice if it does not clearly reflect how much income the taxpayer receives and when he receives it.[3]

Even for cash method taxpayers, determining when the income is received is not always easy. Clearly, when the employee receives cash on payday, he has received income. But if he receives a check instead on December 29, 1983 and cashes it on January 2, 1984 can he claim that he did not receive income until 1984? The law says he cannot. His decision to hold onto the check—to turn his back temporarily on the income—does not postpone his receipt of income. What if he deposits the check in an interest-bearing account? Interest will accumulate on his deposit. If he goes to Nepal for three years can he claim that because he never withdrew the interest from the account he received no income?[4] Here the law says that the taxpayer constructively has received the interest income. His choice not to withdraw the money and spend it does not alter the outcome.

These principles, briefly summarized here, are key to resolving the more difficult variations on the same themes that arise in barter and countertrade transactions. The basic ideas will not change much in such transactions; they simply become more confusing.

Direct Barter or Countertrade Transactions versus Barter and Countertrade Exchanges

The simplest and most well recognized barter transactions involve two parties. Each has something the other wants, so the two agree to swap. This is a direct barter transaction. Likewise, two parties may agree to enter into a countertrade deal. Their decision partially or wholly to offset the cash flow aspects of their transactions is made directly between them.

Both of these direct transactions may involve a great deal of fortuity and substantial transaction costs to at least one of the parties. A dentist who needs his will drawn up may be fortunate enough to run into a lawyer with a toothache; or he may not. At any rate, the dentist's time and energy is not most efficiently spent searching for a barter partner. Companies that actively seek out barter opportunities to conserve on cash may have greater resources to put into the search, but again, it is inefficient for the company randomly to search for a gidget maker who needs the sort of widget that the company manufactures. Likewise, companies that have gone into barter and countertrade deals more reluctantly, and only because the foreign trading partner insisted, also have incurred substantial transaction costs. In either barter or countertrade transaction, if one party has to agree to accept or buy something for which he really has no use, he may involve a third party by selling ("unloading") the unwanted goods, often at a substantial discount, to a broker or distributor better equipped to market the goods.

Barter and countertrade exchanges have arisen largely in response to the inefficiencies of direct transactions.[5] The exchanges invite putative countertraders and barterers to join as members. Both individuals and companies belong to barter exchanges; membership in countertrade exchanges tend to be "companies only." Upon joining, members pay a membership fee up to $200 or $300 depending upon the rules of the exchange. They also pay a commission to the exchange on each transaction. The exchange then does its job by matching barterers—not exactly by helping the dentist find the lawyer with a toothache, but instead by establishing a credit account for both. For example, upon joining the exchange, the dentist may pledge 20 hours of his time to cashless transactions with other members. Assuming that normally he would charge his patients an average of $40 per hour, the dentist has pledged $800 worth of services. He would receive from the exchange 800 credits or scrip totalling that amount. The dentist can spend his units by going to any lawyer who happends to be a member of the exchange—regardless of whether he needs dental work —and asking him to draw up a will. If the lawyer works on the document for ten hours, for which he normally would receive $50 per hour, the dentist's account would be debited 500 units and the lawyer's account would be credited 500 units. Membership in these exchanges needs to be carefully balanced, however, so that all members and prospective members can be reasonably assured of being able to barter for goods that they want. For example, if a department store joins an exchange, it may find that all the other members love to shop at their stores, but find that those members can offer nothing that the department store really wants or needs. Members may thus become disenchanted with membership and leave the exchange. If too many popular outlets leave the exchange, the exchange may have difficulty attracting new members.

This arrangement may or may not be helpful to a company involved in an international barter or countertrade transaction. Many companies are involved in barter and countertrade not by choice but by necessity. They agree to the form of the transaction because they believe that agreeing to those terms may be the only way to cinch the deal or that the transaction will provide important opportunities for market penetration or expansion. Because these companies are not actively seeking opportunities to become involved in barter and countertrade transactions, the barter exchanges' "matching" services would not be particularly useful to these companies. But the exchanges may still provide opportunities for these companies to reduce their transactions costs.

As mentioned above, the reluctant barterer/countertrader often ends up with unwanted goods that he must unload at a discount to a broker or distributor better equipped to handle the merchandise. Companies that become members of exchanges may find this easier and less costly. They can offer their goods to the barter or countertrade exchange for exchange with other members. The exchange's management could provide the same valuable "matching" assistance that it provides to all its members in this secondary barter transaction. The company may incur additional costs it would not otherwise incur by holding the goods while the barter exchange helps the company dispose of the merchandise, but the credit that it receives on its barter account probably will be much closer to the fair market value of the goods than what the company would have received had it sold the goods to a broker or distributor. Even taking into account the commission that the barter or countertrade exchange will collect for its role in the secondary barter transaction, the company may still come out ahead.

With this picture of the two broad categories of transactions in mind, we can move ahead to discuss the tax treatment of barter and countertrade transactions. Exchange transactions are not necessarily treated differently from direct transactions under the code, but they do raise certain valuation and timing issues that do not normally arise in direct transactions. These additional issues naturally tend to complicate the picture.

If, How Much, and When: Taxability, Timing, and Valuation Issues in Barter and Countertrade Transactions

If.

The Internal Revenue Code clearly contemplates that exchanges involving property or services are taxable,[6] notwithstanding the popular misconception that a barter "swap" is not taxable because no money changes hands.[7] In countertrade transactions, these issues have not been raised because, for tax purposes, the transactions have been viewed as two distinct sales for cash. Taxpayers may in fact avoid tax liability by failing to report the value of goods and services they receive in such transactions, but that is illegal. Barter exchanges' credit slips commonly bear a legend reminding exchange members that their transactions are taxable and that taxpayers are required to report such income.[8]

Although the law is unequivocal, enforcement is often difficult, especially in direct barter transactions for which neither party may have kept records. It is doubtful that many, if any, of the large publicly held enterprises now becoming involved in direct barter and countertrade are doing so with the intent of evading taxes, especially considering the high visibility of such deals at present. General Motors, for example, would have great difficulty trying to ignore the value of millions of tons of bauxite on its tax returns. Nevertheless, the IRS apparently suspects that companies and individuals involved in barter and countertrade deals through exchanges may be tempted to ignore the values of goods or services received, or perhaps to fudge the value. The IRS' reporting requirement regulation, discussed below, require the exchanges to make available to the IRS all the data it needs to monitor members' transactions through the exchange, thus reducing the opportunities for tax evasion.

How Much.

Tax liability in a cash sale usually is not difficult to calculate. The taxpayer is responsible for the difference between the amount that he received for the article upon sale and his basis for the article. If, as in a barter transaction, he receives payment in kind instead of cash he will compute his taxable income for the deal by comparing what he received for the article—the fair market value of the good he accepted in payment—and his basis for the article. The regulations define fair market value as the price "at which the property (or services) would change hands between a willing buyer and a willing seller, neither being under any compulsion to buy or sell and both having reasonable knowledge of relevant facts."[9] In some cases it should be relatively easy to calculate the fair market value of the good accepted in payment by referring to the corresponding cash market for that good. If the payment good is a quantity of rice, for example, the fair market value would be the price currently quoted for that quantity on the commodity market. The parties still would need to decide whether, for their deal, it was more appropriate to refer to the spot market for a particular good, or to the "going price" as established in industry supply contracts, but market references will be readily available.[10] This provides an easy standard of reference for the parties, and for the IRS if in the course of an audit it becomes necessary to recompute the taxpayer's tax liability. The issue is less complicated with regard to exchange credits or scrip. In its recently issued regulations, the IRS agreed to defer to the exchange's own valuation of its units, unless the value established by the exchange does not accurately reflect the fair market value of the scrip.[11]

It may not always be so easy, however, to determine the fair market value by a readily available objective standard. For example, there may be more than one fair market value. Goods available in the retail market may change hands between willing, fully informed buyers and sellers at a variety of prices—any or all of which may be appropriately deemed the fair market value for the taxpayer. A manufacturer of electrical supplies may sell his goods to a wholesaler at one price, who in turn sells his goods to a retail outlet for another higher price. The retailer may himself sell identical goods at different prices, one price for the general public and another discounted price for contractors and volume buyers. Which if any of these prices is an acceptable calculation of the fair market value of the goods?

This two-tiered price system presents unique problems in the barter context. If a retailer becomes involved in a barter transaction and accepts in payment goods that he normally would have bought wholesale, it seems inequitable to require him to recognize the retail value of the goods. One commentator suggests an analogy to the area of charitable contributions. Section 170 of the IRC permits deductions when taxpayers contribute property to charitable organizations.[12] The deduction is limited to the fair market value of the

property. The regulations promulgated under the statute recognize
that the fair market value of the propery may mean different things
to different people, because the property may have had one value at
the wholesale level and another at the retail level. The regulations
allow the taxpayer to take a deduction equivalent to the price for
which he would have sold the article in the market had he not made
the donation. If, for example, A, the owner of a stereo equipment
store, donates a sound system to a church, he will be allowed to deduct the price for which he would have sold the stereo at retail in his
store at the time he made the donation. (If he made the donation
during his annual inventory sale, presumably his deduction would be
limited to the sale price of the stereo.) A similar rule could be applied
in barter transactions: If a taxpayer customarily buys goods at wholesale, he must recognize the fair market value of the payment goods at
wholesale; if he customarily buys at retail, he must recognize the full
retail price of the goods as the fair market value received. The same
principle could be applied to determine the value of deductions.

Another sort of valuation problem arises when there is no readily
ascertainable market value for goods received in payment. In a barter
transaction, this problem might arise if an artist swaps a painting in a
barter deal. If he has sold few paintings, valuation of the painting may
be difficult. When prodded on this issue, courts have been willing to
accept even the roughest approximations of fair market value as appropriate proxies.[13] Reluctant taxpayers have argued that the uniqueness
of the goods involved or unusual circumstances surrounding the sale
ought to prevent courts from making such approximations, but courts
generally have been willing to look to the most similar sale as an appropriate substitute. Parcels of land, for example, generally are considered
unique, but that would not prevent a court from establishing the value
of a parcel of land received in a barter transaction by reference to
similar parcels sold nearby the one at issue at about the same time as
the barter transaction. In some cases, for instance when an intangible
is involved, it may be impossible even to approximate in this way the
value of the item received into income. In *United States* v. *Davis*,[14]
for example, as part of a divorce settlement, a husband transferred to
his wife stock certificates in exchange for her relinquishment of all
claims against their marital estate. What amount did the husband realize in this disposition of his stock? He realized the value of the rights
that his wife surrendered. Reasoning that the wife would not have given
up her rights for an amount less than she believed they were worth and
that the husband would not have paid more for those rights than they
were worth, the court held that the husband had realized an amount

equal to the value of the stock he had surrendered.[15] His income was computed by comparing the fair market value of the stock, easily determinable by reference to the stock market, to its adjusted basis.

The idea, then, is always to link the transaction back to a market in which values are readily determinable. Barter transactions undoubtedly will arise that test the limits of a court's ingenuity to find a fair value for income goods, but the general principles outlined here should lead ultimately to the right solution.

As a practical matter, the valuation problem may seldom arise. The IRS regulations regarding barter exchange reporting requirements reflect the Service's judgment that the fair market value of the payment good or the exchange credit issued in lieu of the good almost always will be readily determinable. When all else fails, the government always can offer expert testimony to establish the fair market value of the payment good. This technique has worked well for the government, for example, in its attempts since *Burnet* v. *Logan* to restrict the number of installment contracts eligible for open transaction treatment.[16]

When.

Almost as often and as hotly contested as the issue of how much tax is due is the issue of *when* it is due. As explained in the introductory section, cash basis taxpayers are required to pay tax on income when they receive it and may not deduct expenses until they are actually paid. Accrual basis taxpayers include items in income as soon as they receive the unfettered right to receive the income, even though they may not actually have the cash in hand. Likewise, the accrual basis taxpayer may deduct expenses as soon as the noncontingent obligation to pay arises.

The same principles apply in barter transactions. The taxpayer's obligation to report income arising from such a transaction becomes important as soon as the taxpayer receives the payment good. In direct barter transactions, it is relatively easy to determine when that moment occurs. Even if the payment good is not actually received by the taxpayer, if it is, say, placed in a warehouse until the taxpayer can arrange for its disposition, it still is possible to attribute income to the taxpayer under the doctrine of constructive receipt. In barter exchange transactions, however, determining the moment that the taxpayer has received taxable income may be more complicated. Exchange members typically receive trade units or credits to their account, instead of a payment good as in a direct barter deal. Barter exchanges and their members have long contended that it is inappropriate to say that the member has received income at the moment that the credit is posted to his account. They maintain that exchange members do not have income until they actually use the credit to "purchase" something within the exchange.

The IRS rejects this interpretation of the timing issue. The Service maintains that receipt of anything of value constitutes receipt of taxable income, unless Congress explicitly has exempted that item from taxation or deferred its taxation for some policy reason.[17] Upon receipt of trade units or credits to their accounts, exchange members have received something of value, and that is the appropriate moment for taxation. The exchanges retort that the trade units or credits have only the artificial value assigned to them by the exchange; they are not worth anything outside the exchange and not worth anything inside the exchange until the members use them to "purchase" something.[18] It is therefore unfair and inappropriate, they argue, to tax members on their illiquid accounts.

It is unlikely that either side will convert the other in this continuing debate. Any change in enforcement policy likely will require statutory amendment. If the exchanges continue to grow in popularity over the next decade and if they can convince lawmakers of their legitimacy and "purity of motive," lobbying efforts in this direction are likely to sprout. In the meantime, it appears that the Service has the best of the theoretical arguments. Even if the taxpayers are not in actual receipt when the exchange credits their accounts, they may be in constructive receipt of something of value because they are free to "spend" the credits in their accounts whenever they desire. The doctrine of constructive receipt will not permit taxpayers to turn their backs on income in this way and claim that they have not received the income simply because they have not exercised their right to spend it.

IRS Enforcement Policies

The IRS still views the barter network as an "underground economy." Not too long ago, the epithet probably was deserved. Numerous articles and television features spotlighted barter and nonreporting as the enforcement-free way of avoiding taxes.[19] Barter exchanges have been fighting that image, trying to establish the legitimacy of their organizations and practices. Comments filed in response to the

Treasury Department's barter exchange reporting requirements re-flected this image-building effort. The comments carefully noted, for example, exchanges' efforts to educate members about their responsibility for reporting income on all transactions. The IRS apparently remains skeptical.[20] One comment alluded to IRS audits of barterers' returns.[21]

Most of the barter exchanges have found it necessary to keep some records on behalf of their members simply to keep accounts straight. In regulations promulgated in 1983, the IRS gained access of sorts to the exchanges' records to compare them to returns filed by exchange members, thus increasing their chances of finding non-reporters and discouraging exchange members from trying to evade taxes. The regulations require the exchanges to keep records in greater detail than what the exchanges were accustomed to keeping. Exchanges meeting the definition of "barter exchange" and involved in 100 or more transactions per year are required to report complete information on the details of each transaction, including the "name, address and taxpayer identification number of each member or client providing property or services in the exchange, the property or services provided, the amount received by the member or client for such property or services provided, and the date on which the transaction occurred."[22] The regulation also allows some aggregation of reported information for corporate barterers. Barter exchanges protested the detailed requirements at the time they were proposed as too onerous. Imposing these requirements, they said, would have the same impact on the exchanges as a rule requiring all retailers to report the details of every sale would have on department stores. The exchanges, they claimed, like the department stores, are interested only in aggregate figures.[23] One response to this argument is that barter exchanges *do* have an interest beyond aggregate figures—they need to ensure the accuracy of each individual member's account balance. In this respect they are more like banks than like department stores. To be sure, they are fundamentally different from banks in that they lack fiduciary responsibilities and are not (so far) subjected to the pervasive regulation that governs bank operations. But because they, like banks, must maintain some information on an account-by-account basis for their own clients, and because the opportunities for evasion are enormous, requiring the exchanges to provide at least information on individual account balances does not seem unreasonable. If an exchange member's return is selected for audit, the taxpayer would, as usual, bear the burden of justifying his deductions. This compromise seems reasonable because even though imposing more onerous reporting requirements might make evasion easier to detect, account balance information by itself probably would be adequate for determining which returns deserved closer scrutiny. Additional details would emerge during the audit.

Proper Tax Treatment for a Hypothetical Barter Transaction

The key to determining proper tax treatment for barter transactions is the principle that no matter how exotic the transaction appears, it ought to produce the same net result as a cash transaction involving the same goods and the same parties. As an economic matter, parties who cannot or will not use cash ought not to enjoy any advantage over cash-on-the-barrelhead taxpayers; the tax system operates to ensure that they are in fact treated equally. A few examples will illustrate the point.*

Example 1. The simplest case would involve a commodity for commodity swap. An American export trading company (ETC) agrees to deliver rice to Nigeria in exchange for oil. The parties would agree on some formula to equate the right number of tons of rice with the right number of barrels of oil so that the arrangement represents a fair swap. If oil is currently selling at $33 per barrel, the parties would agree to swap four tons of rice for three barrels of oil. The parties are in effect agreeing to swap $100 worth of goods. Each party's profit will be the margin between its cost of production or procurement and the value of the goods received in the swap, that is, its markup. In a cash transaction, the U.S. ETC would purchase rice for, say, $20 per ton and resell it for $25 per ton on the spot market. It would then use the cash to buy oil from Nigeria. The ETC realizes $5 of income on each ton of rice sold. The ETC has had to spend, however, $80 to acquire the four tons of rice it is offering in the swap. It has realized a gain of $20 on the swap, or $5 per ton, the identical result as in the cash transaction. Even if the transaction does not represent an even swap because one of the parties has made a poor estimate of the value of the goods involved, the tax laws probably will operate to ensure that the cash-barter equivalence principle will apply. The results in

---

*The author gratefully acknowledges the suggestions of Bart S. Fisher and Michael D. Esch in writing this section.

those cases will turn on the particular values adopted by the parties to the sale.

The cash-barter equivalence principle may not produce consistent results, however, when the "price" is different for noncash customers. An example, one involving the burgeoning practice of media barter, will illustrate the point.

Example 2. Typewriter manufacturer, *A*, has been experiencing a sales slump. He believes that additional advertising would end his troubles, but he does not have cash to pay for an advertising campaign. He offers to give an advertising agency typewriters in exchange for their assistance in planning and airing the ads. The agency agrees, but because of the "inconvenience" of having to accept typewriters instead of cash, they insist that the manufacturer delivery $1250 worth of typewriters in exchange for ads worth $1000. In other words, for noncash customers, the agency charges a premium.

This deal represents a distortion of the cash comparison model. The manufacturer is forced to pay more for the ads than they are really worth because of the form of payment he has chosen. *A* will agree to go along because he does not have sufficient cash and the typewriters are not selling well anyway.

Like Kind Exchanges

Section 1031 of the Internal Revenue Code (IRC) provides:

> No gain or loss shall be recognized if property held for productive use in trade or business or for investment (not including stock in trade or other property held primarily for sale, nor stocks, bonds, notes, choses in action, certificates of trust or beneficial interest, or other securities or evidences of indebtedness or interest) is exchanged solely for property of a like kind to be held either for productive use in trade or business or for investment.

The statute itself contemplates deferral of tax liability in the case of certain swaps. No tax is due until a party to the swap later sells the property for cash. The statute thus appears at first blush to offer tax deferral opportunities for barter exchanges. Most barter and countertrade transactions, however, will not qualify for nonrecognition treatment because the requirements of the section probably would be construed to exclude barter and countertrade deals from coverage and because such transactions are outside the rationale of the statute.

The Rationale

The rationale behind the statute is simply that even though an exchange suffices to trigger realization of income, if the taxpayer's position has not actually changed, the exchange is not an appropriate time for recognizing the income realized.[24] A taxpayer who has swapped one tractor for another has not changed his position; he still owns a tractor and holds the same amount of cash that he had before the exchange. Most barterers and countertraders do experience a change in position, however. A barterer generally receives in the exchange a good that is quite different from the good he gave up. A countertrader receives cash just as if he had sold the good. Even though the complete countertrade resembles a barter exchange in that both sides eventually end up with goods, as discussed below, the intermediate cash step probably suffices to take such transactions outside the rationale and the requirements of the statute.

The Requirements

In order for an exchange to qualify for nonrecognition treatment, section 1031 requires that a) the property be held for productive use in the taxpayer's business; b) that there be an exchange of "like kind" property; the section may also require that c) each party exchange his property simultaneously without any intermediate cash step.[25]

Held for Productive Use or Investment. This requirement may pose formidable obstacles for most barterers because the statute specifically excludes from coverage any property held primarily for sale.[26] Thus, even if a typewriter manufacturer could meet all the other prerequisites of the statute, he would not get nonrecognition treatment for exchanges involving his typewriters. Any barterer who seeks to augment his conventional cash sales through barter will encounter this obstacle.

Like Kind Property. At the most general level, this requirement prevents swaps of property "across categories" from qualifying for like kind treatment.[27] A taxpayer cannot swap real property for personal property under § 1031. Beyond that generality, exactly where courts will draw the line and how much similarity they will require is not clear. Courts have approved, for example, exchanges of calves for adult steer, but the statute prevents courts from extending nonrecognition treatment to swaps involving livestock of different sexes.[28] A swap of gold bullion for silver bullion qualifies; an exchange of a partnership interest in a shopping center (which may be considered personal property under state law) and a piece of property will not qualify.[29] Intuitively, it would also seem difficult to argue convincingly that typewriters and advertisements, for example, are of "like kind." Exchanges involving services would be entirely outside the statute.

Simultaneity. Some commentators believe that the statute may also require that the exchange be simultaneous, that is, involve no waiting period or intermediate cash step. The Ninth Circuit addressed this issue in *T.J. Starker* v. *United States.*[30] The taxpayer in *Starker* agreed with a corporation to swap parcels of land.[31] The taxpayer owned a piece of land that the corporation wanted and he was eager to avoid gain recognition on disposition of the property. The corporation, however, did not own any property in which he was interested. The corporation essentially agreed to let the Starkers shop around for a piece of property, which the corporation then would acquire and swap for the Starkers' original parcel. In the meantime, the corporation would take possession of the Starkers' land, paying for it by depositing money in an interest-bearing escrow account. The IRS argued that § 1031 did not apply because even though the taxpayer never handled any cash, the cash step involving the escrow account interrupted the exchange. The Ninth Circuit rejected this argument and held that the transactions did qualify for like kind exchange treatment. The precedential value of the Ninth Circuit's pronouncement, however, is questionable. The IRS plans to continue litigating the issue, hoping for more favorable rulings in other federal courts of appeals. Tax advisers are not counseling clients to rely on the *Starker* decision; to the contrary, they are advising their clients to avoid nonsimultaneous transactions at all costs.[32] Thus, the notion of simultaneity within § 1031 survives.

For barter transactions that can meet the other requirements of the section, simultaneity should present no problem. The thorny theoretical problem will arise in countertrade transactions. There remains some controversy over whether a countertrade deal constitutes two transactions or one. On one hand, countertraders are careful to write *two* contracts that look independent enough to prevent difficulties with one from interfering with performance of the other.[33] On the other hand, the two contracts are integral parts of one deal; one would not have occurred without the other. A countertrader who wants to make his transaction qualify for like kind treatment will be forced to make his deal resemble more and more closely a single barter transaction. This may not fit his business needs, but unless he can eliminate the intermediate cash step that is by definition involved in countertrades, his claimed nonrecognition treatment will be subject to attack by the IRS.

The typical barter transaction, then, that involves swaps from inventory of dissimilar items should not qualify under section 1031. Unless the two goods are dissimilar, there is not much point to the transaction. If the barterer can characterize the swapped goods as held for investment he will improve his chances for success, but for most transactions, in which barterers are merely trying to augment conventional sales, this does not appear to be a practical alternative. Barters involving swaps for services will not qualify for nonrecognition treatment.

Countertraders' main stumbling block, apart from the like kind requirement, will be the intermediate cash step that interrupts simultaneity. Unless countertraders are willing to reform their deals drastically, or do business via escrow accounts, and only in the Ninth Circuit, they probably will not be able to claim like kind exchange treatment with much hope of success.

A Hypothetical Barter Transaction
that Might Qualify for Like Kind Treatment

Taking into account the strict requirements of the statute, it is still possible to hypothesize a transaction, however contrived, that might qualify.

Company *A* has a fancy lathe that it no longer needs because it plans to close down its shop division and have outside contractors perform the more complicated operations. Only routine touch-up jobs will be performed in-house. It would like to acquire a smaller, simpler lathe. *A*'s basis in the lathe is $6,000; its fair market value is $12,000. Company *B* has a basic model lathe that it has outgrown; it would like to acquire a more advanced model. *B*'s adjusted basis in its lathe is $5,000; its fair market value is $8,000. Neither *A* nor *B* is principally engaged in selling lathes, thus lathes would not consitute stock in trade items for either of them. A swap of the two lathes probably would qualify for like kind treatment. The property is held for productive use in business, it is of like kind, and the exchange would occur simultaneously. *A*'s lathe, however, is worth more than *B*'s, so *A* will be unwilling to make an even swap. *B* will have to give *A* its lathe plus

$4000. The involvement of cash here will not disqualify the deal from like kind treatment, but *A* will be liable for tax on its gain to the extent of this cash "boot" of $4000. *A*'s gain on the transaction is the amount realized less the adjusted basis of the lathe it surrendered. ($8000 worth of lathe + $4000 in cash - $6000 = $6000). *A* owes taxes on $4000 of the $6000 gain. Adjustments to *A*'s basis in the basic lathe it received in the exchange will ensure that the additional $2000 in gain not recognized upon the exchange will be taxed later when the lathe is sold for cash.

The general principles of taxation thus govern barter and countertrade transactions, presenting some anomalies but no special advantages or disadvantages to barterers and countertraders. Discerning how these principles ought to apply to these types of transactions is not always clear, and Revenue Rulings (e.g., Rev. Rul. 80-52) thus far published provide meager guidance limited to the peculiar circumstances of the transactions described therein. New legislation is not necessary, but reorganization of existing code sections in a format easily digestible to those advising barterers and countertraders would be a great step forward.

ANTITRUST IMPLICATIONS OF BARTER AND COUNTERTRADE TRANSACTIONS: U.S. AND EUROPEAN COMMUNITY LAW*

Because most barter transactions will be one-time deals, they will usually present few antitrust problems. Countertrade transactions, by contrast, may present formidable antitrust difficulties because they imply a continuing course of transactions that may span a number of years and involve large companies with significant market power.

Antitrust advisers are likely to worry about four elements that may arise in countertrade deals. One element is a natural outgrowth of barterers' and countertraders' haste to dispose of goods that are of no use to them. In so doing, they may offer the goods at substantial discounts, perhaps even below cost to avoid storage costs. If these sales are in sufficient volume, the firm offering them for sale may be held to have violated section 1 of the Sherman Act or section 5 of the Federal Trade Commission Act. It is not inconceivable that countertrade deals could have such an impact since many of them involve a

---

*The author gratefully acknowledges the helpful comments of Stephen J. Narkin with respect to this section.

series of transactions that span several years. The other three elements—reciprocal dealing, tying, and exclusive dealing—have been met with varying degrees of tolerance in U.S. courts. Reciprocal dealing involves an agreement that "I'll buy from you if and only if you'll buy from me." Tying arrangements require that the buyer buy a product he may not want, or may prefer to buy elsewhere, from the supplier of a product that he does want: "I'll sell you my copier only if you'll purchase paper and toner from me also." In exclusive dealing arrangements, one party may agree to purchase exclusively from one supplier. In the countertrade context, this may involve an output requirements contract: "I'll build your snowshoe factory for you; you'll pay me by supplying all my requirements of snowshoes for the next twenty years."[34] Problems of reciprocity and tying may arise not only in the context of the original countertrade deal but also in the context of the firm's efforts to unload the merchandise. Because much of the merchandise received in countertrade deals is of inferior quality or is at least perceived to be so, countertrading firms may feel compelled to "persuade" their suppliers and customers to help dispose of the merchandise.

The objection that has been made to all three of these practices is that each supposedly forecloses competition on the merits. Firms that enter into such agreements are precluded from shopping around for better supply terms. Moreover, to the extent that such arrangements tie up part of the market for the supplied good, they purportedly lock out of the market competitors not party to the arrangement.[35] These objections suggest that the anticompetitive impact of the practices will vary with the market power of the parties and the amount of the market that the arrangement involves. In the United States at least, this has meant that illegality is a matter of degree, the determination turning on the particular facts of each case. The European Community, by contrast, has taken a more liberal approach that upholds many of the contracts that U.S. law probably would strike down.

Throughout the discussion, it is important to keep in mind one important argument favoring even suspicious-looking countertrade deals. They are fundamentally procompetitive. They permit deals to occur in cases in which the transaction might not have taken place at all. For example, they allow for efficient inventory turnover in sales slumps. These procompetitive effects often will outweigh any anticompetitive effects, and should be taken into account, especially in a close case.

Reciprocity, Exclusive Dealings, and Tying Under U.S. Law

Reciprocity

U.S. courts have recognized that reciprocity may be unilateral, coercive, or voluntary (mutual patronage).[36] In unilateral reciprocity, one company decides that it will purchase certain items only from its own customers, not because the customers have insisted, but because they think it is good business to scratch a customer's back. Coercive reciprocity involves a producer's *demand* that companies from whom he buys purchase certain items only from that producer, or the producer will discontinue his purchases. If the producer is a large and important customer, it is easy to see why the "coerced party" would go along. Voluntary reciprocity arises when two parties agree to purchase from one another without any coercion.

Countertrade transactions may involve any of these varieties of reciprocal dealing. But given the reluctance of most American firms to become involved in countertrade deals, it seems unlikely that unilateral reciprocity often would arise. Most firms probably would describe their involvement as coerced or, at best, something to which they reluctantly but voluntarily agreed at the last minute to make the deal work. The focus, then, is appropriately on coercive and voluntary reciprocity.

At one time, U.S. courts held all reciprocal dealing arrangements per se illegal, that is, illegal without regard to the defendant's arguments regarding business justification or procompetitive impact. Now, with regard to some forms of reciprocity challenged in the relatively few reciprocity cases that U.S. enforcement agencies have chosen to pursue, courts are willing to look at the impact of the practice on the market in deciding whether to uphold the arrangement. Under this rule of reason approach contracts involving parties with significant market power and leading to a "not insubstantial" amount of market foreclosure generally are held to be illegal under section 1 of the Sherman Act,[37] section 7 of the Clayton Act,[38] or section 5 of the Federal Trade Commission Act.[39] Coercive reciprocity arrangements, however, generally are still held to be per se illegal because they distort market criteria and have few if any redeeming virtues. As for voluntary reciprocity, at least one federal court, the Southern District of New York in *United States* v. *General Dynamics*,[40] has held that voluntary reciprocity, distinguished from coercive reciprocity, because the parties have relatively equal buying power, is illegal only if there results some not insubstantial amount of market foreclosure. The court reached this conclusion by analogy to tying arrangements. The analogy was appropriate, the court believed, because reciprocity arrangements have a market foreclosure impact similar to that of tying arrangements. The court ruled that market foreclosure of $177,225 worth of merchandise was not a large enough volume to be "substantial."[41] In other tying cases, $500,000 has been held to be "not insubstantial,"[42] and in one recent case, the Supreme Court said that an amount that was more than merely de minimis would suffice.[43]

Would be countertraders reading these decisions must be concerned about whether their deals could be subject to government attack under section 1 of the Sherman Act as contracts in restraint of trade. The risk involved will depend largely on the degree of market foreclosure involved. But even isolating that criterion may not help much; the cases reveal only that something more than a merely de minimis amount is problematic, and that $177,225 apparently is not quite enough. It is important to remember, however, that the limits that this decision seems to impose upon countertraders may not be as strict as they seem.[44] First, the *General Dynamics* district court is the only court to have considered the issue. Because the case was settled before the appeal was heard, the soundness of the district court's logic has not been tested at the appellate level. Second, one commentator argues that the *General Dynamics* court never addressed the culpability of a party who passively and reluctantly accepts the other party's request for reciprocity. U.S. firms presumably would most often find themselves in that position. It is difficult to imagine courts carving out such an exception, however. The anticompetitive effects of substantial market foreclosure are the same, regardless of how either party to the arrangement "felt" about the deal. Holding both parties culpable might in fact bolster the resistance of reluctant participants in such deals. Third, because the *General Dynamics* court actually found no violation of section 1, all of its language about the illegality of voluntary reciprocity is dicta. These limitations on the *General Dynamics* decision are good news for would be countertraders whose deals could easily lock out over $500,000 of a given market. But because of the lack of guidance in this area, planning remains difficult.

Exclusive dealing arrangements

A buyer's agreement to purchase its requirements exclusively from a single supplier may be subject to attack under section 3 of

the Clayton Act or section 1 of the Sherman Act if it results in foreclosure of a "not insubstantial" amount of commerce. In *Tampa Electric Co.* v. *Nashville Coal Co.*,[45] the Supreme Court weighed "the
probable effect of the contract on the relevant area of effective competition . . . and the probable immediate and future effects which pre-
emption of that share of the market might have on effective competition."[46] The Court concluded that such a small percentage of the
relevant market was affected (only .77 percent) and the anticompetitive effects were likely to be so minimal, that it upheld the contract,
which the Court noted might be of great benefit to the parties because
it would provide an assured outlet for the seller and a secure source
of supply for the buyer.

Countertraders entering into turnkey project arrangements thus
will have to be very careful in arranging for payment in kind. A U.S.
company might agree to build a mineral processing plant in a foreign
country and accept payment over an extended period of time by having the foreign factory deliver quantities of the mineral output to the
U.S. company. The larger the duration of the contract and the larger
the volume of supply involved, the more likely that the market foreclosure effect will be viewed as significant, and the more likely the
arrangement is to be attacked. How *much* foreclosure will create difficulties is not clear; by analogy to the tying context, anything more
than a de minimis amount may be problematic, but courts may be
more lenient in the exclusive dealing area because they recognize that
such contracts do have redeeming virtues, including those discussed
by the Supreme Court in *Tampa Electric*.

Tying

Tying arrangements once were held per se illegal under section 1
of the Sherman Act or under section 3 of the Clayton Act. Courts now
follow a rule of reason approach under both statutes, on the rationale
that unless the anticompetitive effects of such arrangements are substantial, there is not much point to disbanding them. Courts therefore
will look to several factors to determine whether the arrangement is
illegal.[47]

*The economic power of the seller in the "tying" product—the one that the buyer
wants or needs.* Courts will seek to determine whether the seller has
sufficient economic power to force the buyer to buy the unwanted
"tied" item in order to get the desirable tying product. A monopolist
or near monopolist has the requisite economic power, but even in the

absence of such overwhelming market power, courts have been willing to infer such economic power if a firm's product is so unique that the buyer will be unable to find suitable substitutes. A firm offering a patented good and insisting that buyers take accessories along with the patented good probably has the requisite market power for the plaintiff to make out a good tying case against him.

A not insubstantial amount of commerce must be affected. The Supreme Court has held that anything greater than a de minimis amount will suffice to meet this requirement.[48]

Lack of business justification. Courts will listen to defendant's business reasons for entering into tying arrangements. For example, a new entrant in a particular market may be able to defend his firm's use of a tying arrangement by explaining that the success of his infant operation will be dictated by the firm's ability to guarantee the reliability of its equipment. For that reason, courts may permit a new entrant to require equipment purchasers also to sign up for a service contract.

Tying will surface infrequently in countertrade deals. In contrast to reciprocity and exclusive dealing arrangements, tying involves an abuse of selling power, not buying power. In most countertrade deals, the U.S. company wants to sell to the foreign country, and the foreign government conditions its purchase upon future purchases by the U.S. firm. A tying issue would arise only if the U.S. company or the foreign country were in a position to tell its partner, "if you want to purchase my machinery, you must purchase all spare parts and service from me also." That is not generally the way that the bargaining works in a countertrade deal.

European Community Law

The European Community Competition Policy takes a much more sanguine view toward these arrangements. Regulation 67/67, for example, grants nonreciprocal exclusive purchasing agreements a "block exemption" from attack under European Community law if at least one of the parties is a small or medium company with an annual turnover of less than 100 million ECU per annum. Thus, while the United States examines these arrangements under a careful rule of reason approach, the European Community regards them as nearly per se legal for at least some categories of companies.[49] The European Community approach may in fact be a proxy for a rule of reason approach that focuses on the degree of market foreclosure. The Regulation may reflect a determination that a small or medium size company could not effect significant market foreclosure. The limited per se approval thus saves tribunals the trouble of a lengthy hearing that reaches the same conclusion. *Reciprocal* exclusive dealing arrangements, by contrast, in which the parties foreclose all other competitors from one another's customer list, do not enjoy block exemption status. The fear is that such practices discourage or preclude "parallel imports" that otherwise would compete with the goods of the parties to the exclusive dealing arrangement. This represents the European Community view towards most reciprocal arrangements; the Competition Policy leaves open the door for rule of reason treatment, but is particularly suspicious of arrangements that circumscribe consumers' alternatives by depriving them of choices among products.[50]

The European Community's attitude toward tying is far more liberal than that reflected in U.S. jurisprudence. Under European Community law, tying arrangements are permitted if the additional goods or services are by their nature or by custom of the trade usually furnished along with the tying product. This notion has a counterpart in U.S. law. A plaintiff challenging a tying arrangement must show that there are two items involved. A defendant may argue that because of custom, trade, or usage what appears to be two products actually constitutes one product. With only one product involved, tying would be impossible. For example, a defendant accused of tying service contracts to his sales of burglar alarms might argue (but probably without success) that there can be no tying arrangement involved because only one commodity is provided: reliable protection, which involves the alarm and the maintenance necessary to keep it functioning correctly. Or a defendant might admit that two commodities are involved but argue that because of customers' preference they are generally provided together. But the rule of reason approach under U.S. law implies probing review; in contrast to European Community law, custom of the trade by itself probably would not justify the tying arrangement under U.S. law.

Extraterritorial Application of U.S. and European Community Law

Would-be countertraders should be aware of these differences between U.S. and European Community antitrust law and policy, but should also be aware that moving the situs of a deal from one jurisdiction to another may not remove the parties from the reach of the other jurisdiction's laws. Both the U.S. and the European Community have been willing to reach beyond their own borders to condemn practices that may have some impact on European or U.S. business.

Under U.S. law, the reach of section 3 of the Clayton Act is confined to U.S. cases and U.S. parties.[51] But most of the practices prohibited under section 3 are also subject to attack under sections 1 and 2 of the Sherman Act. These latter two sections will apply extraterritorially if the arrangements at issue have any effect within the United States—if, for example, the market foreclosure effects of a tying arrangement spill over into the United States.[52] The plaintiff still would need to demonstrate valid personal jurisdiction, of course, but the requisite minimum contacts should not be difficult to establish if a U.S. company or its subsidiary is involved in the foreign deal. Thus, a U.S. firm hoping to escape the reach of U.S. laws by conducting business in the European Community will have to be careful in predicting and controlling the effects of any proposed arrangements.

The European Community has taken what appears to be, at first blush, a more conservative approach. It has not adopted a true effects test, but will try to determine if the conduct complained of involved any behavior within the European Community and whether the arrangement has any impact within the community. In looking for behavior within the community, however, it has been very liberal in piercing the corporate veil and attributing to the corporate parent-defendant the activities of its European Community subsidiary.[53] In other words, it may make no difference that the parent-defendant has never done any business in the European Community; if its subsidiary has done business there, that will suffice to establish the requisite behavior within the community.

Countertraders should not hope, in sum, to avoid antitrust liability on purely jurisdictional grounds. Both the United States and the European Community are likely to try to reach as far as their jurisprudence permits to punish such violations. Angry private plaintiffs are likely to be equally zealous.

Avoiding Trouble

One commentator has suggested several criteria that could help a would-be countertrader determine in advance whether his activities might be subject to attack.[54] Firms that have a large market share in any or all of the products that it sells, or that may have more economic power than their market shares suggest because they sell products for which there are few close substitutes are particularly vulnerable. This criterion goes to the firm's structure and suggests that big, powerful firms ought to avoid countertrade deals involving elements of market foreclosure. Firms that do a large fraction of their business in counter-trade transactions involving market foreclosure increase their antitrust exposure. They may be accused of attempting to monopolize. Firms involved in countertrade transactions also should avoid any hint of coercion in their contracts. Finally, they should avoid excluding competitors from any cooperative countertrade organizations they form. They may, however, charge appropriate fees to defray the costs of taking on additional members who did not share in the initial risks of establishing the venture.

A would-be countertrader can also try to avoid antitrust exposure by applying for preliminary review of his plans. Upon request, the Department of Justice can provide a Business Practice Review and the Federal Trade Commission can issue an Advisory Opinion.[55] These options have been exercised only rarely in foreign commercial transactions, probably in part because even a favorable review will not immunize the firm from government suit. Such preliminary review may be worth the trouble nonetheless because it at least gives the firm an idea of the government's enforcement attitude on the transaction. A similar preliminary review is available in the European Community. If a company does not qualify for a block exemption, it may apply to the Commission for a Negative Clearance that operates much like a Business Practice Review.[56] In both the United States and the European Community, the applicant must submit detailed information about the proposed transaction, which some companies may be reluctant to do because it may expose proprietary information. Moreover, applying for review bears, of course, the risk of receiving a negative determination. If the prospects of suit seem slim and opportunities for early returns seem substantial, and the official answer may be "no," it may not pay to ask.

The Export Trading Company Act of 1982 may provide an antitrust safe harbor for countertraders.[57] Title III of the Act instructs the Department of Commerce, in conjunction with the Department of Justice, to issue Export Certificates of Review to qualified companies. These Certificates may make the prospect of doing business through an ETC especially attractive for countertraders. They provide to a qualified ETC immunity from government suit under the antitrust laws in all matters related to its export activity. The Certificate is available only after the ETC has made extensive disclosures to the Department of Commerce regarding the proposed scope of its operation—which some firms may find objectionable—and only if it appears reasonably certain that the proposed transactions will have no effect within the United States. The Certificate affords much broader protection than did the Webb-Pomerene Act. Antitrust immunity under Webb-Pomerene extended only to transactions involving goods and protected only associations of manufacturers. The Certificate will cover services as well as goods and will cover the full panoply of an exporter's activities. It provides broader and more secure protection for those who will rely upon it.

It is important to note that as broad as the antitrust immunity is, it still covers only *export* activities.[58] A countertrader may still face liability for, say, price fixing on goods he purchases as part of a countertrade deal. Even if the price-fixing activity is carried on abroad, the countertrader may face antitrust liability in the United States if the activity has domestic effects. Moreover, the certificate only precludes suit by the government, and only so long as the firm stays within bounds of its original description of proposed activity. The government may sue if the company diverges from its original plan, and a private plaintiff may sue at any time.[59] A defendant who holds a Certificate, however, enjoys certain advantages in a private suit that make application worthwhile in spite of the invasive disclosure required. The Certificate affords a defendant two crucial presumptions: first, that his activities have *not* injured U.S. competition.[60] From the outset, therefore, the plaintiff has a formidable burden to overcome. Moreover, if the plaintiff loses, he will be liable for the defendant's legal fees. These advantages may discourage private plaintiffs from bringing antitrust suits altogether.

APPLYING U.S. TRADE LAWS TO BARTER AND COUNTERTRADE AGREEMENTS*

Statutory Provisions Applicable to Barter and Countertrade Agreements

There are no statutory provisions in U.S. trade law specifically addressing imports arising from barter or countertrade agreements. A petitioner requesting import relief need not describe the nature of the transaction. Thus, very few cases, only three in fact, actually have been based on a countertrade agreement.

Arguably, one statute indirectly addresses countertrade agreements. Section 406 of the Trade Act of 1974[61] targets imports from

---

*Peggy Mevs and Thomas B. McVey authored this section of the chapter.

nonmarket economies, that is, communist countries. A good deal of East-West trade is done through countertrade agreements and in this way section 406 may apply to countertrade agreements. Two of the trade actions that have arisen from such an agreement have been brought under section 406. And, interestingly, these two cases dealt with the same transaction, a countertrade agreement between Occidental Petroleum Corp. and the USSR. The next section explores the facts and implications of these cases.

Section 406 of the Trade Act of 1974

The Agreement. In 1973 Occidental Petroleum Corp., a U.S. corporation involved in the extracting industry and the refining and marketing of these extractions, arranged a transaction with the Soviet Union. According to the agreement, Occidental would help the Soviet Union build a $900 million ammonia plant and sell it superphosphoric acid. In return, the Soviet Union would sell Occidental ammonia, urea, and potash. The agreement was to span 20 years and would begin in 1978. The sale of the ammonia, urea, and potash would help repay loans obtained from the Ex-Im Bank and other banks to build the plant. Occidental obtained approval for the transaction from the U.S. government before finally going ahead with the agreement. Barely one year after the imports began, the whole agreement was jeopardized when a section 406 petition was filed with the International Trade Commission (ITC) by domestic producers of anhydrous ammonia.

The Investigations. A section 406 investigation is initiated by the ITC when it has reason to believe that imports from a communist country are disrupting a U.S. market. Market disruption occurs when imports of an article like or directly competitive with an article produced in the United States are increasing so rapidly that they are a significant cause of material injury or threat of material injury to a U.S. industry. The ITC has 90 days from the time it receives a petition to make a determination as to whether market disruption is occurring. Recommendations are then made to the president who decides whether to grant relief. If the president does not follow the ITC's recommendation Congress may override his decision and implement the ITC's recommendation. To date, there have been only eight 406 cases brought before the ITC. In none of these cases has import relief ultimately been granted.

In October of 1979 the ITC reached an affirmative determination on the question of market disruption caused by the imports of anhydrous ammonia from the USSR. In a three-to-two decision Commissioners Parker, Bedell, and Moore found that the imports were increasing rapidly, absolutely and relatively, and that despite an increase in domestic consumption of ammonia, domestic producers' share of this increase had decreased. In reaching its affirmative determination the commissioners looked at certain factors such as pricing, market penetration and dependence. They found that U.S. domestic prices were depressed because of these imports. The imports were not priced according to the market forces; prices instead were fixed by rigid forward pricing contracts. The majority also found that Soviet imports had increased their share of the market and that because the agreement ran for 20 years, the imports would capture an even larger part of the market. The United States could become, to a certain extent, dependent on the imports of ammonia from the USSR, an outcome the commissioners viewed as undesirable. They recommended that the president impose a three-year quota that would limit anhydrous ammonia imports from the USSR to 1 million short tons for 1980, 1.1 million for 1981 and 1.3 million for 1982.[62]

President Carter declined to follow the recommendation of the ITC. He found that market conditions did not warrant import relief and that it would not be in the national economic interest to impose such relief.

A few weeks later the Soviets invaded Afghanistan. Shortly thereafter, in January 1980, the president asked the ITC to reinvestigate Soviet anhydrous ammonia imports, stating that he had reason to believe that market disruption existed and that recent events had altered the international economic conditions that had influenced his previous decision.

In this second investigation, however, the ITC found that there was no market disruption. In the second investigation full-year data were available; in the first, only half-year data had been available. But the major factor that caused the reversal was not the additional data but the fact that there was a change in commissioners. Commissioner Parker retired and Commissioner Calhoun took his place;[63] everybody else voted in the same way. The majority in the second opinion found that the increase in imports of Soviet ammonia—from 0 in 1977 to 2 percent in 1978 and to 4 percent in 1979—did not meet the statute's criteria. The Commission did not consider this to be a rapid surge in imports. They also found that although the ammonia industry in the United States had been suffering since 1975 it had rallied in 1978, more or less concurrently with the imports of Soviet ammonia. Further, profits had increased and the few customers that Occidental supplied most likely would have used offshore suppliers anyway.[64]

Criticism and Implications. These investigations have been criticized for their potential effects on domestic importers seeking trading relations with nonmarket economies and domestic producers seeking import relief. Domestic importers are troubled by the political influences exerted on the process. These influences may introduce intolerable commercial uncertainties into any potential countertrade deal. The injury standard adopted in the second investigation makes it almost impossible to prove injury from imports arising out of a countertrade deal. The ITC refused to examine possible long-term market penetration as one of the factors for determining threat of injury. This arguably blinks reality because imports under a long-term countertrade agreement usually do not increase drastically from one year to the next. Generally, they increase little by little or remain quite stable for the duration of the contract. The result, however, is to solidify a market share in the domestic market. Since countertraded goods are usually sold at low prices, this would result in the elimination of some domestic producers who would not be able to compete. Industry investment would fall. For essential or strategic goods, a set market share could lead to dependence and hence vulnerability, a factor that had no place in the ITC's decision. The ITC also failed to consider market penetration capability, marginal pricing, long-term contracting capability and loss of market share.[65] By failing to consider these long-range factors, the ITC has severely handicapped future petitioners.

The decisions are also troubling from the perspective of domestic producers who may need to seek import relief against imports brought into the United States as part of a countertrade transaction. After all, its time, effort, and monetary expense, Occidental came close to having its multibillion dollar deal fall apart. Regardless of the precautions an importer might take, he always faces the risk of a section 406 action when dealing with a nonmarket economy. Occidental discovered that it is difficult to predict the outcome in such a case and the prevailing political situation could make a big difference in the ultimate determination. In *Occidental* an affirmative determination was reached the first time to the delight of the petitioners. When the situation drastically changed overnight Occidental saw itself once more involved in an investigation. Although the determination was ultimately favorable for Occidental it had seen its deal almost fall apart twice in the span of one year. Furthermore, it had had to spend thousands of dollars to defend the case. Occidental's victory was in a sense Pyrrhic.

In part because of the Occidental case, some see section 406 as a deterrent to East-West trade because of its potential disruptive effects on any deal with a communist country. To the extent that non-market economies are the most likely partners for countertrade deals, section 406 may prove to be a powerful disruptive tool for those who feel threatened by the imports.

The importer has very limited recourse to avoid the uncertainty and unpredictability that may surround him in trying to set up an agreement. It is nevertheless important for him to keep in mind all these possibilities before finalizing a deal. Certain steps could be taken to minimize the risks: check with government agencies (ITC, Commerce) on the highlights of the proposal to see if there are any glaring problems that might arise or that might give cause for an investigation, such as a rapid initial surge in imports for the first few years. The importer could also try to protect himself on the contract in the event an investigation were initiated on a 406 action. This could be done by requiring payment of the legal fees or termination and immediate payment of all monies due if the determination were negative.

Antidumping Law

The purpose of the U.S. antidumping law is to prevent the importation of foreign goods priced at "less than fair value" which will result in substantial injury to U.S. industry. A significant problem may arise in countertrade transactions when companies, in pricing their countertraded goods for quick resale, set these prices at levels which are at "less than fair value," that is, below those permitted by the antidumping laws. This is especially pertinent when imports of countertraded goods into the United States involve repeated shipments of the same product, a practice very common in countertrade transactions. If the resulting impact of these pricing practices upon U.S. industry is sufficient, antidumping duties could be assessed upon the imported goods. The unexpected imposition of antidumping duties could significantly affect the resale price of the countertraded goods in the United States, thus jeopardizing their sale as planned and threatening the economic viability of the entire countertrade transaction.

The International Trade Commission has considered at least one antidumping action which pertained to imports arising out of a countertrade transaction. In a preliminary investigation conducted in 1981, the ITC determined that there was "reasonable indication" that imports of truck-trailer axles from Hungary arising out of a countertrade transaction between a U.S. firm and Hungary were causing material injury to other U.S. truck-trailer manufacturers. In this particular instance, however, no duties were assessed since a settlement was reached between the parties prior to a final determination by the Commission.

Section 337 of the Trade Act of 1930

Section 337 of the Trade Act of 1930, as amended by the Trade Act of 1974, is an often overlooked statutory provision which resembles, in part, both the U.S. antitrust laws and the import relief laws discussed above. Like the antitrust laws, Section 337 prohibits certain practices which constitute "unfair methods of competition," including the sale of goods below cost or at unreasonably low prices. The provision differs from the antitrust laws, however, in that it applies specifically to anticompetitive practices in import transactions and provides for only limited forms of relief such as the exclusion of the imported goods from entry into the United States. Moreover, Section 337 differs from the antitrust laws in that cases brought pursuant to this provision are heard before the International Trade Commission rather than in the United States District Courts. As is the case with the antidumping provisions and Section 406 discussed above, Section 337 provides an additional opportunity for disgruntled third parties to interfere with the importation of low-priced countertraded goods, providing additional potential dangers for the U.S. firm which has committed to purchase quantities of countertraded goods.

One advantage of a Section 337 proceeding over an antitrust action is that since the case is before the ITC, the proceedings generally take considerably less time to complete than in a federal antitrust action (often as little as 12 months), thus making it frequently less expensive for a private party to bring action and allowing relief to be granted within a considerably shorter time period. Consequently, in situations where unfair trade violations are occurring but where antitrust actions are deemed impractical, Section 337 provides an additional option through which injured parties could seek redress against "unfair" import practices conducted in connection with countertrade activities.

Section 201, Section 301 and Other Import Trade Measures

Other U.S. import relief and unfair trade laws, including the "escape clause" provisions set forth in Section 201 of the Trade Act of 1974, as amended by the Trade Agreements Act of 1979, Section 301 of the Trade Act of 1974, the U.S. countervailing duty law and the import relief provisions contained in Section 22 of the Agricultural Adjustment Act present similar problems regarding the importation of countertraded goods into the United States. As with other types of import actions described above, these laws are designed to prevent injury to U.S. industry from foreign goods entering the United States by providing for a variety of administrative measures to restrict or prevent the importation of certain goods at harmful price levels found to be creating domestic injury or the potential for such injury. Companies seeking to import countertraded goods into the United States, especially if this import activity involves large quantities of goods or if the goods are offered for sale at extremely low prices, should be conscious of the impact which these laws might have upon their proposed import activities so as to avoid or minimize the disruption caused by import relief actions. Once again, the imposition of duties or other measures to adjust the price or volume of imported goods would most likely complicate the timely sale of the countertraded goods as planned and jeopardize the successful conclusion of the countertrade transaction. While it may be difficult in many cases to predict with certainty the impact of specific import transactions on particular U.S. industries, countertrade planners should at least be aware of the existence of these and similar import relief laws and the potential problems which they could present in countertrade transactions.

Customs Valuation

U.S. customs law contains no special provision for bartered or countertraded goods. Under the transaction method of valuation, applicable in the United States since 1980, duty is assessed on a particular good based on the value that appears in the accompanying invoice.[66] These invoices denote a numerical value and give customs officials no clue as to whether the import is involved in a regular sales transaction or from a barter or countertrade transaction, a distinction that is at any rate irrelevant under present U.S. law. If for some reason the invoice did not denote the monetary value of the good but instead stated that the good was bartered, the value of the imported good would then be equal to the value exchanged for it. This would only apply in a straight barter deal, however.

A special problem arises under the transaction method of countertraded imports, however. Because the prices of the countertraded goods are set by the parties to the deal, albeit with some reference to market values, the price on the invoice may not be the "real" transaction value even though it might have been the price paid nominally.

U.S. Customs is unlikely to investigate such possible discrepancies, however, because of the administrative difficulties involved.

Other Federal Regulatory Concerns

In addition to being subject to laws and regulations which deal directly with import activities, U.S. firms importing countertraded goods will most likely be subject to a variety of separate, highly technical regulatory requirements which pertain to the domestic sales of the imported products once they enter the United States. These provisions, which include labeling, health, safety, environmental, and similar laws, are especially applicable to many commodities common to countertrade transactions, including chemicals (environmental laws), consumer goods (safety and labeling laws), and foodstuffs (health, labeling, and packaging laws). Thus, for example, a U.S. machinery manufacturer which is forced to purchase and import foreign food products into the United States pursuant to a countertrade requirement must not only deal with questions involving quotas, tariff payments, classification, valuation, and antitrust and fair trade laws as discussed above, but also will most likely be required to satisfy a plethora of highly detailed requirements regarding packaging, labeling, sanitation, inspection, and possible federal registration pertaining to the food products which it is selling in the United States. Once again, while firms which are routinely active in import and domestic distribution activities may find these and similar requirements to be fairly routine, these may present greater difficulties for firms engaging in such activities for the first time.

CONCLUSION

This chapter has described only a few of the potential legal, tax, and antitrust difficulties that confront barterers and countertraders. The way is far more certain with regard to tax planning than for antitrust planning, but both areas could benefit from some administrative guidance. Federal regulatory agencies and departments ought to be doing everything possible to promote barter and countertrade transactions. After all, barter and countertrade transactions are fundamentally procompetitive and economy-stimulating. They enable deals to take place that probably would not otherwise occur. Barter and countertrade deals will have no substantial immediate impact upon our balance of trade or our economy, but they often have market-penetration effects that can have important long-term benefits. The growing popularity of barter and countertrade deals is a trend to be seized upon—not only because of the lucrative potential of such deals themselves, but because of these long-range effects that a pattern of such deals might have.

NOTES

1. This example is based upon a transaction between Pepsico and the Rumanian government described in McVey's "Countertrade: Commercial Practices, Legal Issues and Policy Dilemmas" 16 *Law Pol'y. Int'l. Bus.* 1 (1984).

2. For a discussion of the principles governing cash and accrual methods of accounting, see Chirelstein, *Federal Income Taxation*, ¶ 11.01-11.02, 12.01-12.03 (3d ed. 1982).

3. IRC § 446.

4. See Chirelstein, *Federal Income Taxation*, at § 11.01-11.02.

5. For an excellent description of how barter exchanges operate, see Keller, "The Taxation of Barter Transactions" 42 *Minn. L. Rev.* 441, (1982), pp. 480-87. The account in text is drawn from Keller's article.

6. IRC § 1001; Reg. § 1.1001-1(a).

7. See D. A. Simon, *The Barter Book* (1979).

8. Comments of Paul E. Suplizio, Executive Director of International Ass'n of Trade Exchanges, filed in response to proposed Treasury regulation § 1.6045-1 (hereinafter Suplizio's [IATE] comments).

9. Keller, "Taxation of Barter Transactions," p. 450, n. 43.

10. See Memorandum on Tax Implications of Barter Transactions, prepared by Mr. Michael Esch of Patton, Boggs, and Blow (unpublished).

11. 47 Fed. Reg. 51,419 (Nov. 15, 1982) (new § 1.6045-1(e)(4)).

12. See Keller, "Taxation of Barter Transactions," pp. 449-50.

13. Ibid., p. 45.

14. 370 U.S. 5 (1962).

15. Ibid., p. 72.

16. These attempts are described in Chirelstein, *Federal Income Taxation*, at § 14.01.

17. See Rev. Rul. 80-52; 26 C.F.R. § 1.6045-1 (1984), as amended T.D. 7960 (May 23, 1984).

18. Suplizio's (IATE) comments at 3-4.

19. Mamis, "Trade Secrets, Inc.," (Aug. 1982) pp. 69, 72.

20. Suplizio's (IATE) comments at 3-4.

21. Ibid.

22. 26 C.F.R. § 1.6045-1 (1984), as amended T.D. 7960 (May 23, 1984) (describing information required in reports).

23. Suplizio's (IATE) comments at 2.

24. See BNA Tax Management Portfolio (61-4th) *Taxfree Exchanges Under Section 1031*, p. A-1 (hereinafter TPM).

25. IRC § 1031(a).

26. Ibid.

27. TPM, pp. A-7-A-8.

28. Ibid., p. A-8.

29. Ibid.

30. 602 F.2d 1341 (9th Cir. 1979).

31. The case is summarized and discussed by Harroch, "Employing Section 1031 Exchanges: New Opportunities, New Problems and Continuing Risks," *Taxes* 136, (Feb. 1980), pp. 140-42.

32. Ibid., pp. 142, 144.

33. Please refer to Chapter 3 for a more detailed discussion on this issue.

34. For a general discussion of these elements, see J. P. Griffin, U.S. Antitrust Aspects of East-West Countertrade 4-7 (unpublished paper; presented at Interface IV, Philadelphia, October 15, 1982).

35. Ibid.

36. Ibid., pp. 5-6.

37. *United States* v. *General Dynamics Corp.*, 258 F. Supp. 36 (S.D.N.Y. 1966).

38. *Consolidated Foods Corp.*, 62 F.T.C. 929 (1963).

39. *Waugh Equip. Co.*, 15 F.T.C. 232 (1931).

40. 258 F. Supp. 36 (S.D.N.Y. 1966).

41. Ibid., at 59.

42. *International Salt Co.* v. *United States*, 332 U.S. 392 (1947).

43. *Fortner Enterprises, Inc.* v. *U.S. Steel Corp.*, 394 U.S. 495 (1969) [Fortner I].

44. McVey, pp. 52-54.

45. 365 U.S. 320 (1961).

46. Ibid., at 329.

47. *Siegel* v. *Chicken Delight*, 448 F.2d 43 (9th Cir. 1971), *cert. denied*, 405 U.S. 955 (1972).

48. *Fortner I*, 394 U.S. 495 (1969).

49. Commission for the European Communities, Eleventh Annual Competition Policy Report, Brussels (1982); European Commission, The European Community's Competition Policy, Brussels 10 (1976).

50. Ibid.

51. See Handler et al. Cases and Materials on Trade Regulation 353 (1977 & Supp. 1979) (describing extraterritorial application of U.S. antitrust laws).

52. Ibid.

53. See Canenbley, ed. Enforcing Antitrust Laws Against Foreign Enterprises, (1981).

54. See Griffin, pp. 13-14.

55. Ibid., pp. 11-13.

56. Commission for the European Community, Eleventh Annual Report on Competition Policy, Brussels (1982).

57. Pub. L. No. 97-290 (Oct. 8, 1982).

58. Pub. L. No. 97-290, §§ 303, 311.

59. Ibid., at § 306.

60. Ibid.

61. 19 U.S.C. § 2436 (a).

62. See "Anhydrous Ammonia from the U.S.S.R.," USITC Pub. No. 1006, 1-11 (1979).

63. Potter, "East West Countertrade: Economic Injury and Dependence under U.S. Trade Law," *Law & Poly Int'l Bus 13* (1981) pp. 413, 436.

64. See Anhydrous Ammonia from the U.S.S.R., USITC Pub. No. 1051 3-12 (1979).

65. See generally, Potter, "East West Countertrade."

66. 19 U.S.C. § 1401a (b) (1).

10
THE IMPLICATIONS OF COUNTERTRADE UNDER THE GENERAL AGREEMENT ON TARIFFS AND TRADE
R. Michael Gadbaw

INTRODUCTION

The proliferation of countertrade practices and their increasing impact on international trade has prompted serious reviews of the nature and extent of such practices. For the most part, these analyses have focused on the mechanics of countertrade and its economic effects. To date, little attention has been directed at the possible implications of countertrade under the rules currently governing the international trading system and embodied in the General Agreement on Tariffs and Trade (the "GATT").[1] This chapter examines the extent to which countertrade practices are consistent with the generally recognized rules of international trade.

Countertrade practices as such have not been seriously considered in the GATT. This lack of attention may be attributed to several factors. Countertrade is most often used by nonmarket economy countries, few of which have joined the GATT.[2] Moreover, because trade with these countries is relatively modest, private companies and the U.S. government have preferred to encourage trade rather than complain vociferously about countertrade practices where they have arisen.[3] Countertrade has been viewed as a necessary evil to be tolerated because of a desire to encourage trade while accommodating the foreign exchange needs of most nonmarket economies. Recently, however,

Reprinted with permission from the *Journal of Comparative Business and Capital Market Law* 5:355-65. Copyright 1983, Elsevier Science Publishers B.V. (North-Holland).

countertrade has become a matter of serious concern because its use has become more widespread. Countertrade practices are popular in developing countries. Some developed countries have also encouraged such deals, especially with developing countries, in order to secure access to raw material.[4]

Analyzing countertrade with respect to the GATT will prove helpful for several reasons. First, an examination of countertrade in terms of the GATT demonstrates the fundamental incompatibility between countertrade practices and the framework for trade envisioned by the GATT drafters. Second, the GATT rules may provide analogies from which principles may be drawn to govern the use of countertrade. Finally, to the extent that the GATT rules cannot be used to deal with the trade-distorting effects of countertrade, new rules must be developed.

THE STRUCTURE OF GATT

The GATT is essentially a contract among sovereign nations under which they mutually agree to limit their freedom of action to regulate international trade.[5] The centerpiece of this system is a set of tariff schedules specifying the maximum rates that GATT members may charge as customs duties.[6] For almost 35 years and through seven rounds of multilateral negotiations, GATT members have concentrated their efforts on the elimination of tariffs. Their success in this endeavor is evidenced by the generally low level of tariffs, which may be responsible for an increase in international trade.

The elimination of tariffs as a major obstacle to trade has shifted the focus in the GATT to the set of rules that initially were designed to protect the value of tariff concessions.[7] Several attempts have been made over the years to improve the basic framework. The most recent attempt occurred at the Tokyo Round of Multilateral Negotiations during which codes of conduct were developed to augment the rules regarding subsidies, dumping, customs valuation, standards, and government procurement.[8]

Taken together, the rules promulgated under the GATT constitute the legal norms against which any form of governmental intervention in international trade may be tested. In determining whether countertrade is consistent with the GATT principles, both the nature of the countertrade and the extent of governmental involvement in this practice must be examined.

WHAT IS COUNTERTRADE?

For purposes of this analysis, the term "countertrade" refers to the entire range of practices whereby one country requires another to purchase from it as a condition for allowing that country to sell to it. The following aspects of countertrade are relevant to a GATT analysis: (1) the refusal to comply with a countertrade requirement bars a sale from the noncomplying party to the party imposing the requirement; (2) countertrade requirements have trade-distorting effects that are not present in normal transactions in international trade; (3) countertrade practices create risks for sellers that are not compensated for by any significant advantages; and (4) countertrade is used to balance trade on a product, transaction, or country basis. These effects have been identified in the economic literature on countertrade. Although they may or may not be present in a particular transaction, they are taken as given for purposes of the following GATT analysis.

THE NATURE OF GOVERNMENTAL INVOLVEMENT IN COUNTERTRADE

The GATT rules regulate the behavior of governments, not individual business entities.[9] As indicated above, an examination of the consistency of countertrade with the GATT rules requires an examination of the extent of government involvement in countertrade practices.

Two extremes of governmental involvement exist. In the first situation, if a firm decides on its own to discriminate against imports or to impose certain conditions upon importation (for example, barter, buybacks, swaps), the decision cannot be challenged; the GATT does not govern the decisions of commercial entities. If, however, the country where the firm is located has a "buy national" policy, the existence of this policy creates a presumption that some form of state coercion is being used to influence the firm's actions. In such a case, the GATT rules would apply to the government involvement but not to the activities of the private parties.

At the opposite extreme is the state-controlled economy. Although the drafters of the GATT considered this situation, they decided to deal just with the problem of state trading enterprises and not with the problem of state-controlled economies. Article XVII of the GATT imposes upon state trading entities a rule of nondiscrimination and requires them to act solely in accordance with "commercial considerations." Through the provisions of this Article, the drafters attempted to approach state trading in the same manner they dealt with governmental regulation of private trade.

The two situations discussed above raise the question of whether countertrade practices are the results of deliberate state regulation, and, if so, what form that regulation takes. The discussion below focuses on three different contexts in which countertrade practices may arise: (1) those where countertrade is required by law or regulation in an otherwise nonstate-controlled economy; (2) those where countertrade is practised by a state trading enterprise, whose decisions cannot be easily characterized as either commercial or noncommercial, in an otherwise nonstate-controlled economy; and (3) those where countertrade is practised in a state-controlled economy. As state control over the entire economy becomes more pervasive, the GATT framework becomes less relevant because the GATT was designed to allow the free market to function in an unimpeded fashion by placing limitations on government interference with trade.

The GATT does not prohibit governmental protection of private trade agreements, but does require such protection to take the form of tariffs. The GATT also calls upon countries to negotiate the elimination of tariffs. The GATT rules on nontariff measures attempt to restrict the use of other forms of regulation. The more an economy is subject to complete state control, however, the more avenues there are to frustrate the GATT scheme in ways that simply were not anticipated by the drafters.

COUNTERTRADE BY LAW OR REGULATION

Instances in which countertrade is required by law or regulation in an otherwise free market economy are not common. Of the various forms of countertrade, only offsets appear to be a common occurrence in developed market economies. An examination of countertrade in this context is the starting point for any overall GATT analysis because this is the context that the drafters had in mind when designing the rules.[10] If imposed by law or regulation, countertrade conflicts with a number of fundamental GATT rules. Recognition of this fact makes it easier both to appreciate the problems posed for the GATT when countertrade is practised by state-controlled economies, and to understand why a different regime is necessary for managing trade relations between East and West.

The following subsections demonstrate, first, that countertrade practices have economic effects that directly conflict with the framework the GATT was designed to preserve. Such practices are an instrument for direct governmental regulation of trade and can be used to create the same distortions as a quota or a tariff. Second, these sections establish a strong case that countertrade practices violate any of a number of specific GATT Articles, including those designed to protect against nullification or impairment of tariff concessions, those requiring nondiscrimination (most favored nation ("MFN") and national treatment), and those prohibiting quantitative regulations.

GATT Nullification or Impairment

The basis for a GATT member's challenge of the practices of another contracting party is Article XXIII. This article authorizes a complaint in any case in which a member feels that

> any benefit accruing to it directly or indirectly . . . is being nullified or impaired or that the attainment of any objective of the Agreement is being impeded as a result of: (a) the failure of another contracting party to carry out its obligations. . . . or (b) the application by another contracting party of any measure, whether or not it conflicts with the provisions of [the GATT], or (c) the existence of any other situation.

Article XXIII directs the parties to consult about the matter and, if no settlement is reached, the contracting parties, acting in a judicial capacity, may hear the complaints and make recommendations to the parties or give a ruling "as appropriate."[11] If the circumstances are "serious enough," the contracting parties may authorize a specific form of retaliation: the complaining party or parties may suspend the application of "concessions or other obligations" under the GATT to any other contracting party or parties.

Both the GATT precedent and the understanding on the GATT dispute settlement mechanism, embodied in the Framework Agreement reached during the Tokyo Round negotiations, establish that any government measure violating a GATT provision constitutes a prima facie nullification or impairment of a GATT benefit.[12] Once an infringement of a provision is shown, the burden of proof shifts to the offending government to prove that nullification or impairment of a GATT benefit has not occurred. If the accused country fails to produce substantial evidence, the contracting parties must determine whether the circumstances are serious enough to justify authorization of remedial actions.

A more difficult case is presented when a complaining party alleges nullification or impairment as a result of a practice not explicitly prohibited by the GATT. Nevertheless, GATT panels have determined that certain practices constitute nullifications or impairments, even though they do not conflict with any particular rule. Such cases arise where the foreign practice upsets the balance of concessions that have been negotiated in a trade agreement.[13]

Most-favored-nation Treatment

Article I of the GATT requires that contracting parties treat the products of every other contracting party no less favorably than they treat the products of the most favored nation. A strict reading of the language of Article I supports the view that a countertrade requirement applying equally to all foreign countries would not be inconsistent with this obligation because all foreign countries are subject to the same requirement. Despite this view, countertrade practices conditioning access to a country's market on purchases of an equivalent amount of that country's goods are strongly reminiscent of the bilateral arrangements which the unconditional most-favored-nation principle was designed to prevent. Moreover, an extension of the logic of countertrade would allow a country to negotiate a countertrade deal that covered all of its exports to the importing country in return for equivalent purchases. This type of bilateral balancing of trade is fundamentally inconsistent with Article I's purpose of preserving the multilateral character of the GATT system.

Tariff Concessions

Article II, paragraph 1, of the GATT incorporates into the basic agreement the tariff schedules of each contracting party and requires that the protection afforded any product be no greater than that provided for in the member's schedule. Protection provided by countertrade requirements would be contrary to this principle unless the contracting party had included the countertrade requirements as a condition in its GATT schedule.

Article II, paragraph 4, addresses the situation where a contracting party "establishes, maintains or authorizes, formally or in effect, a monopoly of the importation of any product," and it stipulates that such a monopoly cannot be used to provide protection "on the average in excess of the amount of protection provided for in [the] Schedule." This provision could be used against countertrade practices when the government of a country enforces the countertrade requirement through an import monopoly that has been established either formally *or in effect.*

National Treatment of Internal Taxation and Regulation

Article III of the GATT states the basic principle of nondiscrimination in the treatment of imported goods. It requires the taxation and regulation of imports in the same manner as domestically produced goods. The basic rule of paragraph 1 provides that

> laws, regulations and requirements affecting the internal sale of, offering for sale, purchase, transportation, distribution or use of products, and internal quantitative regulations requiring the mixture, processing or use of products in specified amounts or proportions, should not be applied to imported or domestic products so as to afford protection to domestic production.

Countertrade requirements could be construed as quantitative regulations of the use of imported products in specified amounts or proportions: the quantities of products to be purchased and used by the importing country are tied to the foreign country's purchases of the former's locally produced goods. The practice thereby protects domestic producers by forcing the foreign exporter to purchase goods in the domestic producer's own export market rather than from competitors.

Paragraph 5 of Article II provides a more direct basis for challenging countertrade practices. It bans quantitative regulations "relating to the. . . use of products in specified. . . proportions which" require that the specified "proportion of any product. . . must be supplied from domestic sources." This provision has been used to challenge practices requiring a party to purchase a certain amount of a local product as a condition for the party's sale of another product. The European Economic Community in one case required domestic importers and producers of animal feed in member states to purchase specified quantities of dry milk for use in such feed. A GATT panel held this requirement to be a violation of Article III.[14] The same logic could be applied to countertrade requirements.

In addition, paragraph 4 requires that rules forbidding the "internal sale, offer for sale, purchase, transportation, distribution or use" be no less favorable for imports than products of national origin. This provision could be used against countertrade requirements that tie the level of imports to a required level of exports.

General Elimination of Quantitative Restrictions

With the exception of duties, taxes, or other charges, Article XI of the GATT prohibits restrictions on imports and exports, whether made effective through quotas, licences, or "other measures." Countertrade requirements can operate as quantitative restrictions on imports. If a firm is unable to export to a country unless it accepts a countertrade requirement, the effect of the requirement is no different from the effect of a conventional import quota adjusted according to some domestic market criterion. For example, if a country established a quota on the importation of a given product and then adjusted the quota in accordance with the level of exports, the quota would violate Article XI. Countertrade requirements have the same effect on individual firms and, therefore, violate one of the most significant GATT provisions.

STATE TRADING ENTERPRISES

Article XVII of the GATT provides that state enterprises or firms receiving "exclusive or special privileges" from their respective governments must be permitted to make purchases and sales involving imports or exports in a manner: (a) consistent with the "general principles of nondiscriminatory treatment" contained in the GATT, and (b) solely in accordance with commercial considerations.[15]

Paragraph 1(c) of Article XVII applies these principles not only to controls on "state enterprises," but to any firm under the jurisdiction of the host government.[16] This provision is redundant in the context of a countertrade requirement imposed directly by law or regulation. It could, however, be used in situations involving indirect regulations, such as conditioning the receipt of government financing, tax breaks, or other government assistance on acceptance of countertrade obligations.

The GATT and State Trading

The dilemma posed by state trading practices for the drafters of the GATT is comparable to that confronting today's policymakers in their efforts to grapple with countertrade issues. The drafters recognized that state monopolies can exercise their discretion to buy or sell on a discriminatory basis and thereby circumvent the GATT rules.[17] This problem is compounded by the difficulties of detecting and measuring the impact of such practices when decisions are made without public scrutiny or disclosure. Moreover, the drafters faced the practical reality that many countries utilized state monopolies to secure revenue or regulate the trade in certain commodities.

The drafters established some useful principles in Article XVII for dealing with state enterprises, but the rules fall far short in their actual application. Article XVII is drawn from the corresponding provisions of the International Trading Organizations' Charter ("ITO Charter").[18] This Article, also based on an ITO Charter proposal of the United States,[19] reflects an attempt to treat state trading in a manner that is comparable to the GATT treatment of governmental regulation of private trade.

Article XVII and State Trading

As indicated above, the basic rule of Article XVII is that state enterprises are not allowed to discriminate in a manner inconsistent with the principles of nondiscrimination set forth in other parts of the GATT. There is some debate over whether this principle of nondiscrimination is intended to encompass both national and MFN treatment or only MFN treatment. The broader interpretation of nondiscrimination coincides with the basic U.S. objective of subjecting state trading enterprises to the same principles applicable to government regulation of private trade. Although on one occasion the United States argued before a GATT panel for the broader interpretation, it elected to settle the case before a panel decision was issued. The continuing ambiguity in the scope of the nondiscrimination principle is evidence of the desire of the United States and other GATT members to avoid the tough questions in dealing with state trading.

Paragraph 1(b) of Article XVII adds to the principle of nondiscrimination the requirement that state enterprises shall "make any such purchases or sales solely in accordance with commercial considerations. . . . and shall afford the enterprises of the other contracting parties adequate opportunity, in accordance with customary business practice, to compete for participation in such purchases or sales." Application of the principles of "commercial considerations" and "opportunity to participate" to countertrade practices, as well as the application of paragraph 1(a)'s principle of "nondiscrimination," involves some major interpretative difficulties. The principles in both paragraphs are vague and, despite the expectations of the U.S. drafters, no case law involving the interpretation of Article XVII has emerged. Nevertheless, a strong case can be made that countertrade involves both discriminatory effects and considerations alien to those present in normal commercial transactions in violation of Article XVII.

Paragraph 4 of Article XVII could also prove useful in dealing with countertrade. This subsection refers to the disclosure of information relating to the operations of state monopolies. Under this paragraph a GATT member may be called upon to supply information about the operations of any state enterprise related to the administration of the GATT. This notification requirement, adopted as an amendment to the GATT in 1957, has been implemented through a formal notification process. Every three years, countries maintaining state enterprises are called upon to complete a GATT questionnaire designed to elicit detailed information on the operation of state trading enterprises. In particular, the questionnaire requests disclosure of the criteria used by the enterprise to determine the quantities to be exported and imported. This questionnaire, either in its present form or as appropriately amended, could be used to elicit valuable information on countertrade practices: the information could then be used as a basis for a careful scrutiny of such practices under the GATT.

Finally, in addition to Article XVII, two other GATT rules are also applicable to state trading. Article II, paragraph 4, requires that the protection afforded by a state monopoly not exceed that provided for a particular product in a country's Schedule of Concessions. Article XI, which prohibits quantitative and other restrictions, expressly applies to state trading enterprises by virtue of an Interpretive Note in Annex I. Thus, it can be argued that countertrade practiced by state enterprises is inconsistent with the principles of Article II regarding products covered by a tariff concession and Article XI.

STATE-CONTROLLED ECONOMIES

Although the GATT text does not address the problems of accommodating state-controlled economies, except to the extent of imposing certain criteria on the operation of state enterprises, these problems became moot, and the provisions designed to deal with state-controlled economies were eliminated from the GATT draft.[20] This omission was intentional because it was thought that the GATT would not have to address the problems presented by membership of such states because the ITO, with its more comprehensive provisons, was expected to take effect within a short time. The eventual rejection of the ITO meant that the GATT had to accommodate state-controlled economies. In spite of silence in the GATT agreement, ad hoc solutions have evolved to deal with the handful of state-controlled economies that have joined the GATT since 1948.

One proposal, included in the 1946 ITO draft prepared by the United States, but not included in the final ITO draft, required that a country with a complete or substantially complete monopoly of its import trade be willing to undertake global import commitments. The requirements of this provision were imposed on Poland when it sought membership in the GATT in 1967. In its Protocol of Accession, Poland undertook to increase the total value of its imports from other contracting parties by "not less than 7 percent per annum".[21] The Polish formula is significant for purposes of approaching countertrade issues because it represents an alternative to the problematic application of GATT rules to an economic system that does not fit within the GATT framework.

CONCLUSION

Countertrade poses serious issues in terms of basic GATT obligations. The problems are exacerbated by the fact that countertrade is most commonly used by state-controlled economies: the GATT rules are difficult, if not impossible, to reconcile with those countries' extensive government involvement in commercial decisions. From a practical standpoint, it may be desirable to acknowledge this conflict and create an exception for countertrade to the GATT rules to draw these countries into the trading system. One should not ignore, however, the threat that countertrade poses for the GATT system should its popularity spread.

NOTES

1. General Agreement on Tariffs and Trade, *opened for signature* October 30, 1947, 61 Stat. A3, T.I.A.S. No. 1700, 55 U.N.T.S. 187. The GATT has been amended a number of times since 1947. The current version is contained in 4 General Agreement on Tariffs and Trade, Basic Instruments and Selected Documents (1969).

2. Of the nonmarket economy countries only Poland, Hungary, Czechoslovakia, Rumania, and Yugoslavia are currently members of the GATT.

3. This pragmatic view of the importance of trade with nonmarket economies has been an important aspect of the age of detente. For a review of issues affecting East-West trade and U.S. policy, see "East-West Trade, An End to Business as Usual," *The Economist*, May 22, 1982, at 55.

4. See "Bartering Aids Poor Nations," New York *Times*, Jan. 17, 1983.

5. See, generally, R. Hudec, *The GATT Legal System and World Trade Diplomacy* (1975); J. Jackson, *World Trade and the Law of GATT* (1969).

6. GATT Article II states, in part: "[e]ach contracting party shall accord to the commerce of the other contracting party treatment no less favourable than that provided for in the appropriate Part of the appropriate Schedule annexed to the Agreement". GATT, *supra* note 1, at Art. II, para. 1(a). These schedules

have been subject to modification negotiations through successive rounds of negotiation, the latest of which was concluded in 1979 and is embodied in Geneva (1979) Protocol to the General Agreement on Tariffs and Trade, vols. I-IV, June 30, 1979. General Agreement on Tariff and Trade, Basic Instruments and Selected Documents 3 (26th Supp. 1979).

7. Twenty-Fourth Annual Report of the President of the United States on the Trade Agreements Program 39 (1979). These rules are a modest reflection of the Charter of the International Trade Organization that failed to achieve ratification in the U.S. Congress. The official text of the Charter is found in Final Act and Related Documents. United Nations Conference on Trade and Employment. U.N. Doc. ICITO/1/4 (1948) [ITO Charter]. See, generally, C. Wilcox, *A Charter for World Trade* (1949).

8. These agreements are reprinted in Agreements Reached in the Tokyo Round of the Multilateral Trade Negotiations. H. R. Doc. No. 153, 96th Cong., 1st Sess. (1979).

9. See, generally, Jackson, *World Trade and the Law of GATT*, p. 329.

10. The argument against countertrade when imposed by law or regulation is similar to the argument against trade-related performance requirements, such as local content and export requirements. Some of the economic effects of countertrade resemble those resulting from performance requirements. One major distinction between the two is that performance requirements are typically imposed as a condition for foreign investment while countertrade is not. See U.S. Law, *Law & Pol'y in Int'l Bus* 14 (1982) p. 129. Sections of this paper have drawn from that article.

11. Article XXV indicates that "Contracting Parties" refers to the representatives of the GATT members who are acting jointly to implement and further the objectives of GATT.

12. See Uruguayan Recourse to Article XXIII. General Agreement of Tariffs and Trade, Basic Instruments and Selected Documents 100, para. 15 (11th Supp. 1963), GATT Doc. L/1923.

13. See Hudec, "Retaliation Against 'Unreasonable' Foreign Trade Practices: The New Section 301 and GATT Nullification and Impairment." *Minn. L. Rev.* 59 (1975) p. 461.

14. EEC Measures on Animal Feed Proteins. General Agreement on Tariffs and Trade, Basic Instruments and Selected Documents 64, 65, paras. 4.5-4.9 (25th Supp. 1979), GATT Doc. No. L/4599.

15. GATT, *supra* note 1, at Article XVII, para. 1(a), (b).

16. Subparagraph 1(c) states the coverage of the article XVII principle:

No contracting party shall prevent any enterprises (whether or not [a state] enterprise described in sub-paragraph (a) of this paragraph) under its jurisdiction from acting in accordance with the principles of sub-paragraphs (a) and (b) of this paragraph.

Thus subparagraph (c) appears to broaden the scope of Article XVII to all enterprises under the jurisdiction of the state. Jackson, *World Trade and the Law of GATT*, pp. 339, 344.

17. Ibid., p. 333.

18. See ITO Charter, *supra* note 7, at Articles 29-30, 32.

19. U.S. Proposals, Dep't of State Pub. No. 2411, at 17 (1945).

20. See, e.g., Jackson, *World Trade and the Law of GATT*, pp. 334, 335.

21. Protocol for the Accession of Poland, General Agreement on Tariffs and Trade, Basic Instruments and Selected Documents 52, Annex B, para. 1 (15th Supp. 1968).

11
POLICY ISSUES
IN COUNTERTRADE
Thomas B. McVey

As a result of the dramatic increase in the incidence of counter-trade within the recent past, the practice is attracting significant attention outside of the narrow context of the trading room or overseas sales office. Countertrade presents a broad array of complex economic, political, and business issues which are rising quickly on the policy agenda of national governments, international organizations and multinational corporations. It is agreed by most of those familiar with the topic that countertrade will be emerging as one of the most significant and perhaps troublesome international trade policy questions of the decade.

CURRENT POLICY ISSUES RAISED BY COUNTERTRADE

Free Trade Issues

Perhaps the most commonly recognized issue connected with countertrade is the economic or "free trade" question. Countertrade is viewed by many as a coercive, anticompetitive practice which serves as an impediment to free and open trade. Advocates of free trade contend that countertrade requirements serve as a discriminatory, non-tariff trade barrier which distorts the free flow of trade and investment and results in increased costs and other inefficiencies which negatively affect the U.S. and overall world economies. In addition,

---

This chapter is based on Mr. McVey's recent article *Countertrade: Commercial Practices, Legal Issues and Policy Dilemmas*, 16 Law & Pol'y Int'l Bus. 1 (1984) and is included here with the permission of the publisher.

it is pointed out that countertrade transfers the cost of marketing a nation's surplus or undesirable products to the private firm. This transfer provides a valuable benefit to the nation which, some economists will argue, constitutes subsidization of that nation's products by the private firm in the world markets, and creates additional economic distortions and inefficiencies. The overall result of such arrangements is that inefficient producers are allowed to flourish while more competitive producers disappear, to the detriment of the United States and international economies. In a recent economic analysis commissioned by the U.S. Department of Treasury on the topic of the economic ramifications of countertrade, Professor Roy J. Ruffin of the University of Houston concluded that countertrade activities are "uneconomic" and that "all would be served by laws prohibiting such activity."[1]

In response to these trade impediment arguments, countertrade proponents point out that the practice is instrumental in accelerating the industrial and social development of Third World nations. Countertrade facilitates the steady transfer of products and technology to nations with little available investment capital. It is directly responsible for increasing employment, industrial development and export capacity in these nations as well as generating hard currency to finance essential imports including food, medical supplies, and energy resources.

Impact on U.S. Economy

Another sensitive issue involves the impact of countertrade upon U.S. labor and domestic industry. U.S. labor groups have long argued that products imported into the United States as a result of countertrade activities displace U.S.-made products, resulting in significant losses of U.S. jobs and in the deterioration of the domestic work force. In congressional hearings on the topic of military-related countertrade, a representative of the AFL-CIO testified that countertrade deprives the U.S. industrial base of "essential capability and capacity" and urged that "short-term action be taken" to reverse current countertrade policies.[2] Similarly, U.S. business groups are arguing that the displacement of U.S. products created by countertrade practices is inflicting severe damage upon the domestic business community. These groups offer as an example the recent sale of F-16 aircraft by McDonnell Douglas to Canada in which McDonnell Douglas was required to hire Canadian subcontractors to supply components previously manufactured by U.S. firms. Indeed, countertrade may prove to be one of the few issues over which "free-trade" and "protectionist" interests will be in agreement during the course of the next decade.

In response, countertrade proponents point out that most products purchased by U.S. firms pursuant to countertrade requirements do not enter U.S. markets but rather are sold in other nations around the world. This point is directly supported in an analysis conducted by the U.S. International Trade Commission on the impact of countertrade upon the U.S. economy.

Data gathered for this study indicate that the majority of countertrade transactions involving U.S. firms did not result in U.S. imports. Rather, the countertrade products were sold directly or indirectly to developing countries or to the developed countries of Western Europe. This was more often the case where products were obtained through counterpurchase agreements from East European countries.

Even if countertrade does result in an increased level of imports to the United States, this increase generally does not match the increase in U.S. exports which results from U.S. firms responding to countertrade requirements. The International Trade Commission Report estimates that U.S. imports resulting from countertrade during 1980 was $279 million, a small figure in comparison to the billions of dollars worth of U.S. goods exported pursuant to countertrade arrangements.[3] In addition, many companies will often substitute countertrade imports for other imported goods that they normally purchase in sourcing materials for their manufacturing processes. Finally, in support of countertrade, it is argued that both the lower prices and increased quantities of available goods which result from expanded imports are helpful in offsetting U.S. inflationary pressures.

National Security:
Accelerated Communist Industrial and Military Development

As stated above, a significant portion of countertrade requirements are imposed by nonmarket economy nations including the Soviet Union, Eastern European nations and the People's Republic of China. Under such arrangements, significant levels of technology are transferred to these nations by Western firms without the need for the Communist nations to divert currency expenditures from other higher priority uses, including military programs. In essence, the United States and Western European nations are assisting in the accelerated industrial development of the Communist world and underwriting this development as well. Such practices are viewed by many as contradictory to a strong U.S. defense posture since a stronger industrial base enhances the Soviet military capability. Countertrade proponents remind us, however, that while the denial of such benefits to the communist nations might impede their economic and military development, barring Western firms from the lucrative Eastern markets could prove even more detrimental to the economies of Western nations.

National Security:
Dependence upon Foreign Defense Production Capability

A fourth issue involves an additional aspect of national security, that of defense preparedness. As discussed above, a significant level of U.S. countertrade is connected with the export of U.S.-produced military products. Under such arrangements, foreign nations purchasing U.S. military systems request the right to supply materials, produce components, and even assemble military products in cooperation with U.S. defense manufacturers. These practices are referred to as military "offset" requirements. Countertrade opponents point out that offset activities could lead to increased dependence on foreign subcontractors and suppliers by U.S. defense manufacturers and the eventual financial downfall of many U.S. military subcontractors. Such dependence upon foreign production capability could negatively affect overall U.S. defense preparedness. Hearings have been conducted by the Economic Stabilization Subcommittee of the House Committee on Banking, Finance and Urban Affairs focusing on the specific topic of the impact of military-related offset requirements upon U.S. defense preparedness capability.[4] Legislative staff members indicate that further congressional consideration of this issue may be forthcoming in the near future.

In response, supporters of military coproduction and offset requirements argue that such arrangements promote long term efficiencies in military production and result in lower procurement costs to purchasing nations. As a result, such practices actually serve to strengthen the military alliance by spreading both the costs and benefits of a sophisticated defense capability more evenly across the member nations. Additionally, U.S. defense contractors point out that if U.S. firms are prohibited under U.S. law from submitting to foreign countertrade requirements, U.S. industry will be placed at a competitive disadvantage as foreign purchasers will simply turn to non-U.S. defense contractors to fill a significant portion of their defense procurement needs.

Export Competitiveness

Countertrade opponents suggest that countertrade requirements impose a negative impact on U.S. competitiveness and inhibit U.S. export development. By imposing requirements on U.S. exporters to purchase and resell unwanted, and often undesirable, foreign-made goods, the imposing nations are discouraging U.S. firms from expanding their marketing operations into the international arena. Additionally, in light of the fact that U.S. firms are less sophisticated in dealing with countertrade requirements than their Western European and Japanese competitors, U.S. firms are at a substantial disadvantage when competing against these nations in transactions requiring countertrade obligations. In the President's Report to Congress on U.S. Export Competitiveness issued in July 1980, the question of the impact of countertrade is considered:

> Countertrade Encourages Discriminatory Practices. Exporters unwilling to enter into countertrade agreements may be excluded from consideration. An importing country that is short of foreign reserves may select a supplier on the basis of willingness to enter a countertrade deal rather than on the basis of quality or price of the product. The transaction is neither transparent, nor subject to international scrutiny. There have been press reports of countertrade terms which appear to be contrary to the most-favored nation (MFN) and nondiscrimination principles of the General Agreement on Tariffs and Trade (GATT). For instance, countertrade agreements often prohibit competition in a third market by either party or specify the export market(s) to be served by the producer. All countertrade arrangements are bilateral exchanges, often to the exclusion of other competitive exports, and sometimes reflecting other than purely commercial, considerations. *As such, they may impair the United States ability to export.* (emphasis added)[5]

Proponents, however, point out that participation by U.S. firms in countertrade has allowed these companies to increase their international sales and has bolstered the U.S. export position. In most cases, the utilization of countertrade requirements allows the imposing nations to increase their imports through the generation of additional hard currency, consequently opening up greater overseas markets for U.S. firms.

PUBLIC AND PRIVATE RESPONSE TO COUNTERTRADE

Federal Governmental Response

Due to the complexity of the countertrade debate, federal decisionmakers are experiencing difficulty in reaching a consensus regarding how to respond to this new phenomenon. A survey of official and unofficial positions advanced by various federal international trade policy offices on the topic of countertrade discloses a patchwork of inconsistent and at times contradictory policy responses. In the Department of Commerce, for example, despite statements by senior Department officials regarding the undesirable economic effects of countertrade,[6] assistance has routinely been provided for years by officials within the Department's East-West Trade Office to U.S. firms in dealing with foreign countertrade requirements. Similarly, while the Department of Treasury's Office of Trade Finance warns of countertrade's adverse effects upon U.S. production capability, trade, employment, and tax revenues,[7] the International Trade Commission estimates that the practice generates more U.S. exports than it generates in U.S. imports, possibly suggesting that countertrade may be advantageous to U.S. trade.[8] Similar conflicts exist in other federal agencies as well. In short, it is difficult to identify a consistent and precise government view toward countertrade.

As part of the evolution of a federal countertrade policy, numerous studies and investigations have recently been conducted by a host of federal policy offices on the topic of countertrade. In the Executive Branch, for example, such analyses have been undertaken by the Department of Treasury,[9] the Department of Defense,[10] the International Trade Commission,[11] the Office of the U.S. Trade Representative,[12] the Department of Agriculture,[13] and the Department of Labor.[14] These have recently culminated in a comprehensive interagency analysis of countertrade by the federal Trade Policy Review Committee (the "TPRC") under the direction of the Office of U.S. Trade Representative. In this analysis, representatives of 18 federal agencies evaluated the domestic and international ramifications of countertrade and developed a uniform interagency policy on the issue. While the written report setting forth the TPRC findings will most likely not be released to the public, conversations with members of the TPRC indicate that the federal policy sets forth two basic tenets. First, the U.S. government strongly opposes foreign government policies which impose mandatory countertrade requirements. This position is based on the grounds that such practices are uneconomic and distort the free flow of international commerce. Second, despite this theoretical opposition, the U.S. government will not attempt to interfere with and/or discourage U.S. firms from engaging in countertrade. This position is taken so as to enable these firms to remain competitive in the international business environment. It is currently unclear, however, the extent to which the U.S. government will become involved in assisting U.S. firms in dealing with countertrade requirements through activities such as training programs and information exchanges.

In recent congressional hearings conducted on the topic of the federal policy toward barter, additional insight was provided into the TPRC's findings. Carmen Suro-Bredie, representing the Office of the U.S. Trade Representative and the TPRC, presented the following testimony to the House Armed Services Subcommittee on Seapower and Strategic and Critical Materials:

> In the course of this review, U.S. Government agencies found that the recent, increased use of barter is causing distortions in the multilateral trade and payments system. By concealing the *real* prices and costs of transactions, barter may conceal and help perpetuate economic inefficiencies in the marketplace. This lack of transparency is especially troublesome if it makes it possible for a government to subsidize or dump exports when such actions would not be possible through normal channels.
>
> Barter was found to be a return to a bilateral system of trade at a time when the international community is seeking to safeguard and widen a multilateral trading system. Barter transactions are not subject to international rules nor are they subject to multilateral supervision.
>
> The increased use of barter in world trade also has profound effects on the international payments system. If developing countries barter their exports instead of sell them, they reduce the foreign exchange available to repay foreign debt. Barter takes no account of the progress achieved in international settlements. The International Monetary Fund generally has not looked favorably on countertrade and barter. Its loans and rescheduling of private bank loans are conditional on specific programs for increasing exports earnings. These requirements generally are inconsistent with bilateral approaches to trade of the kind typified by barter.
>
> Finally, the Trade Policy Review Group found that barter arrangements increase government intervention in the trading system, thereby raising the possibilities for discrimination and distortion. This intervention is heightened if barter arrangements are formalized by long-term trade agreements or monitored by clearing accounts.[15]

As a result of the distortions which the widespread use of barter could have on the multilateral trade and payments system and the problems experienced by the CCC barter system in the past, the Trade Policy Review Group recommended that the U.S. government exercise caution in the use of its barter authority, reserving it only for those situations which offer advantages not offered by conventional market operations.

On a separate occasion, Richard L. McElheny, Assistant Secretary of Commerce for Trade Development, provided additional insight into the federal government's position toward countertrade in a speech before a meeting of the National Foreign Trade Council Foundation in New York:

> Although figures are difficult to gather, there is substantial agreement that about one-third of world trade today is conducted by countertrade. This is up from an estimated 10 percent in the mid-60's.
>
> Generally, the U.S. Government views all of these forms of countertrade as relatively inefficient means of implementing international trade. The U.S. Government sees countertrade as economically inefficient for those same reasons that trade based on currency replaced the old barter system—i.e., it is more cumbersome, more bureaucratic, less transparent and in general more restrictive than conventional trade. It is viewed as not being cost-effective because it reduces flexibility in purchase and investment decisions, making these too dependent on the partners' willingness to engage in countertrade as compared with product price and quality considerations.
>
> Government-mandated or required countertrade is the major focus on U.S. Government opposition to countertrade. When mandated by a government, it is forced on the trade system. It constitutes a direct government intervention in the marketplace. The dynamics of market forces is minimized and strong political and other non-commerical considerations come into play. It tends to distort.
>
> In addition to concerns regarding bilateralization of trade and the economic inefficiency of countertrade, the U.S. Government is concerned about the problems which may arise with respect to U.S. trade laws. U.S. trade laws, while currently designed to measure foreign subsidies and dumping, do not specifically address the special characteristics of countertrade. As presently constructed, U.S. trade law assistance to a domestic industry injured by imports from countertrade arrangements may to handicapped. For example, the price in a countertrade arrangement can be set at an artifically high level giving the appearance that no dumping exists. Antitrust considerations may also become a greater concern as the practice spreads. Also, in a wider

context, U.S. Customs has difficulty accurately determining transaction value—the determination needed to impose appropriate import duties.

Accordingly, earlier this year, an interagency task force was established to develop a study of U.S. Government policy and countertrade. This has just been completed and, while further study is in progress in other high-level government offices, the task force's study is the basis from which U.S. government policy will be drawn. I would like to take a moment to give you the relevant guidelines. They are as follows:

The U.S. Government generally views countertrade, including barter, as contrary to an open, free trading system and, in the long run not in the interest of the U.S. business community. However, as a matter of policy, the U.S. Government will not oppose U.S. companies' participation in countertrade arrangements unless such action could have a negative impact on national security.

Since U.S. businesses must compete in an environment in which they are voluntarily or involuntarily confronted with countertrade, U.S. Government agencies may provide advisory and market intelligence services. However, U.S. Government officials should not promote the use of countertrade including barter and they should advise U.S. businesses that countertraded goods are subject to U.S. trade laws including quotas. These trade laws include sections 201 and 406 of the Trade Act of 1974, providing import relief from injurious or disruptive imports, as well as the antidumping and countervailing duty statutes.

In addition, the U.S. Government will continue to review financing for projects containing countertrade on a case-by-case basis, taking into account the distortions caused by these practices.[16]

Despite these statements the federal government has actually been engaging in a number of forms of countertrade for years and appears likely to continue to do so for the indefinite future. For example, in the purchase of military equipment from overseas contractors, the Department of Defense frequently imposes offset requirements under which it requests that the foreign suppliers use their best efforts to hire U.S. subcontractors and purchase components from U.S. suppliers. Similarly, the Department of Agriculture has recently concluded the second of two major bilateral barter transactions with Jamaica under which the United States exchanged surplus dairy products for Jamaican bauxite. Such actions depict an inconsistent and confused state of federal countertrade policy.

In the legislative branch, significant activity is also currently underway pertaining to countertrade. In addition to hearings by the House Economic Stabilization Subcommittee as discussed above, an analysis of the economic and political ramifications of countertrade has been undertaken by the General Accounting Office.[17] Similarly, a flurry of legislative activity is currently underway involving the bartering of excess U.S. agricultural commodities for crude oil for the strategic petroleum reserve and minerals for the strategic stockpile. Hearings were conducted on this topic by the Subcommittee on Sea Power and Strategic Critical Materials of the House Armed Services Committee on October 19, 1983.[18]

Responses by Other Public and Private Organizations

The difficulty in developing a consistent policy-level approach to countertrade is present on the international level as well. While most OECD nations, for example, recognize the economic dangers presented by widespread countertrade practices, these nations have not been able to reach an agreement regarding how effectively to deal with this growing phenomenon. An OECD report on East-West countertrade[19] concluded that countertrade causes serious trade distorting effects, introduces unnecessary complications into the transaction process and introduces additional risks for Western firms which are not countered by any significant advantages.[20] Yet, Western European nations have continued their significant involvement in Soviet natural gas development, military offsets, and similar East-West and North-South countertrade transactions. Outside of the OECD, countertrade is the topic of a study of a number of other international fora as well, including the Economic Commission for Europe,[21] the Conference on Security and Cooperation in Europe and the United Nations Conference on Trade and Development (UNCTAD). It appears that economic and business leaders around the world cannot bring themselves to encourage countertrade but, in facing economic reality, cannot condemn it either.

In addition to the government-level countertrade studies and investigations, a number of private interest groups have undertaken analyses of countertrade as well. The Aerospace Industries Association (AIA) and the Electronics Industries Association (EIA) recently conducted a joint study to analyze the impact of rapidly increasing countertrade requirements upon their constituent industries.

Similarly, the "Defense Policy Advisory Committee," a group of thirty chief executive officers of U.S. defense industry firms, has studied the long-term implications of countertrade practices upon the defense industry.[22] Increased attention is also being paid to this topic by the U.S. Chamber of Commerce, the American Association of Exporters and Importers, and the National Foreign Trade Council, among other groups. The establishment of such groups reflects the degree of impact which countertrade practices are having not just upon individual firms but also upon entire industries essential to the U.S. economy.

POLICY OPTIONS AND DILEMMAS

The significant increase in attention to countertrade reflects the fact that many public and private interest groups are becoming concerned about the domestic and international repercussions of countertrade and suggests the possibility of some form of governmental intervention in this area. Options available for a governmental approach to dealing with countertrade include coordinated efforts among developed nations to resist jointly the countertrade requirements of the nonmarket and Third World nations, the imposition by individual Western governments of restrictions upon firms within their jurisdiction to respond to countertrade requirements, the establishment of import laws to prohibit the importation of countertraded goods into individual Western nations and various indirect restraints such as the prohibition of the use of funds of national export financing institutions in export transactions which involve countertrade requirements. All of these options, among others, are currently being considered by federal officials and/or interested private parties as a means of dealing with the increased economic and political effects of countertrade.

As with other issues in international trade, the resolution of the countertrade question involves not just the formulation of a unified U.S. government position, but the development of a consistent multilateral response as well. For example, while many U.S. officials believe that countertrade is an undesirable practice which ought to be discouraged, most recognize that a unilateral U.S. policy prohibiting U.S. firms from responding to countertrade requirements would have little impact upon the use of the practice internationally and would merely render U.S. firms uncompetitive in the international marketplace. Alternatively, while an agreement among developed nations to discourage the use of countertrade may be the most effective and equitable approach to the countertrade issue, this clearly would be difficult to accomplish and would take years, if not decades, to bring to fruition.

While U.S. and foreign officials will be wrestling with this dilemma on the national and international levels, pressures will be mounting from labor and domestic industry groups, free trade interests and national security advocates to quickly come to terms with the phenomenon before the impact upon the U.S. economy is irreparable. At the same time, many U.S. firms involved in international commerce will be concerned that in the rush to develop responses to increased countertrade practices, restrictions will be imposed which will seriously impair their ability to compete in East-West and Third World trade, a substantial share of the international marketplace. A corollary concern will arise out of the government's current problem of a lack of even the most basic economic data regarding the extent of U.S. firms' involvement in countertrade; U.S. firms may become subject to reporting requirements which will force them to reveal confidential information pertaining to their countertrade transactions.

CONCLUSION

Clearly, countertrade presents a set of complex challenges to lawyers, international businessmen and government policymakers. While countertrade might be merely a passing phase in the evolving world of transnational business, it is possible that it is gradually but stubbornly becoming a permanent fixture in world commerce. In light of the far-reaching significance of this new phenomenon, it is crucial that we attempt to understand the long-term ramifications of the practice as vigorously as we attempt to master its technical details.

NOTES

1. R. J. Ruffin, Final Report on Offset Requirements In International Trade, Consultant's Report to the United States Treasury, Order No. 1A-216.

2. *Revitalization and the U.S. Economy, Part 4: Hearing Before the Economic Stabilization Subcomm., Comm. on Banking, Finance and Urban Affairs,* 97th Cong., 1st Sess. 514 (1981) (statement of Stephen Koplan, Legis. Rep., Dep't of Legis., Am. Fed'n of Labor & Cong. of Indus. Orgs.) [hereinafter *Revitalization and the U.S. Economy Hearings*].

3. United States International Trade Comm'n, Pub. No. 1237, Analysis of Recent Trends in U.S. Countertrade, Report of Investigation No. 332-125, Under Section 332 of the Tariff Act of 1930, p. 16 (Mar. 1982) [hereinafter ITC Countertrade Analysis].

4. *Revitalization and the U.S. Economy Hearings*, at 493.

5. Econ. Trade Pol'y Analysis Subcomm. of the Trade Pol'y Staff Comm., Study of U.S. Competitiveness 273.

6. See O'Reilly, *Multinationals Seek Countertrade Deals*, J. Com., Oct. 12, 1982, at 1 (quoting Lionel H. Olmer, Undersec'y of Commerce for Int'l Trade).

7. *Revitalization and the U.S. Economy Hearings*, at 485 (statement of John D. Lange, Jr., Dir., Office of Trade Finance, Treasury Dep't).

8. See ITC Countertrade Analysis, at 25.

9. See, for example, Ruffin, and *Revitalization and the U.S. Economy Hearings*, at 485.

10. *Revitalization and the U.S. Economy Hearings*, at 493 (statement of Col. R.L. Carlberg, U.S.A.F., Dir. for Int'l Acquisition, Off. of the Undersec'y of Defense (Res. & Engineering)) (describes Dept. of Defense Task Group organized to study implications of countertrade for U.S. defense preparedness).

11. See ITC Countertrade Analysis.

12. See infra note #15 and accompanying text.

13. Pursuant to section 210 of the Agricultural Act of 1980, the USDA's Foreign Agricultural Service periodically reports to Congress on the economic consequences of barter and countertrade of U.S. agricultural products.

14. Department of Labor officials have been involved in a number of studies pertaining to the impact of countertrade by U.S. firms upon domestic employment.

15. *National Defense Stockpile Amendments of 1983: Hearings on H.R. 3544, Before the Subcomm. on Seapower and Strategic and Critical Materials of the House Comm. on Armed Services*, 98th Cong., 1st Sess., (1983) (statement of Carmen Suro-Bredie, Dir. of Southeast Asian Aff., Off. of the U.S. Trade Rep.) [hereinafter Stockpile Hearings].

16. Remarks by Richard McElheny, Asst. Sec'y for Trade Development, U.S. Dept. of Commerce, before the Nat'l Foreign Trade Council Foundation on Dec. 15, 1983.

17. The GAO has not decided whether to release the findings of its analysis to the public. See 46 Fed. Reg. 19,323 (1981).

18. See *Stockpile Hearings*.

19. Organization for Economic Cooperation and Development, East-West Trade: Recent Developments in Countertrade (Paris 1981), p. 5.

20. Ibid., pp. 57-66.

21. Economic Comm'n for Europe, United Nations Economic and Social Council, Counter-trade Practices in the ECE Region, 28 ESCOR Comm. on the Development of Trade (Provisional Agenda Item 4(c)), U.N. Doc. GE 79-32495 (1979), p. 4.

22. *Revitalization and the U.S. Economy*, p. 503 (statement of Col. R.L. Carlberg, U.S.A.F., Dir. for Int'l Acquisition, Off. of the Undersec'y of Def. (Res. & Engineering)).

INDEX

Additionality, 98-99, 173-74, 203
Agricultural commodities. *See* Commodities
Agricultural Trade Development & Assistance Act of 1954
barter authority contained in, 174-75, 201-4
barter program pursuant to assessment of, 174-79
commodities in, 175
countries of, 176-77, 179
materials obtained by, 177-79
Albania, 86
AFL-CIO, 268
Annual Materials' Plan (AMP), 191, 194, 213
Antitrust laws
European Community application of, 239-41
Negative Clearance, 242-43
guidelines explaining, 241-43
implications of, countertrade under, 234-35
U.S. application of
Business Practice Review, 242
Clayton Act, 236-38, 241
exclusive dealing arrangements, 237-38
Export Certificates of Review, 242-43
extraterritorial application, 240-41
reciprocity, 236-38
Sherman Act, 236-38, 241, 243-44, 247

[Antitrust laws]
tying, 238-39
Atwood Richards, 165-67

B

Banks
involvement of, in countertrade, 25-26, 44, 50
lending practices of, in counterpurchases, 66-67
Barter
contracts for (*see* Barter contracts)
current impact of, 120-21
development of
Africa and Asia, 95
Latin America, 95
disincentives to
bureaucratic rivalries, 200
cash sales, 199
double coincidence of wants, 124, 184, 197-98
government involvement, 124, 197-98
negotiation, 124-25, 197-98
quality assessment, 125, 198-99
tied sales, 125-26, 199
trade patterns, 125-26, 199-200
transaction costs, 200-1
Eastern Europe and, 85-86 (*see also* specific countries)

ABOUT THE EDITORS
AND CONTRIBUTORS

BART S. FISHER is a partner in the firm of Patton, Boggs & Blow in Washington, D.C. and a Professional Lecturer in International Relations at the Johns Hopkins School of Advanced International Studies. Dr. Fisher received an A.B. from Washington University, a J.D. from the Harvard Law School, and an M.A. and a Ph.D. from the Johns Hopkins School of Advanced International Studies. His recent publications include *The International Coffee Agreement: A Study in Coffee Diplomacy* (Praeger: New York, 1972), *Regulating the Multinational Enterprise: National and International Challenges* (Praeger: New York, 1983) and *Regulation of International Economic Relations: Cases and Materials* (Little, Brown & Co., 1985).

KATHLEEN M. HARTE is a member of the Virginia Bar and currently serves as law clerk to the Honorable Pauline Newman, United States Circuit Judge for the Federal Circuit. She earned a B.A. at the Catholic University of America and an M.S. in Foreign Service and a J.D. from Georgetown University.

THOMAS B. McVEY is a partner in the law firm of Lane & Mittendorf of Washington, D.C., New York City and London. Mr. McVey earned a B.A. at Columbia University and a J.D. at Georgetown University. His recent publications include Countertrade and Barter: Alternative Financing by Third World Nations, 6 Int'l Trade L.J. 197 (1980-1981), and *Countertrade: Commercial Practices, Legal Issues and Policy Dilemmas*, 16 Law & Pol'y Int'l Bus. 1 (1984).

DAVID N. KOSCHIK earned a B.A. at Miami University and an M.S. in Foreign Service and a J.D. at Georgetown University. He is the author of *Foreign Policy Motivated Credit Restrictions: Potential Bases of Authority and a Practical Analysis*, 16 Law & Pol'y Int'l Bus. 539 (1984).

JAMES HIGGISTON is an International Economist with the Grain and Feed Division of the Foreign Agriculture Service, U.S. Department of Agriculture. Mr. Higgiston earned a B.A. in Russian Area

291

Studies at Hunter College and an M.S. in Foreign Service at George-town University.

GERHART VOGT is a graduate of the University for Economics and Business Administration of Vienna. He is a member of the executive board of Centro Internationale Handelsbank A.G. in Vienna, a licensed banking and trading institution that has become a leader in the coun-tertrade field. Dr. Vogt is the author of several publications on special forms of export financing, switch operations, and barter and counter-trade, and has spoken on these subjects at conferences in Europe, Asia and North America.

MILLICENT H. SCHWENK is a Research Scientist at American Uni-versity's Foreign Area Studies program. Ms. Schwenk earned a B.A. at Miami University and an M.S. in Foreign Service at Georgetown University. Her forthcoming publications include chapters on the economies of Greece and Belgium in *Area Handbooks* on those countries.

DONNA U. VOGT is an analyst in Agricultural Policy for the Con-gressional Research Service of the Library of Congress. She is a Ph.D. candidate in Latin American History at Indiana University where she earned an M.A. in Latin American Studies; she earned a B.A. at the Connecticut College for Women. Ms. Vogt's most recent publications include *Barter of Agricultural Commodities Among Developing Coun-tries*, 2 Barter Quarterly 30 (Summer 1984), *The International Coffee Agreement* (Congressional Research Services Report No. 84-224 ENR, Dec. 4, 1984) and *Agriculture in the GATT: Toward the Next Round of Multilateral Trade Negotiations* (with Hanrahan and Cate) (Con-gressional Research Service Report No. 84-169 ENR, Sept. 11, 1984).

R. MICHAEL GADBAW is a partner in the law firm Verner, Liipfert, Bernhard, McPherson and Hand in Washington, D.C. He is former Deputy General Counsel of the Office of the United States Trade Representative and currently practices law relating to international trade and investment, particularly in connection with high technology industries. He earned a C.E.P. at the Institut d'Etudes Politiques, a B.A. at Fordham University, an M.A. in International Relations at the Fletcher School of Law and Diplomacy and a J.D. at the University of Michigan. His recent publications include *Reciprocity and Its Implications for U.S. Trade Policy*, 14 Law & Pol'y Int'l Bus. 691 (1982) and "The Outlook for GATT as an Institution," published as a chapter in *Managing Trade Relations in the 1980s*, (Seymour J. Rubin and Thomas R. Graham, eds.) (American Soc. for Int'l Law 1983).